Special Inspector General Report to the United States Congress

Contents

Special Inspector General Report to the United States Congress

Robert P. Storch, Special Inspector General for OAR Inspector General U.S. Department of Defense

Nimble Books LLC: The AI Lab for Book-Lovers

Fred Zimmerman, Editor

Humans and AI making books richer, more diverse, and more surprising

Publishing Information

- (c) 2024 Nimble Books LLC
- ISBN: 978-1-60888-336-3

Nimble Books LLC ~ NimbleBooks.com

Bibliographic Key Phrases

US government; Operation Atlantic Resolve; Ukraine; Russia; military assistance; humanitarian assistance; economic assistance; sanctions; disinformation; human rights; oversight; accountability

Publisher's Note

In a world increasingly defined by conflict and uncertainty, understanding the motivations, strategies, and outcomes of global power struggles is paramount. This report, a quarterly record of the U.S. Government's activities related to Operation Atlantic Resolve, shines a light on the intricate and far-reaching consequences of Russia's invasion of Ukraine, providing an in-depth analysis of the ever-evolving battlefield dynamics, humanitarian crises, and international efforts to counter Russian aggression. This document delves into the complex landscape of military assistance, humanitarian aid, and economic sanctions, revealing the ongoing challenges and successes in these critical areas. It also sheds light on the Kremlin's sophisticated information warfare tactics, explores the ongoing human rights crisis in Ukraine, and provides a compelling account of the U.S. Government's efforts to address these pressing issues.

This report, a unique compilation of data from across numerous U.S. Government agencies, includes details on the allocation and execution of billions of dollars in supplemental funding, as well as the implementation of various programs and policies. It also features in-depth analysis of the battlefield situation, with insights from the CIA, the DIA, and the Office of the Undersecretary of Defense for Policy, providing a nuanced understanding of the military capabilities and strategic calculations of both Ukraine and Russia.

This is a must-read for anyone interested in the latest developments in the Ukraine conflict, the complex dynamics of international relations, and the challenges of supporting a nation in wartime. Whether you are a researcher, policymaker, or simply an informed citizen, this document offers invaluable insights and a comprehensive overview of the multifaceted U.S. response to Russia's invasion of Ukraine. You will gain a nuanced understanding of the global implications of this conflict and the crucial role of U.S. leadership in shaping the future of the region.

This annotated edition illustrates the capabilities of the AI Lab for Book-Lovers to add context and ease-of-use to manuscripts. It includes publishing information; abstracts; viewpoints; learning aids; and references.

Abstracts

TLDR (three words)

Ukraine War Report

ELI5

This is a book about how the United States is helping Ukraine fight Russia. The United States is giving Ukraine lots of money and weapons. The United States is also helping train Ukrainian soldiers to use these weapons. The United States wants to make sure that the money and weapons it is giving to Ukraine are used properly, so it sends people to Ukraine to check up on things. This book tells about the fighting, the weapons, the money, and the checks.

Scientific-Style Abstract

This report provides an overview of the United States government's response to the ongoing war in Ukraine, focusing on the period from January 1, 2024 to March 31, 2024. The document, a quarterly report from the Special Inspector General for Operation Atlantic Resolve, summarizes the status of military, economic, and humanitarian assistance to Ukraine. The report covers a wide range of topics, including the military situation, U.S. security assistance to Ukraine and other countries, direct budget support to Ukraine, international humanitarian assistance to Ukraine, and U.S. efforts to counter disinformation, protect human rights, and impose sanctions against Russia. The report also describes the challenges faced by U.S. government agencies in overseeing their efforts in Ukraine, specifically highlighting the difficulties in monitoring the use of funds and equipment in a warzone.

Learning Aids

Mnemonic (acronym)

OAR: Operation Atlantic Resolve

Mnemonic (speakable)

Ukraine must **re**solve to **def**eat Russia. **O**peration **A**tlantic **R**esolve helps **Ukraine** defend its **so**vereignty.

Mnemonic (singable)

To the tune of "Mary Had a Little Lamb"

Operation Atlantic Resolve, Operation Atlantic Resolve, To help Ukraine defend, Operation Atlantic Resolve.

With funding from the U.S., With funding from the U.S., To help Ukraine defend, With funding from the U.S.

Excerpts

Most Important Passages

- **Page 3.** "Operation Atlantic Resolve (OAR) is the U.S. contingency operation to deter Russian aggression against NATO and to reassure and bolster the alliance in the wake of Russia's 2022 full-scale invasion of Ukraine. OAR also includes security assistance activities in support of Ukraine."
- **Page 4.** "Multiple factors undermined UAF capability during the quarter. These included the persistent application of legacy Soviet-era warfighting doctrine rather than a joint combat operations philosophy; the impact of attrition on force quality and training levels; limited resources and capabilities; and the tactical and operational situation on the ground."
- **Page 5.** "The United Nations estimated that 14.6 million Ukrainians—nearly half the country's population—will need humanitarian assistance in 2024. Ongoing wartime conditions continued to present serious challenges to humanitarian assistance providers. USAID released new guidance for non-governmental organization (NGO) partners, with recommended precautions for operating in Ukraine."
- **Page 8.** "Operation Atlantic Resolve (OAR) is the U.S. contingency operation in and around the U.S. European Command (USEUCOM) area of operations to deter Russia's aggression against NATO and to reassure and bolster the alliance in the wake of Russia's February 2022 invasion of Ukraine."
- **Page 13.** "Since the full-scale invasion began, USAID has provided direct budget support to the Ukrainian government through three World Bank-managed trust funds: the Ukraine Second Economic Recovery Multi-donor Trust Fund (MDTF), the Special Transfer to Ukraine Single Donor Trust Fund (SDTF), and the Public Expenditures for Administrative Capacity Endurance (PEACE) multi-donor trust fund."
- **Page 24.** "The United States provides security assistance to Ukraine and other European nations under Operation Atlantic Resolve (OAR) and, in some cases, programs funded and managed by State."
- **Page 87.** "The United States, in coordination with the European Union and others, began applying sanctions against Russia following the 2014 invasion of Ukraine. In response to Russia's full-scale invasion of Ukraine in February 2022, the United States greatly expanded its approach, initiating an unprecedented range of comprehensive financial and trade sanctions."

References

Glossary

AEECA - Assistance to Europe, Eurasia, and Central Asia. This is a State Department account used to fund development and economic assistance.

AUSAA - Additional Ukraine Supplemental Appropriations Act. The U.S. Congress has passed multiple supplemental appropriations acts to provide funding for the Ukraine response.

CBRN - Chemical, Biological, Radiological, and Nuclear. This is a common military acronym used to refer to weapons and other materials that could be used in chemical, biological, radiological, or nuclear attacks.

COMSEC - Communication Security. This refers to the measures taken to protect military communications from unauthorized access or interception.

DSCA - Defense Security Cooperation Agency. This U.S. Department of Defense agency manages programs like the Foreign Military Sales program, which provides weapons and equipment to other countries.

EDI - European Deterrence Initiative. This is a U.S. Department of Defense program meant to deter Russian aggression in Europe.

EEUM - Enhanced End-Use Monitoring. This is an extra-strict form of end-use monitoring that applies to especially sensitive technology or equipment.

ESF - Economic Support Funds. These are State Department funds that support economic development and humanitarian assistance.

EOD - Explosive Ordnance Disposal. This refers to the people and activities involved in safely dealing with explosives, such as bombs and landmines.

EUM - End-Use Monitoring. This is the practice of checking to see if weapons or other military equipment are used as agreed by the recipient country.

EXBS - Export Control and Related Border Security. This refers to the practice of controlling the export of certain technologies, especially dual-use technologies, to prevent their use by unfriendly foreign powers.

FMS - Foreign Military Sales. This is a U.S. Department of Defense program for providing weapons and military equipment to other countries.

FMF - Foreign Military Financing. This is a U.S. Department of State program to provide money to other countries for their defense needs.

GAO - Government Accountability Office. This is a U.S. Government agency that provides oversight of federal programs and agencies.

GEC - Global Engagement Center. This is a U.S. Department of State agency that counters foreign propaganda and disinformation.

HIMARS - High Mobility Artillery Rocket System. A rocket-launching system designed to provide accurate long-range firepower.

IDCC - International Donor Coordination Center. This body helps to coordinate military assistance to Ukraine from different donor countries.

IDP - Internally Displaced Person. This refers to someone who has been forced to leave their home because of a conflict, but who has stayed within their own country.

INL - Bureau of International Narcotics and Law Enforcement Affairs. This is a U.S. Department of State agency that fights drug trafficking and organized crime.

IO - Bureau of International Organization Affairs. This is a U.S. Department of State agency that deals with international organizations like the United Nations.

ISN - Bureau of International Security and Nonproliferation. This is a U.S. Department of State agency that tries to prevent the spread of weapons of mass destruction and other sensitive technologies.

MIGA - Multilateral Investment Guarantee Agency. This is an agency of the World Bank Group that provides insurance to companies who want to invest in developing countries.

MDCP - Multi-agency Donor Coordination Platform. This is a forum for donors to coordinate their aid to Ukraine.

MDTF - Multi-donor Trust Fund. This type of trust fund is used to collect money from multiple donors.

MRAP - Mine-Resistant Ambush Protected Vehicle. This type of armored vehicle provides better protection against landmines and roadside bombs.

NADR - Nonproliferation, Anti-terrorism, Demining, and Related Programs. This is a U.S. Department of State account used to fund programs focused on these areas.

NABU - National Anti-Corruption Bureau of Ukraine. This organization fights corruption in the Ukrainian government.

NATO - North Atlantic Treaty Organization. A military alliance of countries in North America and Europe.

NNSA - National Nuclear Security Administration. This is a part of the U.S. Department of Energy that works to prevent the spread of nuclear weapons.

NGO - Nongovernmental Organization. A not-for-profit group that works on a specific issue.

NPU - National Police of Ukraine. The Ukrainian national police force.

OCO - Overseas Contingency Operation. A U.S. military operation conducted outside the United States for more than sixty days.

OECD - Organization for Economic Co-operation and Development. An inter-governmental organization focused on economic and social development.

OFAC - Office of Foreign Assets Control. This is a part of the U.S. Department of the Treasury that administers economic sanctions.

OPG - Office of the Prosecutor General. This is the agency that is responsible for criminal prosecutions in Ukraine.

PATRIOT - Phased Array Tracking Radar to Intercept on Target. A sophisticated air defense system.

PEACE - Public Expenditures for Administrative Capacity Endurance. This is a World Bank-managed trust fund that helps Ukraine to pay for government services.

PEPFAR - U.S. President'2019s Emergency Plan for AIDS Relief. A program to help fight the AIDS epidemic.

PIO - Public International Organization. An international organization that is not a government, for example, the United Nations or the International Committee of the Red Cross.

PRM - Bureau of Population, Refugees, and Migration. This is a U.S. Department of State agency that deals with refugee issues.

PDA - Presidential Drawdown Authority. This law authorizes the U.S. President to transfer weapons and other military equipment from U.S. stockpiles to other countries.

PM/WRA - State Bureau of Political-Military Affairs Office of Weapons Removal and Abatement. This agency manages the U.S. government's efforts to clear landmines and other explosive remnants of war.

PRC - People's Republic of China.

RFE/RL - Radio Free Europe/Radio Liberty. A U.S. government-funded international broadcaster.

RAAM - Remote Anti-Armor Mine System. A weapon that can be used to lay landmines remotely.

SAG-U - Security Assistance Group-Ukraine. This is a U.S. military group responsible for coordinating military assistance to Ukraine.

SAPO - Specialized Anti-Corruption Prosecutor's Office. This agency prosecutes corruption in Ukraine.

SATCOM - Satellite Communications.

SBU - Security Services of Ukraine. Ukraine's intelligence agency.

SDTF - Single Donor Trust Fund. This type of trust fund is used to collect money from a single donor.

SMEs - Small and Medium-Sized Enterprises.

SMR - Small Modular Reactor. A type of nuclear reactor that can be built in modules and is smaller and safer than traditional reactors.

SWIFT - Society for Worldwide Interbank Financial Telecommunication. A system that is used to send financial messages between banks.

TFI - Treasury Office of Terrorism and Financial Intelligence.

UDCG - Ukraine Defense Contact Group. A group of countries that meets to coordinate assistance to Ukraine.

UNHCR - United Nations High Commissioner for Refugees.

USAID - United States Agency for International Development.

USAREUR-AF - U.S. Army Europe and Africa.

USEUCOM - U.S. European Command.

USAGM - U.S. Agency for Global Media.

USAI - Ukraine Security Assistance Initiative. A U.S. Department of Defense program to provide security assistance to Ukraine.

USOSCE - U.S. Mission to the Organization for Security and Cooperation in Europe.

USTRANSCOM - U.S. Transportation Command.

UAV - Unmanned Aerial Vehicle. A drone.

VOA - Voice of America. A U.S. government-funded international broadcaster.

VAMPIRE - Visual Acquisition and Munitions Integration for Responsive Engagement. A weapon system that can be used to track and engage enemy drones.

VPN - Virtual Private Network. A technology that can be used to secure internet traffic.

Timeline

Late 2013: Protests erupt in Kyiv over President Viktor Yanukovych's decision to not sign a cooperative agreement with the European Union at the behest of Russian President Vladimir Putin.

Early 2014: Protests in Kyiv result in the ousting of Yanukovych, who then flees to Russia. Shortly thereafter, Russian troops covertly invade Ukraine's Crimean peninsula, seize government buildings, and hold a referendum in favor of secession and annexation by Russia. This is widely viewed as illegitimate by the international community. Russia then begins massing troops in Crimea and engineering pro-Russian proxy movements in Ukraine's eastern provinces of Donetsk and Luhansk.

February 24, 2022: Russia invades Ukraine on three fronts—land, air, and sea—bombarding the port city of Odesa and moving overland from occupied Crimea and the Donbas, Belarus, and other points of entry along the Ukraine-Russia border.

May 2022: U.S. Embassy personnel begin returning to Kyiv.

August 2023: The U.S. Government updates its integrated country strategy for Ukraine, outlining five mission goals for the U.S. Embassy in Kyiv.

September 2023: USAID makes its most recent obligation to the PEACE fund.

October 2023: Russia begins its winter offensive, with the main objective of capturing Avdiivka.

December 2023: The DoD acknowledges that it has exhausted its replenishment funds for the Presidential Drawdown Authority.

January 11, 2024: The U.S. Embassy in Kyiv expands its movement zone, allowing embassy leadership to approve movements outside but near Kyiv without Washington clearance.

January 16, 2024: U.S. Secretary of State Antony Blinken meets with Ukrainian President Volodymyr Zelenskyy in Davos, Switzerland.

January 21, 2024: Ukrainian forces strike the Ust-Luga Condensate Refinery in Russia, disrupting condensate refining for two weeks.

January 25, 2024: Ukrainian forces strike the Tuapse Refinery in Russia, disrupting refinery operations.

January 26, 2024: NABU touts an 80% rise in prosecutions at a meeting with donor countries.

January 29, 2024: The U.S. Embassy in Kyiv holds a Scenesetter for the OIG Visit to Ukraine.

February 1, 2024: The European Union approves approximately $53 billion in assistance over four years for Ukraine through the EU Ukraine Facility.

February 3, 2024: Ukrainian forces strike the Volgograd Refinery in Russia, damaging one primary processing unit.

February 6, 2024: Ukrainian forces strike the Belgorod 750-kV Substation in Russia, damaging the substation.

February 8, 2024: President Zelenskyy dismisses Ukraine's top military commander, General Valeriy Zaluzhnyy.

February 8, 2024: Valerii Zaluzhnyi publishes an opinion piece expressing restrained optimism that Ukraine could be successful against Russia in 2024.

February 9, 2024: Ukrainian forces strike the Ilsky Refinery in Russia, temporarily disrupting operations at the main processing unit.

February 14, 2024: Ukrainian forces announce that they have destroyed the Russian landing warship, Tsezar Kunikov.

February 18, 2024: Russian forces declare that they have taken full control of the Ukrainian town of Avdiivka.

February 20, 2024: National Security Advisor Jake Sullivan states that the lack of new supplemental funding for Ukraine and shortages in ammunition and air defense systems will deplete Ukrainian defenses.

February 22, 2024: Kremlin internet regulators completely block the website domains of all five of RFE/RL's Central Asian services.

February 23, 2024: State and Treasury announce sanctions for five Kremlin-backed individuals in Ukraine for their connection to the confinement and deportation of Ukrainian children.

February 23, 2024: State and Treasury add more than 300 individuals and entities involved in Russia's aggression against Ukraine to U.S. sanctions lists.

February 23, 2024: State announces new, broader sanctions on three Belarusian government and civil society individuals who had overseen the transfer of Ukrainian children out of Ukraine into Belarus.

February 24, 2024: The U.S. designates Sovcomflot, Russia's state-owned shipping company and fleet operator.

February 25, 2024: A barge collides with and damages a rail bridge crossing the Hunte River, which is the only rail line that services the German seaport used to transit materiel for Ukraine.

February 29, 2024: State invokes the OSCE's Moscow Mechanism to address reports of arbitrary detention of civilians in Russia-occupied Ukraine.

March 1, 2024: The MEASURE contractor submits a draft of its first quarterly report on assistance results to State.

March 5, 2024: Ukrainian forces claim a successful attack on the Russian patrol ship Sergey Kotov.

March 7, 2024: NATO approves Sweden's application to join the alliance, bringing the total number of NATO members to 32.

March 11, 2024: Ukrainian forces strike the Nizhny Novgorod Refinery in Russia, damaging one primary processing unit.

March 12, 2024: National Security Advisor Jake Sullivan announces the provision of a new $300 million security assistance package for Ukraine.

March 12, 2024: Major General Pat Ryder describes the security assistance package as necessary but limited, estimating that it would enable the UAF to continue the fight for a matter of weeks.

March 13, 2024: Ukrainian forces strike the Ryazan Refinery in Russia, damaging two primary processing units.

March 16, 2024: Ukrainian forces strike the Slavyansk Refinery and Syzran Refinery in Russia, damaging one primary processing unit at each site.

March 19, 2024: Delegates from nearly 50 countries attend the 20th Ukraine Defense Contact Group at Ramstein Air Base, Germany.

March 20, 2024: State announces U.S. sanctions against two individuals and two entities involved in spreading disinformation on behalf of the Russian government.

March 21, 2024: SAPO officially becomes a separate legal entity in the justice system of Ukraine, separating operationally from Ukraine's Office of the Prosecutor General.

March 22, 2024: Russia launches an extensive missile and drone campaign that damages critical power generation assets nationwide.

March 23, 2024: Ukrainian forces strike the Kuibyshev Refinery in Russia, disrupting refinery operations.

March 24, 2024: Ukrainian forces strike the Novocherkassk Power Plant in Russia, disrupting two power units.

April 3, 2024: State obligates $255 million for World Bank trust funds to support rebuilding in Ukraine.

April 11, 2024: Russian missiles destroy the Trypilska thermal power plant, the largest power facility in Kyiv oblast.

April 24, 2024: President Biden signs a fifth supplemental appropriation for Ukraine into law.

Index of Persons

OPERATION ATLANTIC RESOLVE
INCLUDING U.S. GOVERNMENT ACTIVITIES RELATED TO
UKRAINE

JANUARY 1, 2024–MARCH 31, 2024

SPECIAL IG MESSAGE

Robert P. Storch

The U.S. Government has responded to Russia's illegal and unprovoked full-scale invasion of Ukraine with a $174.2 billion national-level effort to help Ukraine defend its sovereign territory, bolster the NATO alliance in Eastern Europe, support an enhanced U.S. military presence in the region, and provide direct budget, development, and humanitarian assistance to Ukraine. The Special IG for Operation Atlantic Resolve is responsible for ensuring whole-of-government oversight and transparency of this multi-faceted and resource-intensive effort.

In January 2024, I traveled to Ukraine and other nations in the region with my counterparts from State OIG and USAID OIG to obtain a first-hand update from U.S. and Ukrainian officials. We visited several organizations that receive U.S. assistance— including a health clinic and a power plant—and an enhanced end-use monitoring transfer site. In meetings with senior officials, my colleagues and I expressed the importance of accountability and transparency of U.S. assistance. The Ukrainian officials with whom we met agreed to notify OIG personnel— including our staff at the U.S. Embassy in Kyiv—if there was any hint of fraud or abuse.

In March, we launched UkraineOversight.gov, a new website to provide the public with comprehensive access to a wide range of information regarding the robust interagency oversight effort. The website will be updated regularly with the latest news and reports regarding the independent oversight of the U.S. Ukraine response from the OIGs for the DoD, State, and USAID, the GAO, and the other members of the Ukraine Oversight Interagency Working Group. As detailed in this quarterly report, conducting oversight in the midst of an intense wartime environment is a challenge our offices have risen to meet.

We will continue to report quarterly on the status of OAR and the Ukraine response, other U.S. Government activity in Europe, and efforts to counter Russian aggression. I would like to thank all of the women and men who make this oversight effort possible, especially those stationed in and near Ukraine.

Robert P. Storch
Special Inspector General for OAR
Inspector General
U.S. Department of Defense

We are pleased to present this Special Inspector General report to Congress on Operation Atlantic Resolve (OAR). This report discharges our quarterly reporting responsibilities pursuant to Section 1250B of the National Defense Authorization Act for 2024 and Lead IG reporting responsibilities under 5 U.S.C. 419.

Section 1250B states that no later than 45 days after the end of each fiscal year, the Special Inspector General for OAR shall submit to Congress a report summarizing U.S. programs and operations related to Ukraine.

This report also discusses the planned, ongoing, and completed oversight work conducted by the DoD, State, and USAID Offices of Inspector General, as well as the other U.S. oversight agencies that coordinate their activities through the Ukraine Oversight Interagency Working Group.

This report addresses the following topics specified in Section 1250B:

- USEUCOM operations and related support for the U.S. military: pages 23–45
- Security assistance to Ukraine and other countries affected by the war: pages 23–51
- Economic assistance to Ukraine and other countries affected by the war: pages 13–17, 58–60
- Humanitarian assistance to Ukraine and other countries affected by the war: pages 64–70
- Operations of other relevant U.S. Government agencies involved in the Ukraine response: pages 80, 93–94
- Description of any waste, fraud, or abuse identified by the Special IG: pages 123–131
- Status and results of investigations, inspections, and audits: pages 123–142
- Status and results of referrals to the Department of Justice: page 141
- A description of the overall plans for review by the OIGs of such support of Ukraine, including plans for investigations, inspections, and audits: pages 139–140

Robert P. Storch
Special Inspector General for OAR
Inspector General
U.S. Department of Defense

Sandra J. Lewis
Associate Lead Inspector General
for OAR
Acting Inspector General
U.S. Department of State

Paul K. Martin
Inspector General
U.S. Agency for International
Development

Tanks and infantry vehicles from nine NATO countries assemble in Poland during Exercise Dragon 24, part of Steadfast Defender 24. (DoD photo)

CONTENTS

JANUARY 1, 2024–MARCH 31, 2024

U.S. Airmen service a B-1B Lancer bomber at Luleå-Kallax Air Base, Sweden. (U.S. Air Force photo)

EXECUTIVE SUMMARY

Operation Atlantic Resolve (OAR) is the U.S. contingency operation to deter Russian aggression against NATO and to reassure and bolster the alliance in the wake of Russia's 2022 full-scale invasion of Ukraine. OAR also includes security assistance activities in support of Ukraine.[1] During this quarter:

The prolonged stalemate along the front line began to favor the Russian forces, who benefit from advantages in both manpower and munitions.[2] However, the Ukrainian Armed Forces (UAF) achieved some high-profile asymmetrical successes against Russian forces this quarter by employing unmanned aerial and maritime platforms.[3] After months of heavy fighting, the UAF withdrew from the industrial town of Avdiivka in February, the most significant Russian territorial gain in nearly a year.[4] On February 8, President Volodymyr Zelenskyy dismissed his top military commander, General Valeriy Zaluzhnyy, following increased tensions between the two leaders after Ukraine's failed 2023 counteroffensive and a disagreement over conscription.[5]

Russian forces continued to target energy infrastructure. For the second winter since the February 2022 war began, Russian explosive unmanned aerial vehicles (UAV) and missiles continued to strike civilian targets, such as electricity infrastructure, oil refineries, and district heating facilities across the country.[6] On March 22, 2024, Russia launched an extensive UAV and missile campaign that damaged power generation assets across Ukraine. These attacks denied citizens access to electricity, water, sewage treatment, heat, and communications.[7] They were part of a larger effort to harm Ukraine's economy, targeting key industrial centers, such as Kyiv, Dnipropetrovsk, Kharkiv, and Sumy.[8]

Multiple factors undermined UAF capability during the quarter. These included the persistent application of legacy Soviet-era warfighting doctrine rather than a joint combat operations philosophy; the impact of attrition on force quality and training levels; limited resources and capabilities; and the tactical and operational situation on the ground.[9] The UAF relies heavily on artillery and long-range fires as a primary means of engaging the enemy, rather than to enable maneuver and breaching actions, which has contributed to the UAF's persistent shortage of munitions and overuse of weapon systems.[10] The UAF has limited capability to conduct higher-level maintenance, so some equipment is evacuated to other countries, such as Poland.[11]

Uncertain funding created challenges for both the U.S. military and Ukraine.[12] On April 24, after the quarter ended, President Biden signed the first new supplemental funding bill for Ukraine since December 2022.[13] While the DoD still had authority to transfer existing weapons and material to Ukraine during the quarter, it had run out of funding to replace these items and was thus reluctant to make transfers that could hurt U.S. military readiness.[14] As a result of the diminished international support, the UAF resorted to rationing munitions.[15] On March 12, the DoD announced a new, one-time $300 million security assistance package for Ukraine, supported by funds made available through cost-savings achieved in DoD contracts.[16] The DoD predicted this would extend the UAF's ability to continue the fight for a matter of weeks.[17]

The United States and 18 partner nations continued to train Ukrainian forces. Training courses covered a wide range of capabilities, including artillery, maneuver, air defense, maritime operations, maintenance, medical, and combat leadership.[18] Battlefield demands and legacy training systems have challenged the UAF's ability to train incoming forces, contributing to the UAF's reliance on foreign partners for training before combat deployments.[19] The United States and international partners worked together to develop "capability coalitions," each led by one or two nations with expertise in a specific area of warfighting, such as air defense, artillery, or maritime operations, and focused on building long-term Ukrainian capabilities beyond the current fight.[20]

The Ukrainian government has undertaken efforts to counter public corruption, but it continues to confront obstacles to transparency.[21] The ongoing war with Russia has created new opportunities for corruption, including bribes, kickbacks, and inflated procurement costs within the Ministry of Defense, particularly for procurements of lethal items where there is limited transparency due to classification level of these purchases.[22] The U.S. Government continued to provide technical assistance and training to Ukrainian investigators and prosecutors. Their respective agencies hired more staff and brought more prosecutions during the quarter.[23]

State, Treasury, and other agencies supported enhanced sanctions on individuals and entities for their support to Russia. On February 23, State announced sanctions for five Kremlin-backed individuals in Ukraine for their connection to the confinement and forced deportation of Ukrainian children.[24] The same announcement noted that State and Treasury sanctioned more than 300 individuals and entities involved in Russia's aggression against Ukraine to U.S. sanctions lists—the largest number of sanctions imposed since Russia's full-scale invasion of Ukraine.[25]

> The UAF relies heavily on artillery and long-range fires as a primary means of engaging the enemy, rather than to enable maneuver and breaching actions, which has contributed to the UAF's persistent shortage of munitions and overuse of weapon systems.

The United Nations estimated that 14.6 million Ukrainians—nearly half the country's population—will need humanitarian assistance in 2024.[26] Ongoing wartime conditions continued to present serious challenges to humanitarian assistance providers. USAID released new guidance for non-governmental organization (NGO) partners, with recommended precautions for operating in Ukraine.[27] Since February 2022, USAID has provided more that $2 billion in humanitarian funding, including $60 million thorough sub awards for Ukrainian NGOs working to provide food, healthcare, and other commodities across Ukraine, including in hazardous areas near the front lines.[28]

History of Russia's War Against Ukraine

In late 2013, protests broke out in Kyiv over the then-President Viktor Yanukovych's decision to bow to pressure from Russian President Vladimir Putin not to sign a cooperative agreement with the European Union.[29] This led to the ousting of Yanukovych in early 2014 and his flight to Russia. Shortly thereafter, Russian troops covertly invaded Ukraine's Crimean peninsula, seized government buildings, and held a referendum—widely viewed as illegitimate by the international community—in favor of secession and annexation by Russia. Russia then began massing troops in Crimea and engineering pro-Russian proxy movements in Ukraine's eastern provinces of Donetsk and Luhansk. These groups were partially successful in controlling territory, which afforded Russia an opportunity to deploy regular troops to eastern Ukraine under the guise of protecting pro-Russian populations in the region. This resulted in a low-level armed conflict in that region for the next 8 years.[30]

On February 24, 2022, Russian military forces invaded Ukraine on three fronts—land, air, and sea—bombarding the port city of Odesa and moving overland from occupied Crimea and the Donbas, Belarus, and other points of entry along the Ukraine-Russia border. Within the first month of the large-scale invasion, 19 million people were displaced, almost half of the population of Ukraine, and approximately 575,000 refugees fled Ukraine.[31] Russian forces invading from the north briefly assaulted Kyiv and Kharkiv, Ukraine's second largest city, but were expelled by the UAF. Russian forces soon abandoned their efforts to take Kyiv directly and focused on controlling southern and eastern Ukraine. The UAF's Fall 2022 counteroffensive pushed the Russian forces back from the area around Kharkiv and Kherson. In September 2022, President Putin announced Russia's formal claim of annexation of four Ukrainian provinces—Donetsk, Kherson, Luhansk, and Zaporizhzhia—following a series of dubious referenda held there.[32]

For much of 2023, Russian forces consolidated their control over occupied territory in eastern and southern Ukraine. Russian forces laid extensive minefields, constructed multiple layers of trenches and other fortifications, and conducted other defensive preparations to secure their positions in these regions. Despite heavy fighting and high casualties, both sides made only incremental gains and losses of territory over the course of 2023 as the front lines calcified into relatively static, modern trench warfare.[33] Russian forces achieved limited westward territorial advances during the quarter, including the February seizure of the town of Avdiivka.[34]

A Swedish CB90-class fast assault craft approaches a landing ship during small boat operations in support of Steadfast Defender 24. (U.S. Navy photo)

MISSION UPDATE

A KC-130J Super Hercules prepares to taxi at Andenes, Norway. (U.S. Marine Corps photo)

MISSION UPDATE

Operation Atlantic Resolve (OAR) is the U.S. contingency operation in and around the U.S. European Command (USEUCOM) area of operations to deter Russia's aggression against NATO and to reassure and bolster the alliance in the wake of Russia's February 2022 invasion of Ukraine. OAR also includes security assistance activities in support of Ukraine.[35]

OAR is part of the broader U.S. policy agenda and activities to respond to Russia's continued aggression against Ukraine. The U.S. Government's integrated country strategy for Ukraine, updated in August 2023, outlines five mission goals for the U.S. Embassy in Kyiv. (See Table 1.) Specific objectives related to U.S. security, development, and humanitarian assistance activities are detailed throughout this report.

Table 1.

U.S. Mission Goals in Ukraine

Win the War: Ukraine effectively uses security, humanitarian, economic, and diplomatic tools to prevail on the battlefield and set conditions for a just and lasting peace.

Win the Future: Ukraine strengthens its civil society and democratic and economic institutions and implements anti-corruption, justice sector, and corporate governance reforms to achieve sustainable momentum towards Euro-Atlantic integration to win a secure and just future that delivers prosperity for all its citizens.

Hold Russia Accountable: Ukraine and its allies hold Russia and its enablers accountable for war crimes and damage to Ukraine.

Account for U.S. Taxpayers: Humanitarian, economic, and security assistance delivers effective relief and sustainable results for Ukrainians.

Rebuild the U.S. Mission in Ukraine: Bring back staff to ensure proper execution of administrative objectives.

Source: State, website, "Integrated Country Strategy: Ukraine," 8/29/2023; State, vetting comment, 4/29/2024.

FUNDING

Enacted as part of a larger national security funding bill, the new law provides nearly $61 billion for the U.S. Government's Ukraine response, of which approximately $48.4 billion will be administered by the DoD and $11.6 billion by State and USAID.

As of the end of this quarter, the U.S. Congress had appropriated approximately $113.4 billion in supplemental funding for the U.S. response to Russia's unprovoked, full-scale invasion of Ukraine since February 2022. This includes security, direct budget, development, and humanitarian assistance to Ukraine; security assistance for NATO allies and other partner nations; funding to support enhanced U.S. military presence and activity in Europe; and replenishment of U.S. military stocks transferred to the UAF. This funding was enacted through four supplemental appropriations acts, the last of which was enacted in December 2022.[36]

On April 24, after the quarter ended, President Biden signed a fifth supplemental appropriation for Ukraine into law.[37] Enacted as part of a larger national security funding bill, the new law provides nearly $61 billion for the U.S. Government's Ukraine response, of which approximately $48.4 billion will be administered by the DoD and $11.6 billion by State and USAID.[38] (See Figure 1.) Additional DoD funding for the Ukraine response was provided through base budget appropriations.[39] Since February 2022, USAID has provided $22.9 billion in direct budget support to the Ukrainian government, nearly $2.3 billion in development assistance, and more than $2 billion in humanitarian assistance.[40]

The U.S. Government assists Ukraine and regional partners through a wide range of programs and authorities. (Note that the figures below are as of the end of the quarter and do not reflect the new supplemental funding enacted in April.)

Figure 1.

FY 2022–FY 2024 Ukraine Supplemental Appropriations

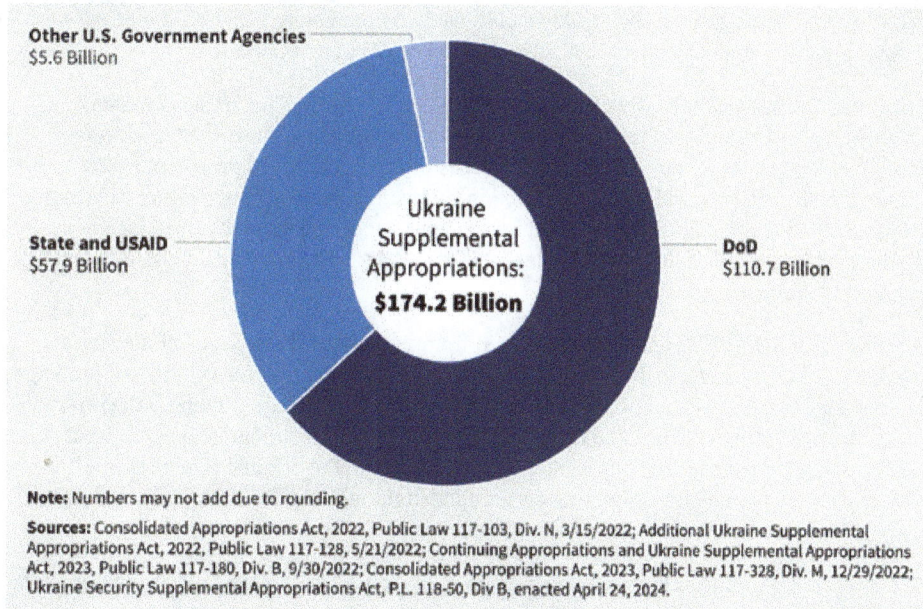

Other U.S. Government Agencies
$5.6 Billion

State and USAID
$57.9 Billion

Ukraine Supplemental Appropriations:
$174.2 Billion

DoD
$110.7 Billion

Note: Numbers may not add due to rounding.

Sources: Consolidated Appropriations Act, 2022, Public Law 117-103, Div. N, 3/15/2022; Additional Ukraine Supplemental Appropriations Act, 2022, Public Law 117-128, 5/21/2022; Continuing Appropriations and Ukraine Supplemental Appropriations Act, 2023, Public Law 117-180, Div. B, 9/30/2022; Consolidated Appropriations Act, 2023, Public Law 117-328, Div. M, 12/29/2022; Ukraine Security Supplemental Appropriations Act, P.L. 118-50, Div B, enacted April 24, 2024.

U.S. Army vehicles are offloaded from a cargo vessel at the port of Alexandroupolis, Greece. (U.S. Army photo)

Presidential Drawdown Authority (PDA): PDA is not a funding source but rather an authority that allows the President to provide military assistance from existing defense articles in the DoD's stocks, subject to a statutory cap.[41] The statutory limit for PDA is $100 million worth of weapons and equipment transferred worldwide per year.[42] However, in response to Russia's 2022 invasion of Ukraine, Congress increased the cap on PDA to $25.5 billion.[43] As of the end of the quarter, the U.S. Government had announced $23.9 billion in PDA drawdowns, of which $19.9 billion had been executed.[44] Supplemental Ukraine funding allowed DoD components to request replacement funds for items transferred to Ukraine, but these replacement funds have been exhausted since the end of FY 2023.[45]

Ukraine Security Assistance Initiative (USAI): Congress created the USAI in 2015 as a funding source for DoD security assistance to Ukraine's military and other security forces, including intelligence support, training, equipment, logistics, supplies, and services. The USAI aims to enhance Ukraine's ability to defend itself from aggression and defend its sovereignty and territorial integrity against Russia and Russian proxy forces.[46] State concurrence is required on all USAI notifications before they are sent to the Congress.[47]

As of the end of the quarter, the DoD had obligated approximately $18.2 billion of its $18.9 billion in supplemental and FY 2022-2024 base USAI appropriations.[48]

European Deterrence Initiative (EDI): The EDI was first established in the National Defense Authorization Act for FY 2015. Originally known as the European Reassurance Initiative, it provides funding to support five lines of effort: increased presence; exercises and training; enhanced prepositioning; improved infrastructure; and building partner capacity. Between 2015 and 2023, EDI-associated investments supported more than $30 billion in requirements to enhance the United States' ability to deter aggression against NATO and to respond should deterrence fail.[49]

Starting in FY 2022, EDI funding transitioned from the former Overseas Contingency Operation (OCO) budget to the base budget. The EDI does not provide centralized funding in a separate account. Recognizing this transition from OCO to base funding, in February 2023, the DoD provided guidance to all DoD Components for continuing to capture EDI-associated investments in their base budgets that align with the original five lines of effort. EDI-associated activities and investments are funded through the DoD's base budget rather than the Ukraine supplemental funds.[50]

Since FY 2022, Congress has appropriated approximately $11.7 billion for EDI, of which the DoD had obligated approximately $7 billion as of March 2024.[51]

Foreign Military Financing (FMF): Through FMF, the Secretary of State may authorize and direct military assistance for a specific purpose, usually in response to a request from the recipient country. FMF funds do not belong to the recipient nation but are executed by U.S. Government agencies and the end items transferred to the recipient country.[52]

State reported that, as of March 2024, it had obligated $4.2 billion and expended $1.4 billion of the approximately $4.7 billion appropriated in the Ukraine supplementals for FMF, which includes some funding allocated for other countries.[53] State said that during the quarter it obligated $60 million in Ukraine Supplemental FMF funds for a loan to Poland in March.[54] State said it expended $400 million in FMF funds during the quarter.[55]

State said that the primary challenges to implementing these FMF programs derive from U.S. industrial base capabilities and resulting production times, which has resulted in weapon systems replenishment failing to keep up with Ukraine and regional partner demands.[56] In addition, State said that uncertainty in follow-on funding negatively impacts necessary planning. Assisting Ukraine to build its own defense industrial base and improve its military capabilities may require identifying co-production opportunities utilizing FMF resources and authorities, which would require building new policies and procedures.[57]

In addition, State said that resources provided to Ukraine through FMF have enhanced the country's near-term warfighting capabilities through U.S.- and partner-provided defense articles, including air defense systems, munitions, maintenance, and sustainment equipment.[58] State also said FMF resources incentivized other countries to donate combat and support equipment (including divesture of Russian-origin equipment) for Ukraine's short-term military needs.[59] State said such incentivization and backfill efforts will enhance future NATO interoperability and encourage countries to invest national resources in interoperable defense articles built to Western standards when upgrading defense capabilities.[60]

Navy Over-Executed its Ukraine Assistance Funding

In March, the DoD OIG issued a management advisory on the Navy's execution of Ukraine response funds, as part of an ongoing audit regarding the DoD's execution of Ukraine supplemental funding. The DoD OIG identified internal control deficiencies that resulted in the Navy over-executing supplemental funds (spending more than it had available). Internal controls are essential for ensuring accountability, integrity, and efficiency in federal spending. Without robust internal controls, the DoD is vulnerable to inefficiencies that jeopardize its ability to achieve its mission and fulfill its financial responsibilities.[61]

The DoD OIG found that the Navy over-executed its Ukraine funding three times during FY 2022 for a total of $398.9 million. This occurred due to the lack of automated controls and the lack of effective manual internal controls. While the Navy was able to redirect funds from other programs to reverse these errors and avoid a potential Antideficiency Act violation, such funds may not be available in the future. Although the Navy has long-term plans to address this issue, the DoD OIG said the Navy should take prompt action to implement preventive controls to avoid over-execution in the future.[62]

European Union Approves New Funding

On February 1, the European Union (EU) approved approximately $53 billion in assistance over 4 years for Ukraine through the EU Ukraine Facility.[63] According to State, about $40.9 billion of these funds will be used for budgetary assistance, $7.5 billion for economic development, $5.2 billion for technical support, and to cover interest accrued on concessional loans. The funding consists of $18.3 billion in grants and $35.5 billion in low-interest loans. Disbursement of these loans and grants will be conditional on Ukraine achieving progress on reforms and investments in public finance, public administration, the justice system, and anti-corruption measures.[64]

State said it works closely with the European Union and other participating countries in the Multi-agency Donor Coordination Platform (MDCP), a long-term initiative that coordinates support from international financial institutions and donor countries for Ukraine's economic recovery and reconstruction needs. The MDCP serves as a platform to facilitate support to Ukraine in an efficient and transparent manner, while avoiding duplicative efforts.[65]

According to State, senior U.S., European Commission and Ukrainian government officials co-chair the MDCP Steering Committee in coordination with the G7 Presidency. The MDCP and its Steering Committee are supported by a technical secretariat, which provides administrative assistance and coordination across the platform.

EU economic assistance is the largest source of economic aid to Ukraine. Prior to the announcement of the EU Ukraine Facility, EU institutions had provided $92.8 billion in financial support.[66] The new aid package will bring total EU commitments to more than $150 billion.[67] Some EU member governments supplement their contributions via the European Union with additional, bilateral economic aid. EU member states provide the majority of European military assistance to Ukraine bilaterally.[68]

Table 2.

Detailed OAR and Ukraine Funding Data

Further details about the use of Ukraine Supplemental, EDI, and other State and USAID funding can be found in the appendixes:

Appendix E **DoD Funding**	• DoD Execution of the First through Fourth Ukraine Supplemental Funds • DoD Execution of European Deterrence Initiative (EDI) Funding
Appendix F **State and U.S.** **Agency for Global** **Media Funding**	• Ukraine Supplemental Appropriations Available to the Department of State • Application of State Ukraine Supplemental Assistance Funds • Administration of Foreign Affairs Funds • U.S. Agency for Global Media Supplemental Funding
Appendix G **USAID Funding**	• USAID Development Funding Related to Ukraine • USAID Humanitarian Assistance Funding Related to Ukraine

Figure 2.

Direct Budget Support to Ukraine Provided Through the World Bank Since February 2022

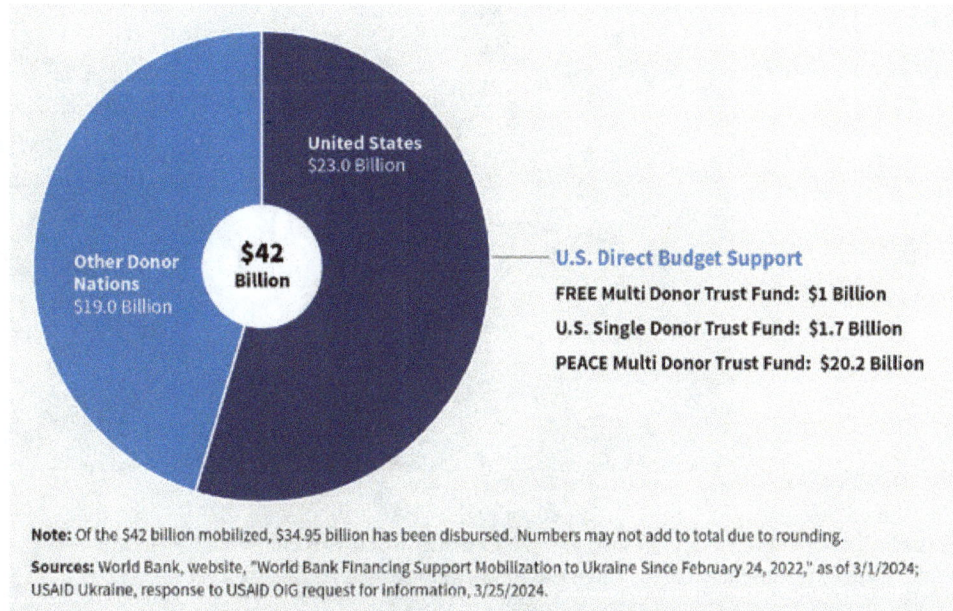

United States
$23.0 Billion

$42 Billion

Other Donor Nations
$19.0 Billion

U.S. Direct Budget Support

FREE Multi Donor Trust Fund: $1 Billion

U.S. Single Donor Trust Fund: $1.7 Billion

PEACE Multi Donor Trust Fund: $20.2 Billion

Note: Of the $42 billion mobilized, $34.95 billion has been disbursed. Numbers may not add to total due to rounding.

Sources: World Bank, website, "World Bank Financing Support Mobilization to Ukraine Since February 24, 2022," as of 3/1/2024; USAID Ukraine, response to USAID OIG request for information, 3/25/2024.

DIRECT BUDGET SUPPORT TO UKRAINE

Since the full-scale invasion began, USAID has provided direct budget support to the Ukrainian government through three World Bank-managed trust funds: the Ukraine Second Economic Recovery Multi-donor Trust Fund (MDTF), the Special Transfer to Ukraine Single Donor Trust Fund (SDTF), and the Public Expenditures for Administrative Capacity Endurance (PEACE) multi-donor trust fund.[69] (See Figure 2.) With the exception of the SDTF, USAID funds are co-mingled in these multi-donor trust funds with the funds of other donor nations. The comingling of funds can complicate efforts to monitor how the funds are used.[70]

According to USAID, the purpose of direct budget support is to provide the Ukrainian government with liquid funds to maintain continuity of operations.[71] The World Bank provides funding to the Ukrainian government on a reimbursement basis, following verification by the World Bank, based on approved expenditure categories.[72]

PEACE Fund Provided Financial Support to Millions of Beneficiaries

The purpose of the PEACE fund was to build resilience, protect essential institutions, and deliver critical services, according to the Ukrainian Ministry of Finance.[73] In addition to mitigating the humanitarian crisis and preserving development gains, the PEACE fund was intended to support the Ukrainian government in maintaining core government functions and protecting its institutional capacity for recovery after the war has ended.[74]

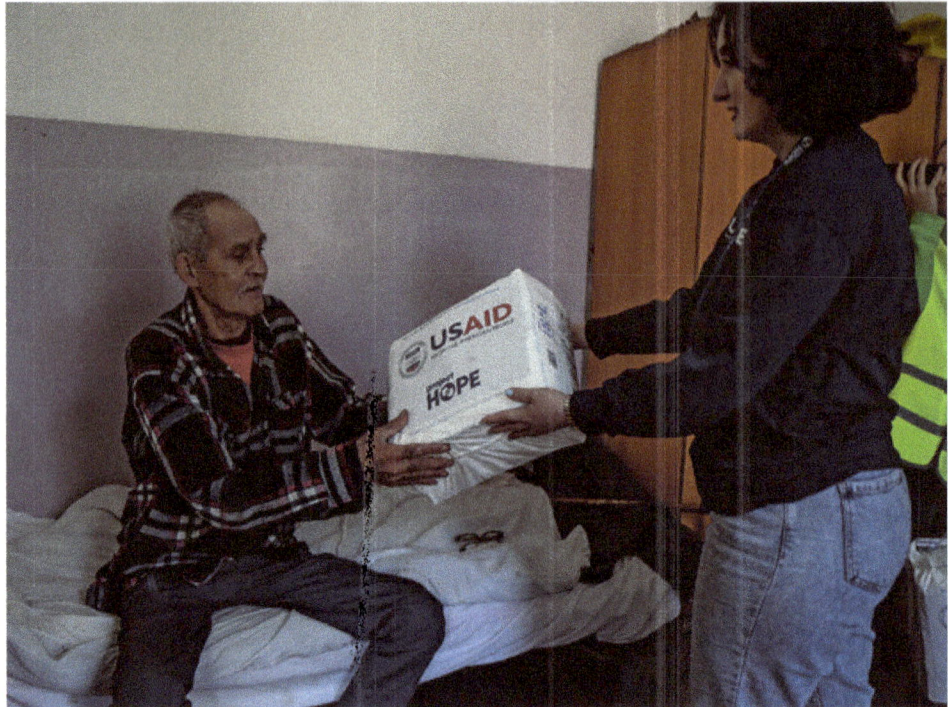

With the support of USAID, Project Hope delivers hygiene items to a hospice with elderly people in Klavdievo, Kyiv region. (USAID photo)

The United States was by far the largest donor to the PEACE fund, with USAID providing $20.3 billion out of $25.5 billion total.[75] USAID made its most recent obligation to the PEACE fund in September 2023, and these funds were subsequently disbursed to the Ukrainian government and expended, according to USAID.[76]

PEACE was designed to provide reimbursement for the salaries of approximately 162,000 Ukrainian government employees, the salaries of 512,000 education employees at the local level, and the total compensation of 60,000 civil protection officers of the State Emergency Management Service of Ukraine.[77] PEACE also provides additional funding for internally displaced persons (IDP). To provide sustained healthcare services to the Ukrainian population, PEACE included the total compensation of approximately 500,000 employees of medical service providers.[78] According to the Ukrainian Ministry of Finance, two-thirds of the civil service employees and more than 80 percent of education sector employees were women.[79] Government employees included those outside of the security/defense sector and education staff of state-owned and municipal education institutions.[80]

PEACE was also designed to provide reimbursement for social safety net payments for senior and other eligible citizens from the Pension Fund of Ukraine.[81] Direct budget support reimbursed transfers from the Ukrainian national budget to its pension fund to cover the budget deficit which ensued from the insufficiency of its own revenues to cover pension payments. These payments included old age pensions, pension supplements, and increases under pension programs, including supplements to minimum pensions, and length-of-service supplements.[82] It also covered pension supplements for people with disabilities, pensioners with dependent children, war veterans, families of troops killed in action, pensions and survivors of the Chernobyl disaster, as well as the cost of social insurance for employees of some mining and agricultural operations.[83] According to USAID, PEACE provided the Ukrainian government funds to cover payments to nearly 8 million pensioners, 1.4 million disability pensioners, and 500,000 survivorship pensioners.[84]

USAID said that it measures the impact of direct budget support by the Ukrainian government's ability to continue providing emergency services and social assistance to its citizens while also paying government salaries that keep schools, hospitals, and civil institutions operational.

In addition, PEACE provided the Ukrainian government funds to support four social assistance programs: the guaranteed minimum income for low-income families (340,000 recipients, 62 percent of whose beneficiaries were children; 73 percent of adult recipients were women), housing and utility subsidies for approximately 2 million households, and social assistance for persons with disabilities (more than 400,000 recipients), and financial assistance to approximately 1.5 million IDPs.[85] Housing and utility subsidies included cash to individuals to pay the cost of utility services, solid and liquid household oven fuel, and liquified gas.[86]

USAID noted that some categories of beneficiaries under PEACE were eligible for payments while residing outside of Ukraine.[87] For example, pensioners were entitled to receive their pensions regardless of their location.[88] Teachers, if legally employed, could potentially provide remote instruction and still be eligible to receive a salary.[89]

USAID said that it measures the impact of direct budget support by the Ukrainian government's ability to continue providing emergency services and social assistance to its citizens while also paying government salaries that keep schools, hospitals, and civil institutions operational. USAID said it also considered indirect benefits based on macroeconomic indicators that reasonably capture the indirect impacts of direct budget support on the fiscal stability of the Ukrainian government and the broader national economy, such as the impact of consumer spending by school employees on economic growth.[90]

Table 3.

Ukraine Government Expenses Covered Through PEACE, as of October 20, 2023, in $ Billions

Type of Support	Amount Covered
Pensions	10.68
School employee wages	3.54
Total compensation for medical service providers	2.09
Social assistance for low-income individuals and families; housing and utility subsidies; disabilities	1.70
Government employee wages	1.47
First responder wages	1.42
Payments for internally displaced persons	1.26
University staff wages	0.55
Family and child allowances	0.30
TOTAL	**23.02**

Note: Totals may not add up due to rounding.

Source: World Bank, "Project Paper on Sixth Additional Financing for Public Expenditures for PEACE in Ukraine.

Independent of these assessments, the Ukrainian Ministry of Finance measured the success of PEACE by assessing the extent to which the Ukrainian government continued to exercise its core functions: online filing of taxes, the payment of its guaranteed minimum income subsidy, issuing of birth certificates, and online requests for housing and utility subsidies.[91] The ministry also tracked the number of government employees outside the security and defense sector paid; the number of education staff paid; the number of schools that remained open through distance, blended, and/or in-person format; the share of pensions paid on time, social payments on time, the number of health service providers operational; and the share of the total compensation of civil protection officers paid on time.[92]

USAID OIG Identifies Challenges in Monitoring Direct Budget Support

USAID reported that it hired a contractor to provide technical assistance to the Ukrainian Ministry of Finance on ways to improve and strengthen its processes and internal controls for paying salaries and benefits supported by direct budget support payments.[93] The contractor conducts spot checks to gather insight into how the Ukrainian government uses funds in the areas supported by USAID's direct budget support contributions, to inform the technical assistance to the Ukrainian Ministry of Finance, according to USAID.[94] (See Table 4.)

A USAID OIG evaluation of the SDTF, published in February, found that while USAID ensured the Ukrainian government adhered to required controls, it did not verify the accuracy

Table 4.

Spot Checks of U.S.-Funded Direct Budget Support and Results

Types of Checks		
Macro	**Institutional**	**Individual**
Review of fund flows from the World Bank to designated Ukrainian banks and on to the Ukrainian government's Single Treasury Account.	Review of fund flows, focusing on payroll and other eligible expenditures, from the Single Treasury Account to agencies and eligible public institutions.	Review of salary payments to individual healthcare employees, teachers and school employees, government employees, and other individual recipients of funds.
Results: Although the majority of these spot checks identified no issues, the contractor did identify several cases where:		

- The percentage of the tax reported by a public institution exceeded the expected level based on the amount of accrued wages and the established tax rate.

- The salary expenditures were financed from the region's local budget but were not excluded from salary expenditures claimed for reimbursement from the World Bank.

- People serving in the military or salary expenditures of people serving in the military were included in the expenditure reports to the World Bank.

- An organization incorrectly included ineligible employees, such as those on unpaid leave, or excluded eligible employees.

- Clinics incorrectly reported the number of people by using a straight headcount calculation instead of a wage basis calculation.

Source: USAID Ukraine, response to USAID OIG request for information, 3/25/2024.

of salary expenditures.[95] For example, USAID ensured that the Ukrainian government submitted monthly healthcare worker salary expenditure reports and corresponding bank statements in accordance with the bilateral agreement.[96] However, the contractor found discrepancies in the reported data and could not easily trace the information the Ukrainian government used to calculate salary expenditures to source documents.[97] Without accurate data and verified expenditures for healthcare worker salaries, USAID relies on Ukrainian government systems to safeguard the integrity of funds provided through direct budget support to support Ukraine's healthcare services during the war.[98]

Despite these identified data quality concerns, USAID did not take additional action to confirm whether the reports were accurate and supported by valid documentation.[99] This occurred because neither the bilateral agreement between USAID and the Ukrainian government nor USAID policies governing direct budget support required that USAID take corrective steps when oversight measures it put in place identified data quality issues.[100]

Additional oversight of U.S. direct budget support is ongoing. USAID has employed another contractor to conduct a full audit of U.S. direct budget support to the Ukrainian government.[101] GAO has an ongoing audit of USAID's oversight of direct budget support to PEACE, and USAID OIG also has a planned audit of USAID's direct budget support to PEACE which was announced in April.

During the quarter, there were approximately 80,000 U.S. Service members in the USEUCOM area of responsibility, of whom approximately 80 percent were permanently stationed there and 20 percent were there on deployments.

PERSONNEL

During the quarter, there were approximately 80,000 U.S. Service members in the USEUCOM area of responsibility, of whom approximately 80 percent were permanently stationed there and 20 percent were there on deployments.[102]

State Raised Staffing Cap at the U.S. Embassy in Kyiv

In response to Russia's 2022 invasion of Ukraine, the U.S. Government initially evacuated the U.S. Embassy in Kyiv. Embassy personnel began returning in May 2022 but with a rigid cap that limited the number of personnel in country due to ongoing security concerns. This staffing cap presented the embassy with a significant challenge to conducting implementation monitoring, evaluation, and oversight of assistance programs, and given the security situation, the cap required constant triage of oversight priorities.[103] The embassy raised the overnight staffing cap several times beginning in May 2022, most recently by 26 percent in January 2024.[104]

State reported that the raised staffing cap allowed the embassy to use temporary duty personnel to supplement vital embassy functions, including for the Health Unit, Regional Security Office, and telecommunications and information management functions.[105] State said that such temporary duty staff fluctuated between 15 percent and 40 percent of all U.S. direct hire personnel during the quarter.[106]

The Office of Defense Cooperation-Kyiv (ODC-Kyiv) reported that the defense attaché's office was often unable to maintain full coverage of its standard portfolios and could only provide limited administrative and logistics support for DoD activities. Approximately

Table 5.

USAID Staff at the U.S. Embassy in Kyiv During the Quarter

	Present	Authorized
Office of Transition Initiatives		
U.S. Direct Hire	27	47
U.S. Personal Services Contractors	7	17
Foreign Service Nationals	85	125
TOTAL	**119**	**189**
Bureau for Humanitarian Assistance–Disaster Assistance Response Team		
U.S. Direct Hire	2	0
U.S. Personal Services Contractors	10	0
Foreign Service Nationals	4	0
Institutional Support Contractors	2	0
TOTAL	**18**	**0**

Source: USAID Ukraine, response to USAID OIG request for information, 3/25/2024; USAID Ukraine, response to USAID OIG request for information, 3/25/2024.

two-thirds of the ODC-Kyiv's U.S. personnel operate from third-country locations, limiting the ODC-Kyiv's ability to interface effectively with their Ukrainian counterparts to review emergent security assistance priorities, perform end-use monitoring (EUM), and coordinate the administrative requirements for UAF personnel conducting U.S.-sponsored training and education. The personnel cap also limits the DoD's ability to meet the UAF's demand for additional high-level advisory support.[107]

As of the end of the quarter, USAID staffing at the U.S. Embassy in Kyiv remained unchanged from the previous quarter. (See Table 5.)

State Loosens Movement Restrictions, but Limitations Remain

Movement restrictions within Ukraine have meant that many projects and activities, particularly those close to front-line areas, received limited direct oversight. Embassy safety guidelines required that all movements outside of Kyiv city be approved by State leadership in Washington, D.C.[108] On January 11, 2024, the embassy, in consultation with State's Bureau of Diplomatic Security, adopted an expanded movement zone within which embassy leadership could approve movements outside but near Kyiv without Washington clearance.[109] No security incidents impacting U.S. personnel occurred during the quarter, State said.[110]

The embassy's motor pool supports all official movements, including transportation to meetings, events, and site and oversight visits. The motor pool also supports high-level visitor transportation and home-to-office transportation, among others. In addition, some sections have self-drive or agency-provided vehicles for some movements. All movements by car must be completed in fully armored vehicles.[111] Embassy staff may walk, cycle, use scooters, or use the underground Metro within the Green Zone, which includes parts of Kyiv city, according to State.[112]

Official travel outside Kyiv city requires coordination with and support from protective services contractors, who provide travel advance survey functions and personal protective services during the planned movement.

According to State, the motor pool supported 1,245 movement requests during the quarter. The majority of these movements occurred within the city of Kyiv in support of daily shuttles, high-level visitors, meetings and events for staff with interlocutors, Deputy Chief of Mission movements, and backup support for the Ambassador's motorcade. In addition, the motor pool also supported movements managed by the Worldwide Protective Services Program, including for the Ambassador's travel to Lviv, Dnipro, and Kryvyy Rih in February, and a U.S. congressional delegation's visit to Lviv that same month.[113]

State noted that despite the expanded movement policy, limitations still exist that can create planning and scheduling challenges. Official travel outside of Kyiv requires logistical preparation and the use of limited available resources. Travel outside Kyiv also requires coordination with and support from protective services contractors, who provide advance survey functions and personal protective services during the planned movement as well as the availability of armored vehicles. State noted that both vehicle and contractor staff may be redirected to support other priority travel or visits.[114]

State also said that waiting for Washington to approve clearances can create challenges. For example, a travel request to Cherkasy, approximately 125 miles southeast of Kyiv, was approved in Washington "in the pre-dawn hours on the day of travel," requiring the travelers to coordinate transportation with the protective services contractor that same day.[115] In addition, State said that the lack of confirmation of planned travel impacts interlocutors, and that canceled trips "translate into broken commitments with implementing partners, Ukrainian government contacts, multi-lateral contacts, and embassy support personnel."[116]

Finally, State said that embassy personnel have been less inclined to submit travel requests, operating under the assumption that travel to certain locations will be denied in Washington, regardless of local need for travel. While not quantifiable, the requirement to seek headquarters clearance on travel beyond the expanded movement zone may also impinge on monitoring travel by preventing requests for in-person oversight visits.[117]

Similarly, the restrictions on USAID staff travel throughout Ukraine continued to constrain USAID's ability to conduct traditional oversight and monitoring techniques.[118] However, USAID U.S. direct-hire staff were able to travel with USAID foreign service nationals (locally employed staff) on five site visit trips during the quarter, including a visit to Zahaltsi village in Kyiv oblast. They conducted a monitoring visit of the Ukraine National Identify Through Youth activity, which is intended to improve innovation, entrepreneurship, and career preparedness skills by youth to expand economic opportunities.[119] USAID uses third-party monitors for oversight of humanitarian assistance and its Energy Security Program in Ukraine. USAID said that it did not receive any third-party monitoring reports during the quarter.[120]

OVERSIGHT OF OAR AND THE UKRAINE RESPONSE

The DoD, State, and USAID OIGs have long-established field offices and personnel in Europe that have initiated audits, evaluations, and investigations of activities related to OAR and the U.S. response to Russia's full-scale invasion of Ukraine. This preexisting footprint in Europe means that the OIGs have deep familiarity with U.S. Government programs and activities in Europe, including pertinent past oversight work on assistance to Ukraine, and established connections with program personnel.

The DoD OIG has more than 200 staff members working full-time or part-time on Ukraine assistance oversight, with 30 of these personnel in Europe, including 2 in Kyiv as of the end of this quarter with plans to increase to 4 in the next quarter. Several staff members based in the United States have made trips to Europe to conduct oversight of security assistance to Ukraine. In January 2024, the DoD, USAID, and Acting State IGs made their second trip to Ukraine since the full-scale invasion, meeting with U.S. and Ukrainian counterparts and viewing examples of U.S. humanitarian and security assistance. State OIG has more than 100 staff members working on Ukraine oversight, with 11 of these personnel in Germany and 5 in Kyiv. USAID OIG has dozens of personnel working at least part time on Ukraine oversight, with 12 in Germany, and 6 in Kyiv as of the end of this quarter.

Additionally, most of the OAR security assistance effort takes place outside of Ukraine in countries such as Germany and Poland, through which equipment is transported and Ukrainian troops receive training. OIG personnel are permitted uninhibited access to U.S. Government operations in these countries.

Since June 2022, oversight organizations from across the U.S. Government have coordinated their activities through the Ukraine Oversight Interagency Working Group. The working group follows a proven interagency oversight model—the Lead Inspector General framework—that the U.S. oversight community employs for overseas contingency operations in Afghanistan, Iraq and Syria, and other locations across the globe. While not all of the agencies that are on the working group were actively conducting oversight related to Ukraine assistance as of the publication of this report, each has equities related to the broader U.S. Government response effort. The Working Group ensures open lines of communication and situational awareness across department and agency boundaries.

Table 6.

Details on Oversight Activity

Further details about completed, ongoing, and planned work by the DoD OIG, State OIG, USAID OIG, and partner agencies can be found in the appendixes:

Appendix H	Completed Oversight Projects
Appendix I	Ongoing Oversight Projects
Appendix J	Planned Oversight Projects
Appendix K	Investigations and Hotline Activity

New Website Integrates Oversight from Across the U.S. Government

In March, the Special IG for OAR launched UkraineOversight.gov as a new website to enhance transparency with regard to the robust whole-of-government effort to oversee U.S. security, economic, and humanitarian assistance to Ukraine. The website was created to bring together oversight work and reporting from the OIGs for the DoD, State, and USAID, the GAO, and the other members of the Ukraine Oversight Interagency Working Group, serving as a convenient, single resource for Congress and the public.

UkraineOversight.gov categorizes work into three Strategic Oversight Areas: Security Assistance and Coordination, Non-security Assistance and Coordination, and Management and Operations. The website also has links to confidential hotlines for the DoD OIG, State OIG, USAID OIG, and the GAO, where whistleblowers can report allegations of waste, fraud, abuse, and mismanagement related to U.S. assistance to Ukraine.

The website will be maintained and updated regularly with the latest information on independent oversight of the U.S. Government's Ukraine response and fulfills a requirement in Section 1250B of the National Defense Authorization Act for Fiscal Year 2024, which requires the Special IG for OAR to publish its unclassified reports to Congress on a publicly available website.

The Special IG for OAR's new website, UkraineOversight.gov.

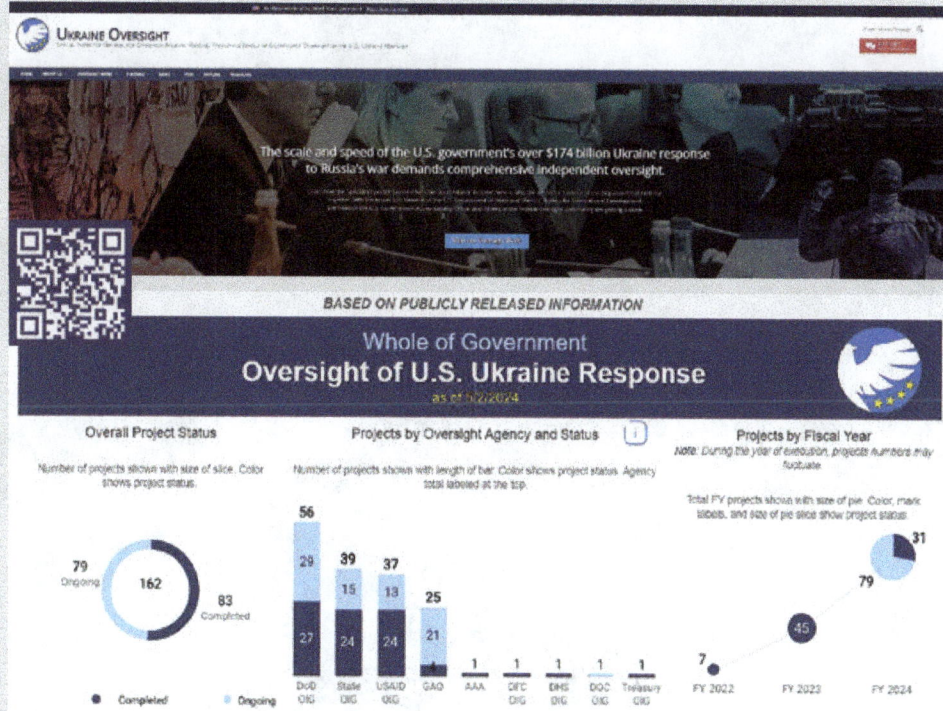

U.S. Army and NATO soldiers maintain a defensive position during a NATO training event at Bemowo Piskie Training Area, Poland. (U.S. Army photo)

SECURITY ASSISTANCE

SECURITY ASSISTANCE

The United States provides security assistance to Ukraine and other European nations under Operation Atlantic Resolve (OAR) and, in some cases, programs funded and managed by State.

The full scope of the OAR mission and related mission goals is classified. OAR began as a U.S. European Command (USEUCOM) effort to provide rotational deployments of combat-credible forces to Europe in the wake of Russia's 2014 invasion of Crimea.[121] Since Russia's full-scale invasion of Ukraine in February 2022, the OAR mission has evolved in line with U.S. policy objectives. The most recent mission statement is outlined in a classified Execute Order dated August 31, 2023.[122] USEUCOM reported that OAR has strategic objectives with associated desired effects.[123] (See Table 7.)

STATUS OF THE WAR

BATTLEFIELD TRENDS

In March, William Burns, Director of the Central Intelligence Agency (CIA), assessed that the Russian government was not serious about negotiating any sort of compromise with Ukraine. He said that Russian President Vladimir Putin believes that time is on his side, and that he

Table 7.

U.S. Goals Related to Security

OAR Strategic Objectives
Support NATO and assure NATO allies in Eastern Europe of U.S. commitment to collective security.
• U.S. efforts to support NATO-led activities in Eastern Europe.
• NATO allies in Eastern Europe are assured of U.S. commitments to collective defense.
Develop combined defensive and offensive capabilities of the U.S. and Eastern European NATO allies.
• U.S. and Eastern allies demonstrate interoperable military capabilities.
Russia is deterred from aggression against Eastern European NATO members.
• Russia perceives NATO as a credible alliance committed to the security, territorial integrity, and sovereignty of its members.
• Russia perceives U.S. commitment to the NATO alliance and its mission to defend the security, territorial integrity, and sovereignty of its members.
• Russia is dissuaded from taking offensive (overt or covert) actions against NATO member states.

Integrated Country Strategy
Ukraine leverages existing partnerships and establishes new ones to ensure continued supplies of military and security assistance and provision of training for new military capabilities.
Ukraine has the tools to protect civilians and critical infrastructure, including the energy grid, heating, cyber networks, media environment and information space.

Source: USEUCOM, response to DoD OIG request for information, 24.2 OAR 007, 4/3/2024; State, "Integrated Country Strategy-Ukraine," 8/29/2023.

can wear down the Ukrainian Armed Forces (UAF) and its international supporters with a protracted campaign. Director Burns added that for serious peace negotiations to take place, Russian leadership would need to be convinced to discontinue the war by understanding that the long-term negative consequences of a drawn-out war are not in their best interest.[124]

Director Burns assessed that—provided continued supplemental assistance—the UAF could maintain its front lines into early 2025 and continue to exact costs against Russia, including penetrating strikes deep into Crimea and against Russia's Black Sea Fleet, which has lost 15 ships in a span of 6 months.[125] According to media reporting, Ukraine has destroyed roughly one third of the Black Sea Fleet, including its former flagship, the Moskva.[126] Director Burns estimated that by the start of 2025, the UAF could put itself in a position to regain the offensive and negotiate from a position of greater strength. However, he said that without additional supplemental assistance, Ukraine's outlook would be considerably less optimistic, and the UAF would likely lose significant ground in 2024.[127]

U.S. Marines use a tactical resupply UAV to conduct a resupply during Exercise Nordic Response 24 in Alta, Norway. (U.S. Marine Corps photo)

Director Burns assessed that Russian military forces have suffered more than 315,000 dead and wounded soldiers as of March 2024—four times the casualties that the Soviet Union experienced in a decade of war in Afghanistan—and the destruction of approximately two-thirds of its pre-war tank inventory. Additionally, long-term economic consequences are increasing Russia's economic dependence on the People's Republic of China, while NATO has increased in both size and strength since the full-scale invasion began, with the accession of Finland and Sweden as well as most member states increasing their military spending.[128]

Ukrainian Forces Retreat from Avdiivka

On February 18, Russian forces declared that they had taken full control of the Ukrainian town of Avdiivka, following several months of heavy fighting. (See map on page 28.) According to media reporting, the capture of Avdiivka represents the largest territorial gain for Russian forces in Ukraine since taking Bakhmut in May 2023.[129] The White House attributed the UAF's withdrawal to "dwindling supplies" and ammunition rationing resulting from a lack of supplemental funding for military support to Ukraine.[130] Ukrainian soldiers who fought at Avdiivka told reporters that their limited supply of rockets and ammunition prevented them from countering the constant bombardment of artillery, aerial bombs, and explosive unmanned aerial vehicles (UAV) from the advancing Russian forces.[131]

The Ukrainian government said it had withdrawn its soldiers to avoid a Russian siege of Avdiivka. The UAF normally tries to rotate soldiers out of front-line positions after several days or weeks of direct combat to rest and resupply, but many of the Ukrainian troops at Avdiivka had been there for nearly a year.[132] The Defense Intelligence Agency (DIA) said that the capture of Avdiivka was the main objective of Russia's winter offensive, which began in October 2023.[133]

According to one analysis, the capture of Avdiivka is unlikely to provide a significant operational advantage to the Russian forces. Russian troops expended a considerable amount of manpower and materiel on their effort to capture Avdiivka and will likely need to engage in a prolonged period of consolidation before attempting a further concerted offensive effort in the area. However, the Ukrainian retreat provides Moscow with a tangible battlefield victory, which supports the Kremlin's messaging that Russia's forces are making progress in the war.[134]

In congressional testimony in March, Director of National Intelligence Avril Haines said that the UAF's retreat from Avdiivka and its struggle to stave off further territorial losses have shown the erosion of Ukraine's military capabilities, the result of declining availability of external military aid. Director Haines added that President Putin has reversed his long-standing reluctance to increase defense spending to support the war in Ukraine, and a surge in Russian ammunition production and purchases from North Korea and Iran threaten to compound the problems caused by Ukraine's ammunition shortage.[135]

UAF Strikes Russian Energy Infrastructure

During the quarter Ukrainian forces employed explosive UAVs to strike multiple Russian energy infrastructure targets connected to the war effort, some of which lay deep inside Russia.[136] (See Table 8.)

In late March, President Volodymyr Zelenskyy indicated Kyiv's efforts to strike Russian oil refineries were the only way to force Moscow into halting its attacks against Ukraine's critical infrastructure. With Ukraine experiencing growing difficulty in protecting its own infrastructure from Russian air attacks, Kyiv almost certainly views its efforts of targeting Russian oil as the best means of inflicting cost with its limited domestic capabilities, according to the DIA.[137]

According to media reporting, the capture of Avdiivka represents the largest territorial gain for Russian forces in Ukraine since taking Bakhmut in May 2023.

Table 8.

UAF Strikes on Russian Energy Facilities

Target	Date	Outcome
Ust-Luga Condensate Refinery	Jan 21	Disrupted condensate refining for 2 weeks.
Tuapse Refinery	Jan 25	Disrupted refinery operations.
Volgograd Refinery	Feb 3	Damaged one primary processing unit.
Belgorod 750-kV Substation	Feb 6	Damage to substation.
Ilsky Refinery	Feb 9	Temporary disruption to main processing unit.
Nizhny Novgorod Refinery	Mar 11	Damaged one primary processing unit.
Ryazan Refinery	Mar 13	Damaged two primary processing units.
Slavyansk Refinery	Mar 16	Damaged one primary processing unit.
Syzran Refinery	Mar 16	Damaged one primary processing unit.
Kuibyshev Refinery	Mar 23	Disrupted refinery operations.
Novocherkassk Power Plant	Mar 24	Disrupted two power units.

Source: DIA, response to DoD OIG request for information, 24.2 OAR SUPP002, 4/16/2024.

Since the beginning of 2024, Ukrainian strikes have disrupted about 14 percent of Russia's oil refining capacity, according to the DIA. As of mid-March, domestic gasoline and diesel prices increased by 20 to 30 percent in Russia. To mitigate the impact of these strikes, Russia banned gasoline exports for 6 months starting in March, began importing refined product from Belarus, planned to import from Kazakhstan, and prioritized shipments of petroleum products by Russian Railways, as opposed to other means of transportation. The strikes have resulted in a negligible disruption of electricity to the Russian military and civilian population. Russia has a robust generation capacity—the third largest in the world— and a high degree of redundancy in its grid, according to the DIA.[138]

Russia has responded to repeated Ukrainian attacks on its oil and gas infrastructure by conducting large-scale bombardment of Ukraine's energy production and transmission networks, according to the DIA. In March and April, Russia launched hundreds of missiles and one-way attack UAVs, striking electric grid infrastructure, such as substations and energy production facilities, including the Dnipro Hydroelectric Power Plant.[139]

Russia depends on its oil exports and energy industry, which make up approximately 30 percent of the country's budget revenues and are crucial for the funding of the war in Ukraine, according to media reporting.[140] The Office of the Undersecretary of Defense for Policy (OUSD(P)) said that it is the policy of the United States not to encourage or enable attacks inside Russia, and the DoD remains focused on finding ways to provide Ukraine with the equipment and training to retake its sovereign territory.[141]

UKRAINE CONFLICT TRENDS

During the quarter, the front lines of the conflict remained mostly unchanged and attacks continued at similar pace—what some analysts have called "positional warfare." Apart from the Ukrainian retreat from Avdiivka, neither side reported any significant gains. According to data compiled by the Armed Conflict Location and Event Data Project (ACLED), air and UAV strikes constitute an increasingly larger portion of attacks in Ukraine, while shelling and missile attacks have decreased.

Attacks by Quarter and Type, February 24, 2022–March 31, 2024

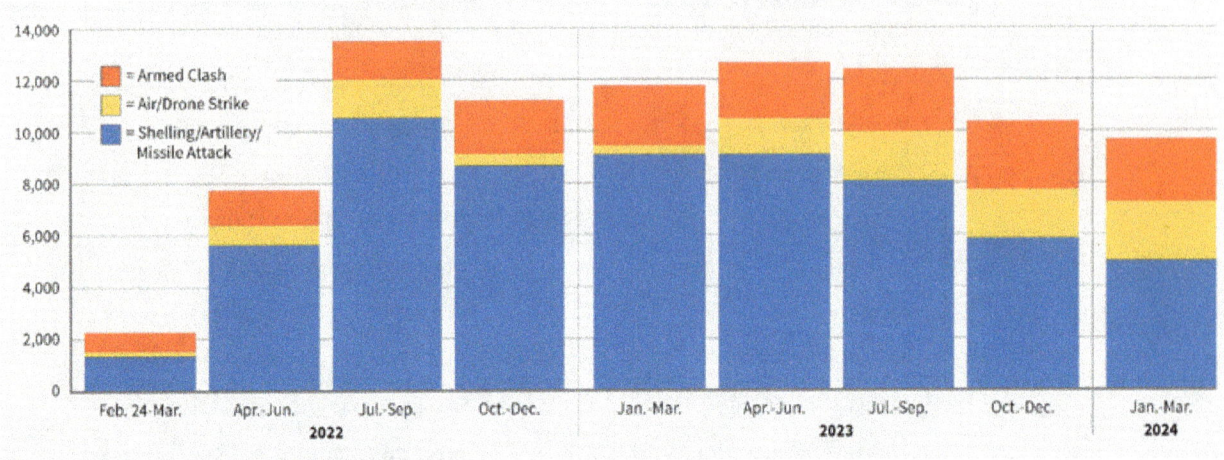

Locations of Attacks during the Quarter, January 1–March 31, 2024

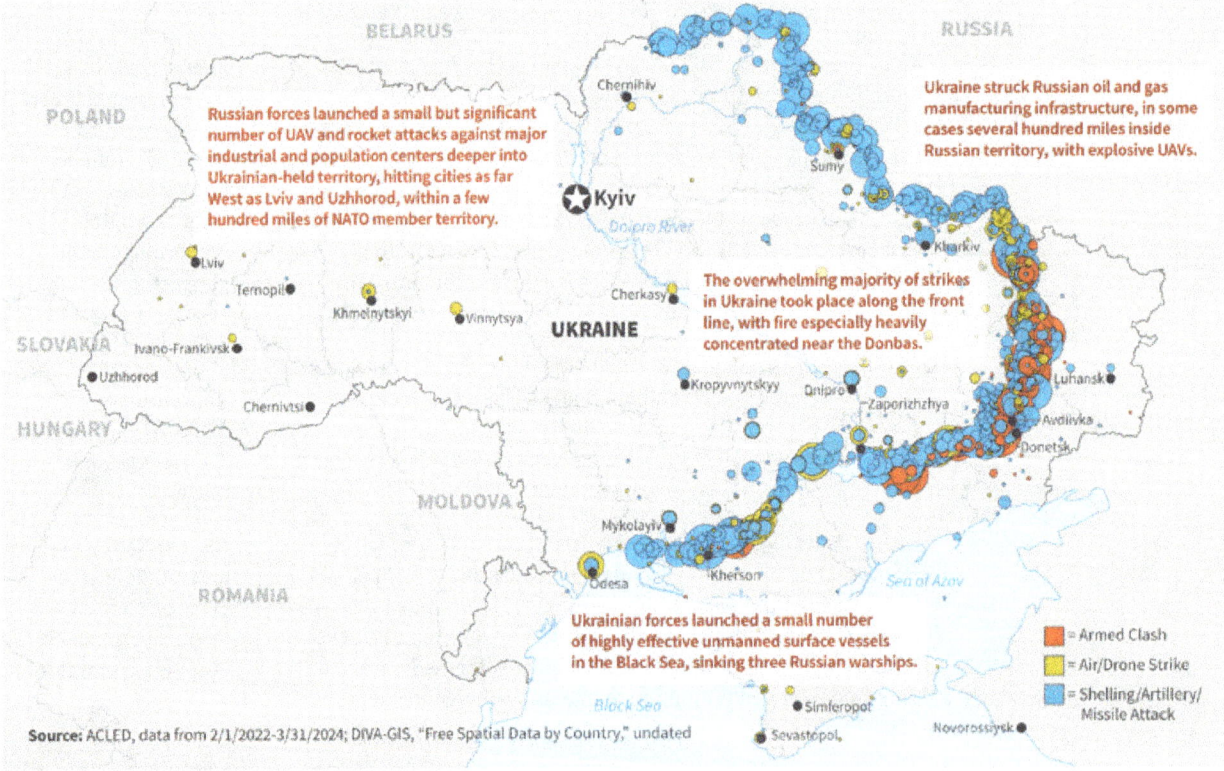

Russian forces launched a small but significant number of UAV and rocket attacks against major industrial and population centers deeper into Ukrainian-held territory, hitting cities as far West as Lviv and Uzhhorod, within a few hundred miles of NATO member territory.

Ukraine struck Russian oil and gas manufacturing infrastructure, in some cases several hundred miles inside Russian territory, with explosive UAVs.

The overwhelming majority of strikes in Ukraine took place along the front line, with fire especially heavily concentrated near the Donbas.

Ukrainian forces launched a small number of highly effective unmanned surface vessels in the Black Sea, sinking three Russian warships.

= Armed Clash
= Air/Drone Strike
= Shelling/Artillery/Missile Attack

Source: ACLED, data from 2/1/2022-3/31/2024; DIVA-GIS, "Free Spatial Data by Country," undated

UAF Employs Unmanned Surface Vessels to Strike at Russian Fleet

Ukraine has increasingly employed unmanned surface vessels packed with explosives to wage asymmetric naval warfare. This tactic has limited the effectiveness of Russia's Black Sea Fleet and made it possible for Ukraine to maintain a shipping corridor along a key sea lane for grain exports. According to media reporting, Ukraine currently has no large naval ships and deliberately scuttled its own flagship at the beginning of Russia's full-scale invasion to prevent the possibility of it being captured by Russian forces.[142]

The UAF employed unmanned surface vessels to sink at least three major Russian warships this quarter. On February 1, the UAF announced that it sank the Russian guided missile ship, Ivanovets. On February 14, the UAF announced that it had destroyed the Russian landing warship, Tsezar Kunikov. Ukrainian military intelligence reported that the Tsezar Kunikov was likely fully loaded when it sank, having just spent approximately 10 days at a loading site used by the Russian military. On March 5, the UAF claimed a successful attack on the Russian patrol ship Sergey Kotov. The UAF released video footage of the three operations, all of which took place off the coast of occupied Crimea and involved swarms of unmanned surface vessels striking the enemy vessel at the waterline and exploding on impact.[143] According to media reporting, UAF operations have destroyed or disabled 24 Russian warships and 1 submarine, amounting to roughly one-third of Moscow's Black Sea Fleet, since the start of the full-scale invasion.[144]

These Ukrainian strikes against the Black Sea Fleet have changed Russian naval operating patterns, according to the DIA. The Black Sea Fleet has begun avoiding the Ukrainian coast and moving some ships away from its main base in occupied Sevastopol, Crimea. The Russian Navy is also facing obstacles conducting its core operations in the northwestern part of the Black Sea. The Black Sea Fleet has attempted to improve its defenses against UAF strikes, increasing defenses at its bases and reducing the time its ships spend at sea, according to the DIA. It has also moved some ships from Sevastopol to Novorossiysk on Russia's Black Sea coast.[145] (See map on page 28.)

President Zelenskyy Dismisses Top General Amid Dispute over Strategy

On February 8, President Zelenskyy announced the dismissal of Ukraine's top military commander, General Valeriy Zaluzhnyy. This announcement, which raised strong public controversy among the Ukrainian public, followed increased tensions between the two leaders after the failure of Ukraine's 2023 counteroffensive to meaningfully move the front line of the war. Zelenskyy had previously rebuffed comments by Zaluzhnyy describing the state of the war as a stalemate. Zelenskyy also disagreed with Zaluzhnyy's calls for a mass mobilization of up to half a million draftees.[146]

Despite such strategic setbacks, Zaluzhnyy enjoyed overwhelming popularity and trust from the Ukrainian public, while polling indicated declining public trust in Zelenskyy's presidency.[147] Media reports have cited Zelenskyy's concerns with Zaluzhnyy's increasing public and political support as reasons for Zaluzhnyy's dismissal, even as Zelenskyy retained the trust of the majority of the Ukrainian public.[148] Following the dismissal, Zelenskyy appointed Zaluzhnyy to be Ukraine's ambassador to the United Kingdom.[149]

In a February 8 opinion piece written before his dismissal but published after it, Zaluzhnyy expressed restrained optimism that Ukraine could be successful against Russia in 2024 but noted that this would require the adoption and mastery of new technologies, such as UAVs, and related training.[150] He wrote that Ukraine's inability or unwillingness to increase its military manpower through mass mobilization left it unable to compete with Russia's significant manpower advantage.[151]

Zaluzhnyy's dismissal came at a point when the UAF is facing a renewed Russian offensive while Ukrainian manpower and ammunition were running short. Zaluzhnyy was replaced by General Oleksandr Syrskyy, who served as the Commander of Ukrainian Land Forces since 2019. Upon taking command, General Syrskyy said he recognized that the challenges facing Ukraine in 2024 are different from those at the start of the war and that the UAF will need to change and adapt to the new realities on the ground.[152]

UKRAINIAN CAPABILITY

UAF Demonstrates Ingenuity but Lacks Some Operational Capabilities

Multiple factors impacted UAF capability during the quarter, the U.S. Army Europe and Africa (USAREUR-AF) reported, including the persistent application of Soviet doctrine; the impact of attrition on force quality and training levels; limited resources and capabilities; and the tactical and operational situation on the ground.[153]

Command and Control: Changing the mindset of a UAF still reliant on legacy Soviet-era warfighting doctrine is one of the key challenges for U.S. and NATO-nation trainers advising the UAF, USAREUR-AF said. For example, UAF corps headquarters have not historically structured their staff elements by warfighting function in a way that supports joint combat operations. USAREUR-AF said that UAF corps headquarters' have demonstrated limited proficiency in synchronizing operations above the brigade level.[154] Assessing the full impact of reliance on Soviet-era doctrine across 25 months of the war and a 700-mile front remains challenging. Observations from the early stages of the full-scale invasion in 2022 suggested that some UAF units and commanders had adopted a post-Soviet doctrine and more of a mission command philosophy, but attrition has reduced force quality over time.[155] DoD doctrine defines mission command as the conduct of military operations through decentralized execution based on orders, emphasizing trust, force of will, initiative, judgment, and creativity.[156]

Combined Arms Operations: The UAF relies heavily on artillery and long-range fires as a primary means of engaging the enemy rather than enabling maneuver and breaching actions. The few attempts UAF made to conduct breaching operations were not successful. The reliance on artillery has contributed to the UAF's persistent shortage of munitions and overuse of weapon systems, according to USAREUR-AF.[157] In addition, the lack of significant air power and engineering capabilities undermines the ability of the UAF to

> **Upon taking command, General Syrskyy said he recognized that the challenges facing Ukraine in 2024 are different from those at the start of the war and that the UAF will need to change and adapt to the new realities on the ground.**

maneuver against a prepared defense. Persistent Russian intelligence, surveillance, and reconnaissance of the battlefield and quantitative Russian advantages in artillery and other long-range fires capabilities also limit the UAF's ability to mass combat power.[158] According to USAREUR-AF, the absence of a significant UAF offensive in Summer 2023 afforded Russian forces the opportunity to continue emplacement of land mines and other defenses, which will increase the challenges faced by the UAF in any future offensives.[159]

Armor: The UAF has demonstrated increasing ability to employ and operate NATO-standard armored assets such as tanks and infantry fighting vehicles. The Security Assistance Group-Ukraine (SAG-U) reported that Western-provided equipment provides greater battlefield protection for UAF personnel.[160]

Air: New munitions deliveries slightly improved UAF air capability during the quarter, though a shortage of Western munitions remains a gap, SAG-U reported. UAF air capability can still be greatly improved by filling critical requirements through donations, funding, and expert advisors.[161]

Maritime: Overall, UAF maritime capability improved this quarter, due to donations of various types of maritime equipment as well as an expansion of various types of maritime related training, SAG-U reported.[162] However, the UAF continues to lack the numbers of equipment, needed to accomplish their 2024 Maritime Campaign Objectives. In particular, the UAF needs a continuous supply of anti-ship cruise missiles for its coastal defense brigades. It also requires various types of UAVs and unmanned underwater vehicles for mine counter measure operations to keep its sea lanes open.[163]

UAV: This quarter, the UAF has demonstrated superior proficiency and innovation in certain areas, such as employment of small commercial UAVs for reconnaissance and attack, and difficulty in others, like the effective employment of combined arms to breach enemy defenses and exploit a breakthrough. The UAF has demonstrated the ability to rapidly adapt commercial UAV technology at scale. Both sides are employing electronic warfare capabilities to counter the other's use of UAVs and defend their own. According to USAREUR-AF, the UAF has proven its ability to operate in this complex battlefield, employing technology to improve the survivability of its forces. The creation of mobile fire teams to counter Iranian-made one-way attack UAVs shows another innovation in the use of resources and capabilities to address tactical and operational challenges, according to USAREUR-AF.[164]

In addition, the UAF has experienced manpower challenges that limit its ability to rotate forces out to rest, refit, and train.[165] The average UAF soldier's age is now over 40.[166] Women are exempt from the draft, and Ukraine's martial law prohibits most men between the ages 18 and 60 from leaving Ukraine unless they are deemed unfit for military service for health reasons or some other exemption.[167] According to media reporting, this law could potentially provide about 50,000 new troops for the UAF, though President Zelenskyy did not publicly state how many conscripts the army would call up immediately. Lowering the conscription age has been controversial in Ukraine due to concerns that taking more young adults out of the civilian workforce could further challenge the country's already fragile economy.[168]

> This quarter, the UAF has demonstrated superior proficiency and innovation in certain areas, such as employment of small commercial UAVs for reconnaissance and attack, and difficulty in others, like the effective employment of combined arms to breach enemy defenses and exploit a breakthrough.

RUSSIAN CAPABILITY

Russian Military Aims to Grow and Modernize While Trench Warfare Continues

In March, Director of National Intelligence Avril Haines stated that President Putin likely believes Russian forces have the advantage of time and that developing a larger, better equipped military will deter Western powers from opposing his regional aims. Russia also continues to modernize and fortify its nuclear, space, and cyber capabilities. She said that Putin's strategic goals remain unchanged. He continues to see NATO enlargement and Western support to Ukraine as reinforcing his long-held belief that the United States and Europe seek to restrict and undermine Russian power.[169]

This quarter, Russia reorganized its domestic military structure, splitting its Western military district into the Moscow and Leningrad military districts. According to the DIA, Russia most likely did this in response to Sweden and Finland's NATO accession.[170]

In 2023, following the attempted rebellion by the Wagner Group, the Russian Defense Ministry established its Volunteer Corps.[171] The DIA assessed that this reorganization was probably done to centralize administrative and command control of all private military companies and volunteers fighting in Ukraine. In Ukraine, the Volunteer Corps probably assigns these private fighting units to Russian military combat units so that the Russian military commanders maintain tactical and operational control of volunteer units, while the Volunteer Corps maintains administrative control, including contract terms and pay.[172]

As of February, some Wagner Group units were almost certainly subordinated under the National Guard of Russia, forming a volunteer unit distinct from the Defense Ministry's Volunteer Corps to reinforce Russia's war effort in Ukraine. The DIA said it was unclear whether former Wagner fighters who sign contracts with the National Guard will retain independent command structures or Wagner branding.[173]

Volunteer Corps units probably enable the Russian military to meet its manning requirements in Ukraine without unpopular mass mobilizations. Additionally, the use of these units enables Moscow to better protect its core units by holding them in reserve and deploying volunteer units for initial phases of offensive operations.[174] However, Russia probably has challenges fielding volunteer units capable of achieving tactical success without experiencing overwhelming personnel losses. Consolidation of volunteer units under the Defense Ministry's Volunteer Corps also directly links these units and their battlefield actions irrefutably to the Russian government, thus diminishing the credibility of Russia's denial of responsibility for war crimes and other atrocities committed by volunteers, according to the DIA.[175]

As of February, some Wagner Group units were almost certainly subordinated under the National Guard of Russia, forming a volunteer unit distinct from the Defense Ministry's Volunteer Corps to reinforce Russia's war effort in Ukraine.

Kremlin Disinformation Campaigns Target Both Western and Ukrainian Audiences

Russia has intensified its online efforts to increase opposition to military funding for Ukraine in the United States and Europe, according to media reporting. Russian disinformation campaigns have employed increasingly difficult to trace technologies to influence the debate over support for Ukraine ahead of the U.S. elections. These techniques are sometimes more subtle and skillful than the fake social media accounts that Russia's disinformation campaigns employed to influence the 2016 election, according to the media.[176]

While many voices opposed to additional aid are genuine, according to media reporting, Russian military intelligence aims to amplify these arguments for isolationism, actively supporting candidates who oppose aiding Ukraine or who call for pulling the United States back from NATO. Russian online proxies replicate and distort legitimate news sites in the United States, Israel, Germany, Japan, and other countries in order to undermine continued aid to Ukraine, media reported. While the parties involved may be subject to sanctions, much of the content they promote is protected as free speech.[177]

This quarter, Moscow continued its use of artificial intelligence technologies, including tools that generate believable fake text dialogue and video content, to complement Russia's information warfighting capability, according to the DIA. These tools can quickly and cheaply craft disinformation and propaganda content, generate unique text, images, and videos, and reach a wider audience for disinformation with the veneer of believability. Additionally, Russia increased its information operations efforts directed toward the West with rhetoric that agitates existing socio-political divisions, aggravates divisions between NATO member states, and argues against additional lethal aid to Ukraine.[178]

On March 20, the Department of the Treasury imposed sanctions on two Russian companies as well as on their founder and Chief Executive Officer. According to Treasury, these companies, acting on behalf of the Russian government, operate a network of more than 60 websites that impersonate genuine news organizations in Europe, then use fake social media accounts to amplify the misleading content as part of state-directed deception campaigns.[179]

Additionally, the Russian government continued to operate its more traditional international propaganda networks. Despite the EU's suspension of Kremlin outlets Sputnik and RT (formerly known as Russia Today) in March 2022, both channels remain easily accessible via web and streaming platforms 2 years later, according to a report by Radio Free Europe/Radio Liberty (RFE/RL).[180]

An RFE/RL forensic team, testing the effectiveness of Sputnik and RT's suspensions, successfully accessed the channels in 20 out of 27 EU countries through the use of virtual private networks. According to the RFE/RL report, both Sputnik and RT were available in the "European Quarter" of Brussels, Belgium, including inside the premises of both the European Council and European Commission. This suggests that the Kremlin—through its media and the false narratives that frequently appear on these channels— has the access necessary to influence EU decision-making bodies.[181]

Russia Maintains Ad Hoc Partnerships with PRC, Belarus, Iran, and North Korea

In March, Director of National Intelligence Haines informed Congress of an evolving relationship between the governments of Russia, the People's Republic of China (PRC), North Korea, and Iran. Increased collaboration and willingness to exchange aid in military, economic, political and intelligence matters enhances their individual capabilities. It also enables these governments to cooperate on actions aimed at undermining the rules-based international order and to resist external international pressure, Director Haines said. Parochial interests, desire to avoid entanglements, and wariness of each other's instability will likely limit their cooperation, absent direct conflict between one of these countries and the United States.[182]

Belarus continues to provide military and economic assistance to Russia, including the facilitation of Russia's forced deportations of children from occupied Ukraine, according to the DIA. As of March, Belarus was supporting Moscow's war effort with assistance from the Belarusian defense industry, such as repair services and production of electronics. Belarusian President Lukashenka stated that Belarus and Russia were jointly attempting to avoid Western sanctions, with Belarus becoming a gateway for sanctioned goods to enter Russia.[183]

China continued to maintain a discreet, flexible, and cautious approach to providing materiel assistance to Moscow.[184] In March, CIA Director Burns assessed that the PRC's leadership's ambitions with regard to Taiwan have been sobered by Russia's experience in Ukraine thus far, both in terms of the local population's tenacity and the considerable outpouring of support from the United States and others. In this regard, he said, U.S. support to Ukraine has improved the state of great power competition in the Pacific.[185]

This quarter, Iran continued to provide military UAVs to Russia for combat in Ukraine, and North Korea has transferred ammunition to Russia, sending at least one million rounds of 122mm and 152mm artillery ammunition. In late December, Russia began using North Korean-provided surface-to-surface missiles against targets in Ukraine, launching approximately 50 this quarter.[186] According to the DIA, Russia was able to offset its domestic ammunition shortages in part by importing artillery rounds and short-range ballistic missiles from North Korea.[187]

SUPPORT TO UKRAINIAN FORCES

The United States and its partners and allies coordinate security assistance to Ukraine through a variety of international mechanisms ranging from high-level Ukraine Defense Contact Group meetings to informal discussions between the SAG-U, the International Donor Coordination Center (IDCC), and representatives from donor nations. At SAG-U and the IDCC, staff evaluate Ukrainian requests for training and equipment, identify which partner nation can provide the assistance, and ensure that the assistance is delivered in a timely manner.[188]

The DoD established SAG-U in November 2022 to provide a long-term, focused organizational structure to coordinate and oversee the full-spectrum of U.S. security assistance to the UAF. SAG-U is a dedicated U.S. military joint service headquarters located in Wiesbaden, Germany, under the operational control of USAREUR-AF. It consists of approximately 500 joint and

> Belarus continues to provide military and economic assistance to Russia, including the facilitation of Russia's forced deportations of children from occupied Ukraine, according to the DIA.

multinational service members, including personnel from more than 22 nations.[189] SAG-U said that its three lines of effort are to train, advise and assist, and sustain the UAF.[190]

SAG-U reported that it continued to communicate daily with its Ukrainian counterparts in the remote advise and assist capacity. SAG-U described its current system of communication with the UAF as effective and reliable, though several challenges exist. These include a lack of in-person discussions, inability to work face-to-face with UAF counterparts to build trust and relationships to gain additional situational awareness, and difficulty with consistent information flow during periods of intense operations.[191] SAG-U predicted that it will continue to face challenges as it focuses efforts on urgent requests from the Ukrainian government toward defense of contested areas.[192]

The IDCC is the primary coordinating body for international military assistance to Ukraine.[193] Established in March 2022, the IDCC coordinates lethal and nonlethal security force assistance from 44 contributing nations to enable donor countries from around the world to provide military equipment, training, and aid to the UAF.[194] The IDCC is collocated with SAG-U in Germany.[195] In addition to its staff of military personnel from donor nations, the IDCC includes several UAF liaison officers, who communicate Ukrainian government requests for assistance.[196]

The IDCC is not a multinational command like those led by the United States in Iraq and Afghanistan. Led by a U.K. Brigadier General, the IDCC is a coordinating entity through which partner nations voluntarily share information and synchronize efforts toward common goals.[197] SAG-U staff refer to the IDCC as a "coalition of the willing," as the IDCC (and the U.S.-led SAG-U) do not exercise any sort of multinational command and control. The IDCC itself does not deliver assistance nor provide training but rather facilitates the bilateral provision of both from individual donor nations.[198]

Established in March 2022, the IDCC coordinates lethal and nonlethal security force assistance from 44 contributing nations to enable donor countries from around the world to provide military equipment, training, and aid to the UAF.

EQUIPPING

DoD Announced New Aid Amid Lack of Replenishment Funds

According to a media report, the DoD sent $10 billion worth of weapons to Ukraine through Presidential Drawdown Authority (PDA) that it did not have funds to replace at the time. The $10 billion deficit was due to a combination of factors, including inflation and the difference in the value of the equipment sent to Ukraine compared to the cost to replace it, such as when the Army replaces older munitions with newer versions that cost more.[199]

This quarter, the DoD OIG was working on an ongoing audit of the estimates used in valuing assets provided to Ukraine under PDA. The DoD still had $4.4 billion in PDA authority remaining to send aid to Ukraine as of the end of the quarter, but without funds to replenish these items, such transfers could risk weakening U.S. military readiness, and the DoD is unable to transfer funds from other accounts to replace items sent to Ukraine.[200]

On March 12, National Security Advisor Jake Sullivan announced the provision of a new $300 million security assistance package for Ukraine. The weapons, ammunition, and equipment will be drawn from existing U.S. military stocks under the DoD's remaining PDA authority. As the DoD has no remaining funds to replenish PDA stocks, this package will be supported by funds made available through cost-savings in contracts that the DoD negotiated to replace equipment previously sent to Ukraine under PDA. Sullivan said this limited, one-time saving would allow for the provision of a modest amount of new security assistance without impacting U.S. military readiness.[201]

This is the first PDA package for Ukraine since December 2023, when the DoD acknowledged it had exhausted its replenishment funds.[202] On February 20, National Security Advisor Sullivan said that the lack of new supplemental funding for Ukraine and shortages in ammunition and air defense systems will deplete Ukrainian defenses and enhance Russia's advantage as it continues to press into Ukrainian territory.[203]

This new security assistance package includes additional ammunition for HIMARS, 155 millimeter artillery rounds, including high-explosive and cluster munitions, 105 millimeter artillery rounds, anti-armor systems, small arms ammunition, spare parts, maintenance, and other ancillary equipment. This comes at a time when Russian forces are increasing their attacks in the east and in other parts of Ukraine. The DoD Press Secretary, Major General Pat Ryder, described this assistance as necessary but limited, estimating that it would enable the UAF to continue the fight for a matter of weeks. He said that it will be impossible to support Ukraine's battlefield needs without additional supplemental appropriations.[204] Ukrainian military personnel have told reporters that they began rationing their artillery shells this year due to limited supply.[205]

Polish tank crews operate U.S. M1A2 Abrams tanks at Fortress Range, Nowa Deba Training Area, Poland. (Polish Armed Forces photo)

End-Use Monitoring

Federal law requires End-Use Monitoring (EUM) of certain transfers of defense equipment and services to foreign entities to ensure that the items are being used in accordance with the terms and conditions of the transfer agreement and applicable federal law.[206] The DoD, through the Golden Sentry program, conducts EUM of items that were transferred via FMS or other U.S. Government security cooperation programs on a government-to-government basis. State, through the Blue Lantern program, conducts EUM of articles and services exported through direct commercial sales that may be funded by means including FMF.[207]

The U.S. and Ukrainian governments signed an updated EUM concept of operations in November 2023, and process improvements are underway with the Ministry of Defense and General Staff of the UAF to streamline data management and business rules for Ukrainian self-reporting on the status of U.S.-provided defense articles, according to the Office of Defense Cooperation-Kyiv (ODC-Kyiv). These developments clarify defense article disposition status and data input requirements to expedite UAF self-reported inventories into the database by the ODC-Kyiv.[208]

Certain defense items are subject to Enhanced EUM (EEUM) if they incorporate sensitive technology; are particularly vulnerable to diversion or other misuse; or whose diversion or other misuse could have significant consequences for U.S. national security. Of the 19 types of designated defense articles that required EEUM, 8 had been provided to Ukraine as of the end of the quarter.[209] (See Table 9.)

The ODC-Kyiv said that its main challenges for conducting EUM during the quarter were the embassy personnel cap and movement restrictions.[210] Force protection and logistical constraints due to wartime conditions have limited the DoD's ability to conduct in-person EUM/EEUM site visits at locations far outside of Kyiv or Lviv. Most EEUM-designated articles are forward-deployed to front-line units outside of approved travel zones.[211]

The Defense Security Cooperation Agency (DSCA), which administers the Golden Sentry program, has modified standard EEUM requirements to account for the non-permissive conflict environments. In Ukraine, U.S. representatives may accept reports from Ukrainian forces about the status of defense articles in lieu of direct observation by U.S. personnel.[212] Ukrainian forces self-report their EEUM inventories on a quarterly basis to complement the ODC-Kyiv's on-site inspection regime.[213]

Based on information provided by the ODC-Kyiv, at the end of the quarter, 88 percent of defense articles were compliant and 12 percent were "delinquent" or unaccounted for. This would represent a 13 percent increase in the compliance rate compared to the previous quarter.[214] The DoD OIG continues to conduct an ongoing series of evaluations regarding compliance with the

Table 9.

U.S.-origin Defense Articles Provided to Ukraine Subject to EEUM

- **Communication Security (COMSEC) Equipment**
- **Javelin Missiles**
- **Stinger Missiles**
- **Stinger Gripstocks**
- **Advanced Medium-Range Air-to-Air Missiles (AMRAAM)**
- **Air Intercept Missiles-9X (AIM-9X)**
- **Switchblade Unmanned Aerial Systems**
- **Night Vision Devices (NVDs)**

Source: ODC-Kyiv, response to DoD OIG request for information, 24.2 OAR 048, 3/26/2024.

(continued on next page)

End-Use Monitoring *(continued from previous page)*

requirements for tracking EEUM in Ukraine.

The ODC-Kyiv reported that it leverages relationships within Ukraine's Ministry of Defense, General Staff, Logistics Command, and other subordinate units to monitor U.S.-provided material after its transfer to the Ukrainian government. These key relationships provide the ODC-Kyiv access to Ukrainian logistical records, which enhance the EEUM self-reporting system.[215] The DoD OIG has documented improvements in the EUM process and delinquency rates since February 2022.[216]

The DoD OIG and the Government Accountability Office (GAO), in reports released during the quarter, documented several ongoing weaknesses in the EUM program in Ukraine. (See Table 10.)

Additionally, State reported that under the Blue Lantern program, it worked closely with law enforcement partners to conduct EUM of priority items provided by State INL, including defense and dual-use items. According to State, INL has prioritized the inspection of weapons, UAVs, vehicles, and explosive ordnance disposal equipment, among other sensitive equipment. State INL has developed a risk-based approach to EUM to monitor the most critical equipment while accommodating for logistical challenges presented by a war-time environment.[217]

Table 10.

EUM Challenges in Ukraine

- The DoD has established new entities in Europe to deliver military assistance to Europe, but it has not fully documented the roles and responsibilities of these new entities.

- DoD guidance on PDA does not clearly define at what point in the delivery process defense articles are officially considered delivered: DoD officials sometimes record defense articles as delivered while they are in transit, weeks before they arrive in Ukraine.

- The ODC-Kyiv does not always receive timely notification of EEUM defense articles delivered to third-country logistics nodes prior to transfer to Ukraine.

- The ODC-Kyiv and DSCA are sometimes unaware of third-party transfers of U.S.-origin defense articles (such as by a partner nation).

- Many articles are immediately deployed to the front lines where these articles are inaccessible for monitoring.

- DSCA has not consistently tracked allegations of EUM violations in Ukraine.

- State INL's rapidly growing inventory is also overwhelming its existing EUM database for EUM, slowing the process for adding information and tracking items.

Sources: GAO, "Ukraine: DOD Should Improve Data for Both Defense Article Delivery and End-Use Monitoring," GAO-24-106289, 3/2024; DoD OIG, "Evaluation of the DoD's Enhanced End-Use Monitoring of Defense Articles Provided to Ukraine," DODIG-2024-043, 1/10/2024; State, vetting comment, 5/10/2024.

USEUCOM Had Limited Oversight of Equipment Transported Via Rail in Europe

In February, the DoD OIG completed an evaluation of the DoD's implementation of security and accountability controls for the transportation of equipment bound for Ukraine, from European seaport to ground transportation. DoD policy establishes security requirements for equipment transportation based on equipment classes. For sensitive items, DoD policy requires the equipment to be protected by armed escorts at all times. For less sensitive items, tracking devices should be used while transporting equipment through Europe.[218]

This evaluation identified that USEUCOM personnel had limited oversight of the execution of transportation via German rail service, which could have negative operational impacts, such as incorrect planning for rail transport or delays in rail shipping. This was due to USEUCOM lacking an English translation of German rail service requirements, as the command relied on local national employees to manage those requirements.[219]

Introduction of F-16s to the UAF Planned for Summer 2024

In Europe and the United States, training of Ukrainian F-16 pilots continued this quarter.[220] The U.S. Air Force, with oversight by the OUSD(P), is responsible for the development and management of U.S.-provided F-16 pilot training, which was underway this quarter at an Air Force base in Arizona. The UAF pilots selected for this training were vetted prior to course entry and entered the course with significant prior aviation experience, according to the ODC-Kyiv. This course is the standard Air National Guard course that provides F-16 pilots with basic proficiency in air-to-air and air-to-surface operations. During the quarter, more than a dozen Ukrainian pilots were training on the F-16 in Denmark and the United States. These pilots will fly aircraft to be donated by Denmark in summer 2024 and other allied donations planned for later in 2024.[221]

Allied nations at Fetesti Air Base in southeast Romania continued preparations to train additional Ukrainian pilots on the F-16 in the coming months. According to media reporting, the jets had arrived, and flight instructors were ready to begin training. However, training of Ukrainian pilots had not yet started as of the end of this quarter.[222]

The ODC-Kyiv said that the duration of training will depend on student experience, English language skills, and progression through the training program. Pending available resources and Ukrainian demand, the U.S. Air Force plans to continue to support Ukraine's F-16 program and future training.[223] Dozens of Ukrainian personnel were preparing for or undergoing maintenance and support training in Europe and the United States this quarter. In addition to allied and partner nation training of Ukrainian personnel, Western defense contractors will ultimately need to accompany the jets into Ukraine and remain there until enough Ukrainian crews are trained, a process that could take years, according to media reporting.[224]

The need for these new aircraft remains high as Russian forces have increasingly employed more aggressive air support to gain ground in eastern Ukraine, using its warplanes to send guided bombs over long distances into the Ukrainian front lines. On March 1, President Zelenskyy said that the integration of F-16 fighters was necessary to help the Ukrainian forces defend against Russian guided bombs, aircraft, and missiles. However, U.S. National Security Advisor Jake Sullivan told reporters that there were not very many Ukrainian pilots able to fly these aircraft.[225]

The OUSD(P) said that the introduction of the F-16 aims to improve the effectiveness, survivability, and sustainability of the Ukrainian Air Force. The F-16s will also replace some of the aircraft lost or damaged in combat while strengthening the capabilities of the Ukrainian Air Force in the long term.[226]

SAG-U said that the UAF continues to operate its fleet of legacy aircraft, which will continue to play an important role in the defense of Ukraine and provide capabilities that are often more cost effective than ground combat, according to SAG-U. While new munitions deliveries slightly enhanced the UAF's capability this quarter, these were not necessarily the Western-produced munitions that would enable the greatest efficiency in Ukrainian air operations.[227]

OAR Has Had Minimal Impact on DoD Global Logistics

According to the U.S. Transportation Command (USTRANSCOM), the greatest logistical challenge associated with OAR this quarter was the instability of funding to purchase and ship aid to Ukraine.[228]

This quarter, USTRANSCOM support to OAR included strategic airlift and sealift for personnel and cargo. Tactical-level formations, enablers at all levels, aviation units, and command and control nodes were all deployed and redeployed as necessary in support of the operation. Items to be transferred to Ukraine were prepositioned to USEUCOM in advance of this quarter's PDA approval to shorten the delivery time. [229]

USTRANSCOM said that it maximized sealift and commercial airlift to minimize the impact on military air requirements. However, activation of Military Sealift Command vessels incurs the costs associated as well as depleting available capacity for any unexpected contingency requirements.[230]

USTRANSCOM said that this quarter's logistical support of OAR had minimal impact on other operations, and the limited amount of equipment moved was covered by USTRANSCOM's commercial partner capacity.[231]

At the same time, OAR is competing for specific military weapons and equipment that are required by U.S. military forces and partners in the Middle East and the Pacific, resulting in a lack of or delay in the requested support for OAR. Beyond lift capacity concerns, readiness to available forces is also reduced due to increased mission requirements, reduction of available training, and required down-time for maintenance, according to USTRANSCOM.[232]

Rail Bridge Closure Forces USEUCOM to Find Alternate Port

On February 25, a barge collided with and damaged a rail bridge crossing the Hunte River, which is the only rail line that services the German seaport used to transit materiel for Ukraine. Until that time, this was the only northern European sea port receiving all munitions destined for Ukraine. As of the end of the quarter, the timeline to repair the bridge was uncertain. Shortly following the event, another seaport in Poland was approved to receive shipments containing a net explosive weight of up to 3 million pounds. USEUCOM said that ultimately having two seaports capable of receiving munitions will be a long-term benefit when the Hunte River bridge is repaired, but the situation highlights the need to be proactive in securing multiple seaports for accepting large shipments of explosives to mitigate future issues.[233]

According to the U.S. Transportation Command, the greatest logistical challenge associated with OAR this quarter was the instability of funding to purchase and ship aid to Ukraine.

MAINTENANCE

The DoD has stressed the importance of training UAF maintenance crews on providing in-country support, according to the SAG-U. Currently, damaged Western equipment is evacuated to other countries, such as Poland, for major repairs and maintenance. Limited funding for spare parts and skilled technicians has been a key challenge for UAF armor maintenance.[234]

SAG-U reported that Ukraine is often able to overhaul and rebuild many of their weapon systems using parts produced domestically. However, the UAF has limited capability to conduct higher-level maintenance. In some cases, instructions for certain sensitive types of maintenance have not been approved for release to the UAF.[235]

The DoD Provided Ukraine Equipment Without Plans for Long-Term Sustainment

In February, the DoD OIG published two evaluations related to sustainment of major weapon systems provided to Ukraine. These evaluations found that the DoD had not developed or implemented a plan to sustain the Bradley, Stryker, and Abrams armored vehicles or the Phased Array Tracking Radar to Intercept on Target (PATRIOT) air defense systems provided to the UAF between January and September 2023. These reports concluded that without deliberate and planned sustainment support, including proper spare parts, ammunition, and maintenance support, the UAF would not be capable of maintaining these weapon systems in their ongoing fight against Russia's full-scale invasion.[236]

The evaluation of armored vehicles found that the DoD provided supply packages containing consumables and spare parts, as well as personnel and facilities to conduct field-level maintenance. However, DoD officials acknowledged that the existing efforts did not constitute a sustainment plan and had not yet identified how to provide spare parts, ammunition, and other necessary supplies beyond FY 2024. The evaluation also found that the DoD had not developed a plan to provide depot-level maintenance for these vehicles, either by training Ukrainian maintainers or by providing U.S. personnel and facilities to meet depot level maintenance requirements.[237]

Similarly, the evaluation of the PATRIOT system found that DoD officials provided basic operation and maintenance training courses for the UAF as well as initial parts and supplies. However, the DoD did not establish advanced training to address lifecycle maintenance tasks, a process to anticipate sustainment needs, a supply system for providing replacement parts, or facilities necessary to perform lifecycle sustainment activities. This was due in part to limitations of the PDA program's ability to meet requirements for ongoing sustainment.[238]

Both evaluations found that the DoD provided Ukraine with armored vehicles and air defense systems without a plan to ensure their long-term usefulness. This puts at risk Ukraine's ability to fight effectively using the U.S.-provided equipment, as well as the DoD's readiness to address other national security threats if needed. While the DoD is currently working on developing such plans, greater foresight should be employed in the future provision of such major weapon systems.[239]

Providing weapon systems to the UAF without a plan to ensure sustainment creates additional risks. Specifically, the UAF may not be able to independently sustain these systems in the future. Additionally, the DoD cannot accurately predict sustainment costs or assess long-term readiness impacts to other U.S. missions. These evaluations contained recommendations, which, if implemented, will enhance the DoD's readiness and its capability to provide more effective support to the UAF.[240]

In January, the DoD OIG released a management advisory on the Army's provision of remote maintenance and distribution of spare parts for the UAF. This provides interim results on the audit of the extent to which Army contracting personnel followed federal policies to award a contract for maintenance of equipment for Ukraine and effectively monitor contractor performance. So far, the DoD OIG's ongoing audit has found that Army contracting personnel adequately planned the task order and properly supported the award decision. Overall, the Army contracting personnel complied with the procedures designed to ensure the selection of the most qualified contractor to repair and return critical equipment to the UAF as they defend against Russia's full-scale invasion.[241]

UAF Uses 3D Printing to Generate Spare Parts

The UAF employs industrial-sized 3D printers provided by the U.S. Government at multiple engineering and maintenance activities across Ukraine, according to SAG-U. This capability allows the UAF to produce select spare parts for weapons and equipment and enhances UAF capabilities. At least three other partner nations plan to provide additional 3D printer capability throughout 2024 to increase the UAF's manufacturing capacity and flexibility.[242]

SAG-U said that, while the UAF tests 3D printed parts for safety, this technology has limitations with respect to the quality and durability when compared to parts from the manufacturer. UAF attempts to reverse engineer critical parts to 3D print may result in specifications not being fully up to standard, which could damage equipment and pose safety risks. SAG-U said that the DoD was working with industry to make technical data available to the Ukrainians to prevent the need for such reverse engineering.[243]

TRAINING

The DoD continued to support the UAF's ability to operate U.S.-provided weapons and equipment in accordance with U.S. training and doctrine, according to SAG-U. This includes training Ukrainian personnel to serve as instructors with the goal of enhancing the UAF's self-sufficiency, though U.S. advisors continue to assist the UAF in its daily operations.[244]

Battlefield demands and legacy training systems have challenged the UAF to allocate sufficient experienced capacity to train incoming forces, contributing to the UAF relying on foreign partners for basic, platform, and collective training before combat deployments, USAREUR-AF said.[245]

The types of training that the U.S. and international partners provide to the UAF have evolved over the course of the war. (See Figure 3.) The ODC-Kyiv reported that it works with SAG-U and U.S. Military Service component commands to facilitate and coordinate training requirements for the UAF based on feedback from Ukrainian training coordinators in the UAF General Staff and to reflect changes on the front lines.[246]

The UAF employs industrial-sized 3D printers provided by the U.S. Government at multiple engineering and maintenance activities across Ukraine, according to SAG-U

Figure 3.

Evolution of Training for Ukrainian Forces

FIRST YEAR

Focus on **platform-specific training**: training the UAF to operate U.S. and other Western equipment

SECOND YEAR

Focus shifted to **collective training** for newly generated combat units.

THIRD YEAR

More system **maintenance training** courses provided.

Training for the F-16, small boat operations, and Marine Corps company collective training are more prevalent.

Specialist training focuses on combat engineer, medic, explosive ordnance disposal, marksmanship, and chemical, biological, radiological, and nuclear, (CBRN) training.

Source: ODC-Kyiv, response to DoD OIG request for information, 24.2 OAR 059B, 3/26/2024.

Expanded Training Includes Command and Control, Maritime Skills

This quarter, international trainers remained at the training areas for multiple iterations to ensure continuity and coherence in the training. Specialized training for new weapons systems has decreased significantly over the last quarter due to the lack of new systems being introduced to the UAF.[247]

SAG-U reported that the UAF employed U.S.-provided weapons systems and equipment properly to achieve tactical objectives throughout the quarter. SAG-U attributed defensive setbacks not to how the weapons were used but to limited supplies.[248]

Command and Control: Recent training events have focused on Ukraine's ability to conduct effective command and control in coordination with international partners. The SAG-U supported the UAF's efforts to onboard and train personnel in employing commercial, off-the-shelf mobile IT equipment, such as tablets, smart boards, and televisions to perform functions such as planning, directing, coordinating, and controlling forces and operations in the accomplishment of the mission. This capability was trained, integrated, and employed during this quarter's training events overseen by United States and international partners, according to SAG-U, though limited funding for new equipment remained a constraint to growing this capability.[249]

UAV: The DoD and its allies and partners continued to provide proven, tested systems that Ukrainian operators and maintainers can integrate without requiring significant additional training. Training efforts have developed a cadre of Ukrainian personnel who are now able to serve as UAV instructors.[250]

Maritime: UAF Marines began NATO-level Marine Corps training at the Maarneward training facility in the Netherlands with plans for a U.K. Royal Marine training facility in Romania to open in July 2024. UAF maritime capability improved this quarter due to donations of equipment and an expansion of maritime training, according to SAG-U. Partner nations trained the UAF on operations, maintenance, and tactics for donated maritime equipment, including small and riverine boats.[251]

Reconstitution: In October 2023, USAREUR-AF planned to conduct reconstitution training for three Ukrainian brigades during the quarter in response to UAF requests made in consultation with SAG-U. Reconstitution refers to the effort to build a unit back to a desired level of operational readiness, particularly in terms of personnel and materiel, following battlefield losses. In January, USAREUR-AF conducted a 30-day reconstitution training program for a UAF brigade and its three subordinate battalion tactical groups. Reconstitution training for a second brigade was cancelled by the UAF due to operational demands on the battlefield. Reconstitution training for a third brigade is tentatively scheduled for Fall 2024.[252]

DoD Had Limited Ability to Ensure Ukrainian Trainees' Compliance on Human Rights

In January, the DoD OIG released a management advisory that highlighted limitations in the DoD's ability to demonstrate compliance with the Leahy Laws, which prohibit the United States from providing assistance, such as DoD training, to a unit of a foreign security force if credible information indicates that the unit committed a gross violation of human rights. Examples of gross violations of human rights include torture, extrajudicial killing, enforced disappearance, and rape.[253]

When reviewing data from August to December 2022, the DoD OIG found that the DoD's vetting process initially lacked the necessary data to ensure full compliance, which increased the risk that foreign troops may have been or may be allowed to attend DoD training who were legally prohibited from doing so. For example, officials in the ODC-Kyiv and SAG-U were unable to verify which UAF units had been vetted and authorized to send personnel to specific training events. The ODC-Kyiv and SAG-U were also unable to fully verify whether UAF personnel arriving at the Grafenwoehr Training Area in Germany belonged to a Leahy-vetted unit.[254] The ODC-Kyiv took corrective measures by immediately changing how it documented units that received Leahy vetting and were approved to send personnel to training.[255]

International Partners Aim to Build Long-Term UAF Capabilities

The Secretary of Defense-led Ukraine Defense Contact Group (UDCG), which includes ministers and chiefs of defense from more than 50 countries, meets regularly to identify how the international community can best assist the Ukrainian forces in defending their territory.[256] The DoD established "capability coalitions," under the UDCG construct, through which partner nations aim to help the UAF address its long-term warfighting requirements, while SAG-U and the IDCC address their immediate needs.[257]

According to USEUCOM, the UDCG operates capability coalitions focused on providing long-term development in air defense, air force, armor and maneuver, artillery, and maritime capabilities. Additionally, other nations have independently established coalitions on demining, information technology, and UAVs. Each coalition is led by one or two nations with expertise in that area along with Ukrainian partners. Each coalition is also tasked with addressing issues related to the defense industrial base, production issues, and backfill. Unlike SAG-U and the IDCC, which focus on current combat operations, the capability coalitions aim to address mid- to long-term, big picture goals. USEUCOM said that the UAF's demands exceed available international support, so donor nations must figure out how best to allocate the resources at their disposal.[258]

The UDCG is distinct from the IDCC in that it is a ministerial level group that consists of chiefs of defense for all nations working to support Ukraine. The UDCG meets monthly, either in-person or virtually, to discuss overarching efforts and pledge contributions, including funds, equipment, training, and other support to Ukraine. The IDCC, by contrast, is the working group that operates on a day-to-day basis to receive UAF requests and attempt to match them with available donor resources. According to SAG-U, donor nations are not required to operate through the IDCC, and the IDCC does not report to the UDCG. UDCG is the top tier of leadership, Capability Coalition Leadership Groups are the second tier, and each Capability Coalition Steering Group constitutes a third tier, with working groups operating below them. Neither the IDCC nor SAG-U is included in this hierarchy, according to SAG-U.[259]

Figure 4.

Countries Training the UAF by Type

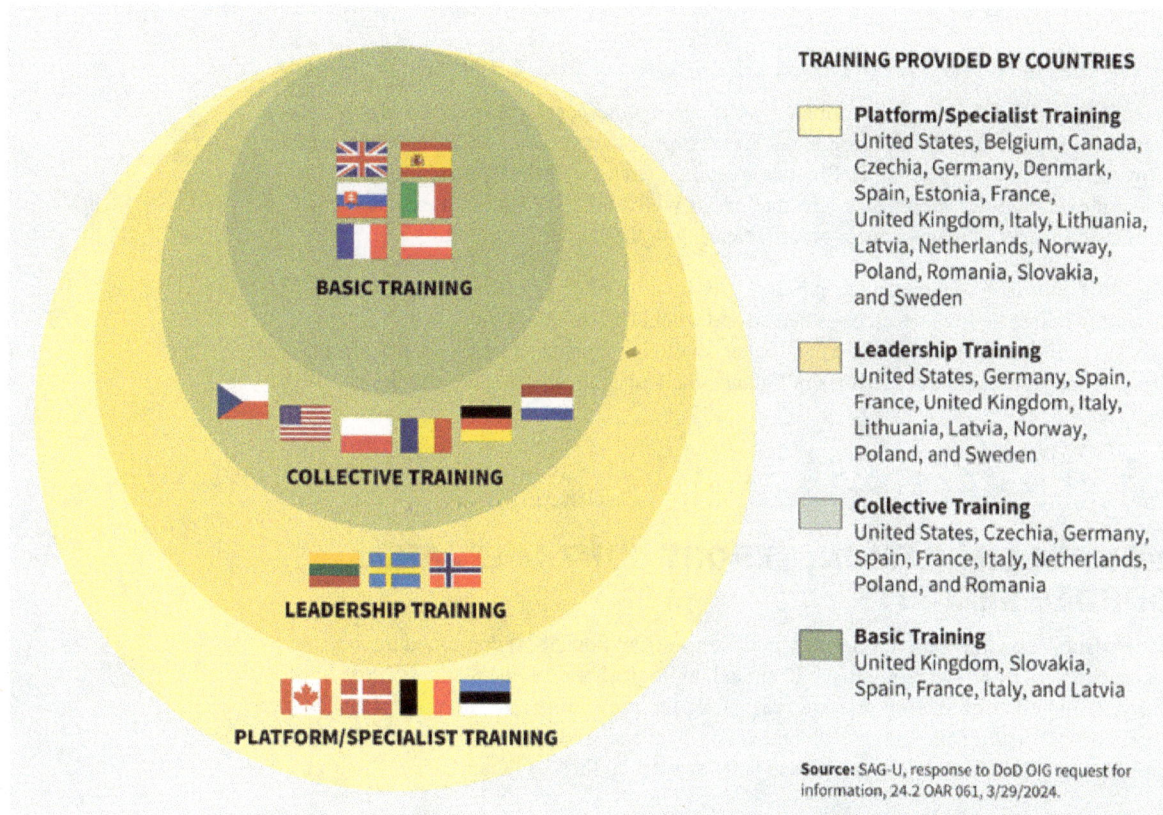

TRAINING PROVIDED BY COUNTRIES

Platform/Specialist Training
United States, Belgium, Canada, Czechia, Germany, Denmark, Spain, Estonia, France, United Kingdom, Italy, Lithuania, Latvia, Netherlands, Norway, Poland, Romania, Slovakia, and Sweden

Leadership Training
United States, Germany, Spain, France, United Kingdom, Italy, Lithuania, Latvia, Norway, Poland, and Sweden

Collective Training
United States, Czechia, Germany, Spain, France, Italy, Netherlands, Poland, and Romania

Basic Training
United Kingdom, Slovakia, Spain, France, Italy, and Latvia

BASIC TRAINING

COLLECTIVE TRAINING

LEADERSHIP TRAINING

PLATFORM/SPECIALIST TRAINING

Source: SAG-U, response to DoD OIG request for information, 24.2 OAR 061, 3/29/2024.

SAG-U reported that it was unable to provide detailed information on international support for UAF training, as the DoD does not exercise command over the IDCC nor any other donor nation. All information on allied and partner nation contributions is reported voluntarily to SAG-U.[260] Many donor nations do not share information on the totality of their contributions, which makes it difficult or impossible to calculate total numbers for international training support. However, SAG-U estimates that approximately 17 percent of UAF troops trained outside of Ukraine were trained by the U.S. military, while the rest have been trained by the partner nations and allies.[261] This quarter, approximately 20 nations trained UAF troops within their respective borders.[262] (See Figure 4.)

Since 2022, IDCC partner nations have completed training for more than 123,000 UAF troops in approximately 1,800 courses. As of the end of the quarter, there were roughly 7,200 UAF troops engaged in 142 ongoing training courses. These courses covered a wide range of warfighting capabilities, including artillery, maneuver, air defense, maritime, maintenance, medical, and leadership.[263]

Most of this collective training was at the company level and took place in eight countries: Czechia, Germany, Spain, France, Italy, the Netherlands, Poland, and Romania, with battalion-level training conducted in Germany and Poland. The United States trained one corps headquarters staff in late December 2023. The DoD also provided individual and collective training to one air assault brigade headquarters with three battalions.[264]

U.S. Training Aims to Build Ukrainian Maintenance Capacity

According to the ODC-Kyiv, Ukrainian institutions and defense personnel are highly capable of repairing and sustaining many Western-provided vehicles and weapons systems. However, one limitation is the fact higher level maintenance manuals often contain original manufacturer proprietary information for which the U.S. Government must obtain permission from the manufacturer before releasing to the Ukrainians.[265]

The DoD aims to fill maintenance gaps in UAF capability through tele-maintenance, providing real-time maintenance assistance and troubleshooting. SAG-U said it leverages existing USEUCOM capabilities when higher-level maintenance is required, performing depot-level maintenance at facilities in Poland when possible and transporting items to other facilities when necessary.[266]

OTHER SECURITY ASSISTANCE

NONPROLIFERATION, EXPORT CONTROLS, AND BORDER SECURITY

State's Bureau of International Security and Nonproliferation (ISN) continued to provide assistance under two strategic pillars: chemical, biological, radiological, and nuclear (CBRN) and nonproliferation scientific response; and preventing arms diversions and border security.[267] Overall, State ISN has obligated $69.5 million and expended $31.4 million appropriated in the Ukraine supplemental acts for work in these pillars.[268] (See Table 11.)

> Since 2022, IDCC partner nations have completed training for more than 123,000 UAF troops in approximately 1,800 courses.

Table 11.

State ISN Programs Related to Ukraine, as of March 2024

Pillar	Activity
Chemical, Biological, Radiological, and Nuclear Scientific Response Obligated: $38.6 million	• Trained 24 participants from several Ukrainian government agencies on best practices for chemical-related infrastructure protection and security vulnerability assessments. • Completed a gap analysis for the Ministry of Health's Rapid Response team to support future chemical sampling and forensic analysis cooperation and training. • Trained Ukrainian government IT personnel on CBRN infrastructure and cybersecurity threat prevention, detection, and response. • Engaged dual-use scientists through fellowships, microgrants, or training to aid their research, search for new employment, and reduce exploitation risks by proliferator states
Border Security Obligated $30.9 million	• Made the first large-scale deliveries of micro-cameras to improve the State Border Guard Service's operational capabilities on Ukraine's Russian and Belarusian borders. • Continued its training for the Customs Service on basic enforcement for newly established customs teams. • Conducted end-use monitoring efforts in Kyiv, as well as in Chernivtsi, Khmelnytskyy, Lviv, and Lutsk.

Source: State, response to State OIG request for information, 3/24/2024.

State noted that ISN provides direct assistance to Ukraine, generally in the form of training and equipping Ukrainian government units. State said ISN has obligated approximately $69.5 million to address CBRN concerns and to counter conventional weapons diversions.[269] The programs generally involve training and providing equipment to a wide variety of Ukrainian government organizations, including the Ministry of Defense and National Security Defense Council, Ministry of Health and National Health Service of Ukraine, State Border Guard Service, State Emergency Service, State Customs Service, State Emergency Service, State Special Communications Service, Security Service of Ukraine, and Department of State Protection of Ukraine.[270]

In January, State's Bureau of International Narcotics and Law Enforcement Affairs (INL) Air Wing sent aviation experts to assess the current capability and capacity of the Ukrainian State Border Guard Service 24th Separate Aviation Squadron, located near Lviv. State INL found Border Guard counterparts to be extremely capable, rating them as one of the best aviation programs they have evaluated globally. They also found that the Border Guard's fleet is sufficient for its mission, and maybe under-utilized for the mission.[271]

Also in January, State INL sponsored drone training for the Border Guard and other Ukrainian law enforcement agencies. State INL stated that drones are critical for law enforcement and border guard surveillance and monitoring.[272] State INL also supported a hostage negotiation class for police in Lviv.[273]

In March, State provided 62 dugout shelters to the Border Guard to replace infrastructure destroyed by Russian artillery. State INL stated these shelters are essential to forward deploying guards to protect Ukraine's border. State INL said it traveled to Cherkasy twice in March to confirm the full delivery of all elements of the shelters, including beds, lights, solar panels, and ventilation systems.[274]

In addition, State INL stated it traveled to Stare in Kyiv oblast to evaluate the National Guard's International Interagency training center's potential for consolidating training support for all the various Ministry of Internal Affairs agencies. State INL also traveled to Rivne in Western Ukraine to evaluate the patrol police training capability, and to Sokyrychi, also in Western Ukraine, to evaluate a potential new training site for the patrol and community police.[275]

DEMINING

The Russian military has made extensive use of land mines in Ukraine, especially in areas formerly occupied by Russian forces. According to media reporting, approximately 30 percent of Ukraine's territory—an area larger than Florida—may be covered with minefields, which would make Ukraine the most heavily mined country in the world. These mines range from anti-tank and anti-vehicle mines to anti-personnel mines and booby traps. Land mines have proven a significant obstacle for the UAF and slowed the pace of counter-offensive operations. They have also proven deadly for Ukrainian civilians. Land mines and other explosive remnants of war will present a serious challenge to post-war reconstruction. An anti-land mine NGO assessment attributed 677 civilian fatalities in Ukraine to mines and booby traps as of July 2023.[276]

Several U.S. Government agencies support demining efforts in Ukraine. State said it had obligated approximately $153 million and expended approximately $76 million in Ukraine supplemental funds to implement demining programs in Ukraine as of the end of this quarter.[277] State obligated an additional $9.9 million and expended an additional $7.3 million in supplemental funding this quarter.[278] Of the $9.9 million in newly obligated funds, $8.4 million extended an existing demining program, State reported.[279] The remaining $1.5 million supported a new grant with a demining NGO.[280]

State's Bureau of Political-Military Affairs' Office of Weapons Removal and Abatement (PM/WRA) is responsible for implementing State's humanitarian demining assistance in coordination with the political-military unit of the U.S. Embassy in Kyiv.[281] State PM/WRA implements these programs through a U.S.-based contractor to provide training and equipment to Ukrainian government demining operators and deploy survey, clearance, and explosive ordnance risk education teams. State PM/WRA implements these programs through grants to a range of international nongovernmental organizations, State said.[282] These NGOs deploy survey, clearance, and explosive ordnance risk education teams to strengthen the Ukrainian government's demining capacity. The current completion dates for active awards are between April 2024 and March 2027, with several projects ending in late 2024.[283]

During the quarter, State PM/WRA's contractors and awardees provided training and equipment for Ukrainian government demining operators; operated a training facility in western Ukraine; conducted manual and mechanical clearance operations; conducted

According to media reporting, approximately 30 percent of Ukraine's territory—an area larger than Florida—may be covered with minefields, which would make Ukraine the most heavily mined country in the world.

non-technical survey to identify hazardous areas; provided in-person and digital explosive ordnance risk education; and provided technical guidance and advisory support to key Ukrainian government stakeholders responsible for overseeing demining efforts, State said.[284]

State PM/WRA's new grant with the Geneva International Center for Humanitarian Demining follows a recently expired award with the same organization. Its purpose is to enhance Ukraine's national mine action capacity through increasing operational efficiency and coordination, which advances State's goal of improving civilian security and facilitating Ukraine's economic recovery. The grant's purpose is to assist Ukrainian government demining stakeholders in Kyiv and Chernihiv by strengthening long-term demining capacities; develop and implement effective frameworks, systems, tools, and processes to improve coordination and operational efficiency; and provide training and technical assistance for refining operational methods and processes.[285]

State INL said it continues to equip and train the Ukrainian National Police (NPU) Explosive Ordnance Disposal (EOD) Department to improve their professional capabilities to safely protect the public. The NPU's EOD Department has been actively engaged in demining activities across Ukraine. Much of their work focuses on demining liberated areas littered with Russian explosive ordnance that endangers Ukraine's law enforcement and civilians.[286]

INL said it provided EOD emergency assistance which has consisted of vehicles, UAVs, metal detectors, anti-mine boots, blasting machines, X-ray machines, hook-and-line kits, uniforms, personal protective equipment, field gear, and medical supplies worth more than $7.5 million to support demining activities throughout Ukraine.[287]

According to State, demining activities in Ukraine produced a variety of incremental results during the quarter, amid ongoing efforts and project timeframes.[288] U.S.-funded demining programs returned land to productive use in areas of Ukraine liberated from Russia's forces, improving civilian security and setting the stage for economic recovery and the return of displaced persons.[289] Non-technical surveys improved the Ukrainian government's knowledge of explosive hazard contamination, helping it to prioritize areas with the highest contamination. Explosive ordnance risk education activities resulted in safer civilian behavior around explosive hazards, mitigating the risk of accidents. Training and equipment for Ukrainian government demining operators increased the safety and efficiency of their operations and advanced the Ukrainian government's plans of scaling up its demining response, State reported.[290]

State said its demining efforts have returned approximately 2,320 acres of land to productive use, 1,980 acres previously recorded as suspected contaminated areas, and 320 acres through actual clearance and technical survey. Additionally, State-funded non-technical surveys in liberated areas found no evidence of contamination in approximately 252,000 acres, allowing the Government of Ukraine to better prioritize its demining resources.[291] The Ukrainian government claimed that 4.4 million acres were returned to productive use in 2023.[292]

State aims to ensure that grant funding is used only for approved program purposes through oversight practices, such as monthly and quarterly reports.[293] U.S. embassy staff directly met with implementer staff in Kyiv and, when possible, conducted site visits. State was not able to conduct any field visits to directly observe implementation during the quarter.[294]

State INL said it continues to equip and train the Ukrainian National Police (NPU) Explosive Ordnance Disposal (EOD) Department to improve their professional capabilities to safely protect the public.

While USAID in Ukraine does not work directly on demining, it participates in quarterly U.S. Government interagency calls on demining facilitated by State PM/WRA.[295] This quarter, USAID distributed informational leaflets created by a State PM/WRA implementer to farmers in formerly occupied and front-line communities who also received seed donations facilitated by USAID.[296] State PM/WRA also informs farmers that receive demining assistance about USAID programs and where to look for assistance opportunities.[297]

During the quarter, USEUCOM's Humanitarian Mine Action program provided explosive ordinance device training for 23 Ministry of Interior personnel. It was the first of five planned training programs for the State Emergency Services of Ukraine and the National Police of Ukraine.[298]

REGIONAL DETERRENCE

Sweden Joins the NATO Alliance

On March 7, NATO approved Sweden's application to join the alliance, bringing the total number of NATO members to 32. Both Sweden and Finland, which joined NATO in April 2023, have historically pursued military neutrality in their foreign policies, aiming to balance relations between Russia and the West. However, Russia's full-scale invasion caused the two nations to change course, and they both applied for NATO membership in May 2022.[299]

As member nations, Sweden and Finland will both enjoy protection under Article 5 of the NATO treaty, which obliges all members to come to the aid of any ally whose territory comes under armed attack.[300]

The accession of a new nation to the alliance requires the consent of all existing NATO members, and Sweden's membership had been delayed due to objections by Türkiye and Hungary. The Turkish government expressed concern that Sweden was harboring and not taking enough action against Kurdish groups that the Turkish government regards as terrorists, and Hungary's populist President Viktor Orban, known for his pro-Kremlin sentiments, has been skeptical of support for Ukraine. However, after months of discussions, Türkiye ratified Sweden's admission in January, and Hungary did so in March.[301]

Both Sweden and Finland come into the alliance with modern militaries. Finland has already reached NATO's agreed-upon defense spending target of 2 percent of GDP, and Sweden has plans to do so by 2026. Finland's conscript military is large and highly trained, according to media reporting. The Finnish military has a reserve force of 900,000 personnel, and an estimated wartime force strength of 280,000 personnel. Sweden's military is smaller, with approximately 57,000 personnel. Sweden reinstated conscription at the start of 2018 after suspending it in 2010.[302]

On March 7, NATO approved Sweden's application to join the alliance, bringing the total number of NATO members to 32.

Steadfast Defender Exercise Aims to Demonstrate NATO's Capabilities in Northern Europe

USEUCOM reported that during the quarter, it conducted exercises, training, and influence activities as part of a persistent presence along NATO's eastern boundary. These activities, USEUCOM said, "bolstered regional force readiness, increased interoperability, and enhanced the bonds between ally and partner militaries."[303] USAREUR-AF leads land-based efforts using rotational units who come to Europe on 9-month deployments. [304]

This quarter, U.S. and NATO forces participated in the Steadfast Defender exercise, which began in January and is expected to run until May 2024. This exercise involves more than 90,000 troops from all 32 NATO allies, including new members Sweden and Finland. The first part of the exercise focused on reinforcing maritime security in the Atlantic Ocean and as far north as the Arctic, and the second part focused on moving troops across Europe, from the High North to Central and Eastern Europe to demonstrate NATO's ability to defend the territory of all its member states.[305]

The various components of Steadfast Defenders involved a total of more than 50 ships—including aircraft carriers, frigates, corvettes, and destroyers—and more than 80 different air platforms—including the F-35, F-18, F-15, Harrier jet, helicopters, and UAVs. A total of 1,100 combat vehicles, including tanks, infantry fighting vehicles, and armored personnel carriers participated in the ground phases of the exercise.[306]

From March 4 to 15, U.S. and allied forces participated in Trojan Footprint, a special operations exercise led by USEUCOM every 2 years since 2016. Part of the larger NATO global exercise, Steadfast Defender, Trojan Footprint included approximately 2,000 troops from Albania, Bulgaria, France, Georgia, Greece, Italy, Montenegro, North Macedonia, Portugal, Romania, Spain, the United Kingdom, and the United States. It is the largest special operations exercise in the European theater in which the United States participates.[307]

Art and yoga classes are held for IDP women and children at the Zaporizhzhia mental health center, Ukraine, implemented by Project HOPE and provided through the USAID Bureau for Humanitarian Assistance. (USAID photo)

DEVELOPMENT AND HUMANITARIAN ASSISTANCE

DEVELOPMENT AND HUMANITARIAN ASSISTANCE

In addition to security assistance, the U.S. Government provides development and humanitarian assistance to support Ukraine and its people. State's Integrated Country Strategy for Ukraine outlines mission objectives related to a variety of U.S.-funded activities in Ukraine.[308] USAID's Country Development Cooperation Strategy for Ukraine further identifies objectives and intermediate results related to U.S.-funded development activities in Ukraine.[309]

GOVERNANCE AND COUNTERING CORRUPTION

State and USAID operate several activities in Ukraine that seek to strengthen anti-corruption institutions, implement key criminal justice reforms, and increase transparency throughout the Ukrainian government. (See Table 12.) State's INL provides technical assistance to the National Anti-Corruption Bureau of Ukraine (NABU), Specialized Anti-Corruption Prosecutor's Office (SAPO), Office of the Prosecutor General (OPG), HighAnti-Corruption Court (HACC), and other Ukrainian institutions that investigate, prosecute, and adjudicate cases of high-level corruption.

USAID works with the National Agency for the Prevention of Corruption to improve policy frameworks to prevent corruption through legislative action; support watchdogs and investigative journalists; and improve the e-governance and digitization capacities of the Ukrainian government to prevent corruption.[310] USAID said that all of its activities in Ukraine include aspects to counter corruption.[311]

Table 12.

U.S. Goals Related to Counter-Corruption

Integrated Country Strategy
Ukraine implements sustainable reforms of its institutions, with a focus on anti-corruption laws, regulations, and enforcement; transparent financial and fiscal systems; and the justice sector.
Ukraine builds its capacity for regulatory oversight and holds accountable those responsible for committing malfeasance or misfeasance.
Country Development Cooperation Strategy
Increased health system transparency.
Economic impact of corruption reduced in likely sectors
Strengthened anti-corruption systems and practices

Source: State, "Integrated Country Strategy-Ukraine," 8/29/2023; USAID Ukraine, "Ukraine Country Development Cooperation Strategy 2019-2024, Extended Through Jan 9, 2026," 1/4/2024.

Ukrainian Anti-Corruption Progress Highlights Complexity of the Corruption Challenge

According to State, Ukraine's corruption and rule-of-law concerns are the country's greatest challenge for post-war economic recovery and attracting foreign investment.[312] In January, Transparency International released its 2023 annual global Corruption Perceptions Index, finding that Ukraine had climbed 40 positions in the global rankings since the 2014 revolution and is now ranked 104 out of 180 countries, compared with 144 out of 177 countries in 2014.[313] The rankings, coming amidst the latest in a series of corruption scandals, highlight the complexity of Ukraine's struggle with corruption and its efforts to demonstrate its commitment to tackling it, as it seeks continued U.S. and Western aid in the third year of war against Russia's full-scale invasion of Ukraine.[314]

Since 2014, Ukrainian authorities have undertaken anti-corruption reforms as part of Ukraine's desire to move closer to Europe.[315] The Ukrainian government touts its digitization of public services and online registers as a major step toward improving transparency and accountability in government activities.[316] President Volodymyr Zelenskyy won the presidency in 2019 promising greater reforms and a departure from the outside influence of oligarchs. Reforms have continued even in wartime, as a result of strong conditionality on assistance.[317]

While reforms continue, endemic corruption persists. Bribes, kickbacks, and inflated procurement costs are common risks for corruption within the Ministry of Defense, particularly for lethal procurements.[318] The ongoing war with Russia has created new opportunities for corruption, with several recent scandals within the defense sector revealing the misuse of wartime resources and weapons procurement funds.[319] These practices lead to the purchase of inferior equipment or the diversion of funds intended for food, ammunition, and other military needs.[320]

There are also significant corruption concerns more broadly with regard to the operations of the Rada (parliament) and in other sectors of the government. Some ministries have taken steps to counter corrupt practices and instill western standards of accountability while others have not. Low salaries contribute to corruption risks.[321]

Ukrainian Anti-Corruption Bodies Show Progress

State INL has operated a long-running rule of law program and dedicated more than $50 million since February 2022 to help Ukraine strengthen the capacity of anti-corruption institutions, including NABU and SAPO.[322] State INL highlighted ways during the quarter that NABU, in collaboration with other anti-corruption bodies, investigated a range of criminal actors, including several high-ranking officials in the government and judiciary accused of accepting bribes and embezzling worth more than $100 million, State said.[323] During a January 26 meeting with donor countries, NABU touted an 80 percent rise in prosecutions, while acknowledging ongoing challenges.[324] It also arrested two members of the Rada for attempting to bribe officials. In 2023—the latest period for which data is available—NABU launched 641 new investigations and indicted 100 individuals. NABU and SAPO secured guilty verdicts against 63 individuals in 2023, compared to 35 in 2022 and 27 in 2021.[325]

In December 2023, as a condition to open EU accession talks, the Ukrainian national parliament passed legislation authorizing NABU to hire 300 new detectives and granting SAPO operational independence from the Office of the Prosecutor General.[326] State INL said that during the quarter, it assessed and started the process for procuring general skill tests and a psychological evaluation for new hires to assist NABU in the selection process of new personnel. State INL also noted that as part of its interagency agreement with the Federal Bureau of Investigation (FBI), an International Corruption Special Agent arrived in Kyiv in March. The new agent would embed within NABU.[327]

On March 21, SAPO officially became a separate legal entity in the justice system of Ukraine, separating operationally from Ukraine's Office of the Prosecutor General (OPG). State INL said this reform allows SAPO to manage its own assets, premises, human resources office, accounting staff, and technical workers, which will improve operational security and prevent information leaks. The Ukrainian government introduced this reform in December 2023 and later implemented it with the support, advocacy, and coordination from State INL and its implementing partners. State INL supported SAPO with services and equipment that OPG had provided. According to State, INL also assisted with the selection of a communication team and is purchasing additional computers and other IT equipment.[328]

In addition, Ukraine undertook a selection process with international and Ukrainian members to install a new head of the National Agency for Corruption Prevention through what USAID characterized as "a strong, transparent process."[329]

The Ukrainian government needs to take further anti-corruption measures as part of the country's EU accession process and to fulfill conditions for U.S. assistance, State said.[330] Such measures include the ability for NABU to conduct wiretapping independently of the Security Services of Ukraine (SBU), and have independent forensic capabilities.[331]

Hiring of Judges to Address Judicial Backlog

During the quarter, also as a result of EU conditionality, a State INL-funded implementer began applying a model for merit-based and transparent vetting to assist with the selection process for High Council of Justice (HCJ) judicial disciplinary inspectors.[332] In September 2023, the Ukrainian parliament passed new regulations to establish the Service of Disciplinary Inspectors and restore the HCJ's disciplinary function. This restoration will allow for the review of more than 12,000 judicial misconduct cases after a 3-year pause, including cases involving imprisoned former Supreme Court Chief Justice Knyazev and U.S.-sanctioned former Kyiv District Administrative Court Head Pavlo Vovk.[333] The implementer will assist with the HCJ's first round of selection of candidates for interviews.[334]

According to State, Ukraine's judiciary currently has approximately 2,500 vacancies.[335] During the quarter, State INL awarded a grant to increase civil society participation in ensuring that candidates for judicial positions meet integrity and professional ethics criteria. This is done through the Public Integrity Council, which assists the High Qualification Commission of Judges in Ukraine (HQCJ) in evaluating judicial candidates' integrity and backgrounds.[336] A State INL implementer assisted the HQCJ with organizing interviews with 12 candidates for the new Public Council of International Experts, which will play a key

According to State, Ukraine's judiciary currently has approximately 2,500 vacancies.

role in carrying out vetting for HACC candidates. The implementer assisted the HQCJ with organizing selection of candidates for vacant HACC positions.[337] The first interviews for the positions were held in April 2024.[338]

Table 13.

Selected State and USAID Anti-Corruption Activities Completed During the Quarter

Objective	Activity
Training and support to Ukrainian anti-corruption units (State INL, in partnership with the Department of Justice)	• Completed the final session for the nine-month **NABU CryptoEdge training program** for detectives to combat high-level financial corruption by to tracking and analyzing crypto-assets and blockchain activities. The program trained 272 NABU detectives. • Held the first of eight planned trainings on **human intelligence** for NABU detectives. • Facilitated travel to Paris for a group of representatives from Ukrainian anti-corruption agencies to participate in the **Organization for Economic Cooperation and Development's (OECD) Global Anti-Corruption Integrity Forum** as part of the effort to help Ukraine join the OECD. • In collaboration with the CEELI Institute in Prague, conducted a **training and roundtable** session for **SAPO prosecutors, NABU detectives, and HACC judges** focused on the **intricacies of plea bargaining**. • Began an interagency agreement with the **FBI agents** to mentor NABU, SAPO, and other key law enforcement partners on improving capacities to investigate and prosecute corruption cases. • Funded the participation of U.S. and Ukrainian officials in a **DoJ-FBI Black Sea Anti-Corruption Working Group meeting in Tbilisi, Georgia**, which brought together prosecutors, police, and financial investigators from Bulgaria, Georgia, Moldova, Romania, and Ukraine to discuss unique concerns related to the Black Sea region. • Funded **DoJ's Trial Advocacy Training**, which trained SAPO prosecutors on opening statements and direct and cross examinations.
Support to the Moldovan criminal justice sector (State INL)	• Provided **technical assistance and training** to the Anti-Corruption Prosecution Office and National Anti-Corruption Center, and other anti-corruption institutions. • Continued to support the Prosecutor Vetting Commission's development of policies and processes and logistical requirements for the **extraordinary vetting of current prosecutors and external candidates**.
Help establish an anti-corruption enforcement architecture (State INL)	• Helped Ukraine establish a **transparent, merit-based selection processes** for the heads of NABU, SAPO, and HACC. • Assisted in **vetting candidates** for the High Council of Justice and High Qualifications Commission of Judges, which has responsibility for judicial oversight and appointments. • **Provided technical assistance** on key anti-corruption legislation, passed in December 2023, to strengthen SAPO's independence, reinstate mandatory asset declarations for government officials and members of parliament, and relaunch key judicial bodies.
Improve Transparency of Public Procurement (USAID)	• Funded Prozorro, Ukraine's **electronic public procurement system** where state and municipal customers announce tenders to purchase goods, works and services, and business representatives compete for the opportunity to become a state supplier, since 2016. This system was developed by the international anti-corruption organization Transparency International Ukraine with a help of volunteers, NGOs, the business community and state bodies of Ukraine. Prozorro is a result of the collaboration between the Ukrainian and American government, the business sector, and civil society. USAID estimates that Prozorro has generated approximately **$8 billion in savings** for Ukrainian taxpayers compared to the previous systems, which were susceptible to corruption risks.

Sources: State, responses to State OIG request for information, 4/12/2024 and 4/28/2024; USAID Ukraine, response to USAID OIG request for information, 12/15/2023; and U.S. Mission to the EU, cable, "Scenesetter for Special Representative Penny Pritzker's February 15-16 Visit to Brussels," 24 USEU BRUSSELS 142, 2/12/2024.

ECONOMIC GROWTH

ECONOMIC DEVELOPMENT

As part of State's on-the-ground monitoring efforts, contract evaluators are tasked with identifying projects with an outsized potential to enhance Ukraine's economic recovery. State-funded monitors will focus on these projects' revenue-generating activities, thereby contributing meaningfully to the Ukrainian recovery overall.[339]

In January, State's Bureau of Energy Resources (ENR) obligated $2.2 million of recovered prior-year funds under the Assistance to Europe, Eurasia, and Central Asia (AEECA) account to support Ukrainian stakeholder agencies with understanding Ukraine's critical mineral resources and prioritizing them for commercial and sustainable exploration and development.[340] A goal of this project is to help Ukraine develop its mineral resource sector for long-term national benefit, including integrating the sector with global critical mineral supply chains and investment.[341] State ENR noted that at the time of its response, the contract's scope of work was under discussion, and that it planned to add another $2 million in Ukraine supplemental funds to the contract.[342]

New Law Seeks to Improve Management of State-Owned Enterprises

During the quarter, Ukraine's parliament passed two laws that seek to improve the management of state-owned enterprises and increase the transparency of their activities.[343] USAID assisted in drafting the legislation. In February, the parliament passed a draft law on the corporate governance of state-owned enterprises. President Zelenskyy signed the law in March, bringing Ukrainian legislation into compliance with the OECD's corporate governance guidelines.[344]

The second law, which awaits the President's signature, addresses market integrity. It will allow Ukraine to sign a memorandum of understanding with the International Organization of Securities Commissions to implement an instrument across 131 jurisdictions to share information and coordinate its efforts across borders, improving the ability of regulators to ensure that markets operate transparently, according to USAID.[345] Passage of the laws will help Ukraine to receive further financing from the European Union, the International Monetary Fund, and the World Bank.[346]

Table 14.

U.S. Goals Related to Economic Growth

Integrated Country Strategy
Ukraine rebuilds a transparent and competitive post-war economy through corporate governance, legislation to achieve de-oligarchization, especially in the energy and metals sectors, attract foreign investment, and generate sustainable government revenue.
Ukraine implements international best practices and continues decentralization while rebuilding social, physical, and critical infrastructure.

Country Development Cooperation Strategy
Strengthened subject matter expert competitiveness.
Increased productivity of agricultural SMEs through market systems.
Inclusive, innovative finance expanded.

Source: State, "Integrated Country Strategy-Ukraine," 8/29/2023; USAID Ukraine, "Ukraine Country Development Cooperation Strategy 2019-2024, Extended Through Jan 9, 2026," 1/4/2024.

AGRICULTURE

Disruptions to Agriculture Sector Remain, Despite Increase in Grain Exports

Russia's full-scale invasion caused economic challenges and logistics disruptions that have reduced agricultural producers' access to services, including those related to exporting goods.[347] Russia's attacks on Ukraine's agricultural infrastructure continued during the quarter, with attacks in March on the Odesa port and the destruction of a grain elevator in Dnipropetrovsk oblast.[348] According to USAID, the biggest threats to Ukraine's agriculture sector that USAID activities are addressing include the difficulty of assessing critical inputs such as seeds and fertilizer; inadequate export logistics networks and export infrastructure; limited access to affordable finance; and inadequate drying, storage, and value-added processing services.[349]

More than 1,100 ships passed through Ukraine's Black Sea corridor since August 2023 and grain exports increased to near pre-war levels, according to USAID.[350] However, Polish farmers continued to block border crossings with Ukraine, as well as Slovakia and Germany, to protest reduced grain prices.[351] In addition, Ukrainian grain was vandalized within Poland, including an incident during which 180 tons of Ukrainian corn was dumped from rail cars headed to Poland's Gdansk port.[352]

Although experts from the Institute of Public Finance in Poland refute the claim that Ukrainian grain is responsible for agricultural market volatility, Polish farmers believe that this influx will cause negative economic impacts on their market share, according to USAID.[353] These blockades and protests have reduced revenues to the Ukrainian government by approximately $167 million to $180 million per month, according to the head of the tax committee in the Ukrainian parliament.[354] In January and February, Ukrainian exports to Poland dropped by 32 percent compared to the previous year.[355] Ukraine and Poland are trying to negotiate a resolution.[356]

Fertilizer Distribution, Border Crossing Enhancements Seek to Boost Agriculture Exports

USAID continued to support micro, small, and medium-sized enterprises through seed and fertilizer distribution, expanded access to processing and value-adding processes, and increased access to finance.[357] In January, a USAID contractor distributed fertilizer to 7,600 farmers.[358] Land reform efforts continued, although at a smaller scale. Ukrainian legal entities gained the right to buy and sell agricultural land in January, part of a long-awaited land reform effort, unlocking significant financing estimated at more than $12 billion in loans that can be provided against land as collateral.[359]

Through private and public sector partnerships, USAID also supported the provision of export-facilitating equipment to Ukrainian ports and border crossings.[360] Equipment delivered this quarter included lighting systems, prefabricated buildings, dynamic scales, and bogie exchange lifts for overcoming differences in track gauges.[361] By the end of 2026, USAID expects that these efforts will increase Ukraine's truck cargo traffic by approximately 1,700 trucks per day.[362]

USAID also reported that it helped nearly 1,500 Ukrainian businesses generate more than $25 million in export sales, attract $5.6 million in investment, and create and retain nearly 7,400 jobs, and supported $23.2 million in financing for Ukrainian micro, small, and medium-sized enterprises.[363]

State Applied Global Food Security Programs to Build Agricultural Resiliency

State reported that, as of March 2024, it had obligated $145 million and expended $47.7 million of the ESF funds appropriated in the Ukraine supplementals for global food security programs.[364] These funds supported programs to address food insecurity in countries affected by Russia's invasion of Ukraine and its resultant disruption of world grain, fertilizer, and fuel markets. The programs aim to build resiliency, protect livelihoods, and improve productive agricultural capacity in low-income and food-deficit countries.[365]

State's Bureau of Oceans and International Environmental Science Affairs (OES), which managed $104 million of these funds, reported that during the second quarter, it did not obligate or expend additional Ukraine supplemental funds for existing programs, nor did it implement new food security programs.[366] However, OES also reported it conducted monitoring and oversight activities via email and phone communication, and it reviewed grant award implementers' financial reporting for the first quarter of FY 2024. OES stated it tracked these programs using both standard and award-specific indicators.[367]

State's Bureau of International Organization Affairs (IO) reported that it obligated $10 million in the second quarter to expand an existing soil mapping program implemented by the UN Food and Agriculture Organization (FAO).[368] This new funding builds on $20 million that the bureau previously obligated for the program to improve soil mapping, soil health, fertilizer use efficiency, and agriculture productivity in Zambia, Guatemala, and Honduras. The $10 million obligated in the second quarter added two additional countries, Ghana and Kenya, to the program.[369] State IO noted that these programs were implemented through FAO in the form of direct monetary support, and that progress is monitored through the U.S. Mission to the United Nations in Rome and country embassies in close coordination with USAID Missions.[370] In addition, State IO stated that during the quarter, it met with FAO officials in Washington to discuss program progress to date. State IO officials traveled to Guatemala in early March to attend a week-long technical FAO-led soil mapping workshop to coordinate program actions and define specific project outcomes.[371]

State reported that, as of March 2024, it had obligated $145 million and expended $47.7 million of the ESF funds appropriated in the Ukraine supplementals for global food security programs.

INFRASTRUCTURE

Russia Continues to Attack Ukrainian Infrastructure

For the second full winter since the onset of Russia's full-scale invasion, Russia's drone and missile strikes continued to strike electricity transmission and distribution grid substations, Ukraine's oil refineries, and district heating facilities.[372] Russia's winter campaigns intended to cripple Ukraine's energy infrastructure at a time when the country's population depends on such facilities for heating.[373]

In particular, State said, Russia sought to harm Ukraine's economy by targeting the energy grid of key industrial regions, specifically Kyiv.[374] While previous attacks focused on freezing millions of Ukrainian civilians, this past winter's attack campaign focused on industrial centers and the broader Ukrainian economy.[375]

In January, Russia launched a mass missile attack against Ukraine that damaged energy infrastructure in Kyiv, Dnipropetrovsk, Kharkiv, and Sumy, including transformer substations, a distribution point, cable lines, and gas pipelines.[376] In February, Russia carried out a massive UAV attack on the southern and central regions of Ukraine that damaged multiple substations and left communities temporarily without power.[377] Russia launched the largest attack ever on Ukraine's energy infrastructure in March, according to Ukraine's Minister of Energy.[378] USAID reported providing equipment, supplies, materials, and other support to assist Ukraine's energy institutions repair and rehabilitate energy infrastructure damaged by Russian attacks.[379] This support included the provision of autotransformers, repair materials, and pipes, generation equipment, mobile boiler houses, and protection for field personnel.[380]

Beginning on March 22, Russia launched an extensive missile and drone campaign which damaged critical power generation assets nationwide and targeted Ukraine's largest underground natural gas storage facility for the first time. On April 11, Russian missiles destroyed the Trypilska thermal power plant, the largest power facility in Kyiv oblast.[381]

Russia's attacks on the power sector have sought to not only deprive citizens access to reliable electricity, water, sewage treatment, heat, and communications, but to harm Ukraine's economy by reducing available power to key industrial regions, such as Kyiv, Dnipropetrovsk, Kharkiv, and Sumy.[382] While previous attacks focused on the electricity transmission system which Ukrainian energy workers have proven adept at repairing and strengthening, the recent damage to critical power plants may result in long-term electricity deficits resulting in load shedding and curtailment of industrial production.[383]

Table 15.

U.S. Goals Related to Infrastructure

Integrated Country Strategy
Ukraine implements international best practices and continues decentralization while rebuilding social, physical, and critical infrastructure.

Sources: State, "Integrated Country Strategy-Ukraine," 8/29/2023.

As of December 2023, 2 years of Russia's attacks have caused approximately $152 billion in direct damage to Ukraine's infrastructure, according to an assessment by World Bank, the Ukrainian government, the European Union, and the United Nations.[384] Released in February, the assessment found that the most affected infrastructure sectors are housing, transport, commerce and industry, agriculture, and energy.[385] (See Figure 5.)

Figure 5.

Estimated Damage to Infrastructure by Sector, in $ Billions, as of December 2023

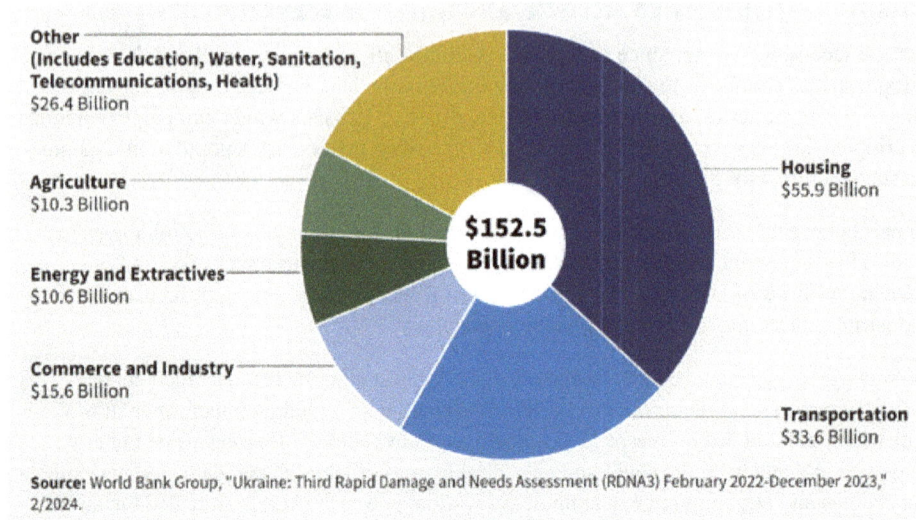

Other
(Includes Education, Water, Sanitation, Telecommunications, Health)
$26.4 Billion

Agriculture
$10.3 Billion

Energy and Extractives
$10.6 Billion

Commerce and Industry
$15.6 Billion

$152.5 Billion

Housing
$55.9 Billion

Transportation
$33.6 Billion

Source: World Bank Group, "Ukraine: Third Rapid Damage and Needs Assessment (RDNA3) February 2022-December 2023," 2/2024.

Efforts Continue to Secure Energy Infrastructure

During the quarter, the U.S. Government continued to assist the Ukrainian government to secure energy infrastructure, including nuclear sites. USAID provides equipment, supplies, materials, and other support to help Ukraine's energy institutions repair and rehabilitate energy infrastructure damaged by Russian attacks.[386] USAID assistance has provided autotransformers, repair materials and pipes, generation equipment, mobile boiler houses, and protection for transformers and field personnel.[387] USAID OIG currently has an ongoing audit of USAID Energy Activities in Ukraine that aims to assess USAID's oversight of the implementation of the Energy Security Project procurement. The audit also aims to determine whether USAID verified that the Energy Security Project delivered selected equipment and materials to recipients as intended.

The Department of Energy's National Nuclear Security Administration (NNSA) donated a vehicle to Ukrainian authorities to transport equipment and personnel as the country manages radioactive materials in crisis regions or near front lines.[388] Ukraine's law enforcement agencies will use the vehicle to secure more than 400 open sources of radiation, State said, which were abandoned at the Metrological Institute of Kharkiv following the area's recovery from Russian occupation.[389]

During the quarter, State ENR provided $210,000 to the Bureau of Administration to cover transportation costs for 47 pallets of HESCO barriers, donated by State's Bureau of Overseas Buildings Operations, for Ukraine to enhance passive protection of the energy infrastructure against shrapnel and indirect damage.[390] The DoD also provided some equipment and limited logistics support to help secure energy sites in Ukraine. The Ukrainian government managed transportation, delivery, and construction within Ukraine.[391]

State Continues Efforts to Advance Ukraine's Energy Transition

During the quarter, State ISN obligated $10 million in Ukraine supplemental ESF funds for two grants to implement Project Phoenix, an initiative to transition Europe and Eurasia off coal-fired power plants to secure and safe small modular reactors (SMR), while retaining local jobs through workforce retraining.[392] This funding was used to expand Project Phoenix to Ukraine and support government stakeholders with technical assistance, feasibility studies, and comprehensive analyses of Ukrainian fossil fuel power generation facilities, with the goal of identifying and supporting priority projects for conversion to safe and secure SMR technologies.[393] State's Bureau of International Security and Nonproliferation (ISN) issued two grants during the quarter, one to provide technical and advisory services to Ukrainian partners for coal-to-SMR conversions, and the second to evaluate the feasibility replacing coal-fired power plants with secure and safe SMR technology.[394]

State ISN also obligated a total of $4.1 million for energy security programs. These funds contributed to the development of a user manual and ammonia module for a hydrogen pilot plant simulator.[395]

In addition, State ENR allocated $7 million in Ukraine supplemental funds for a planned gas program and another $2.8 million in supplemental funding for a planned advanced decarbonization project, including implementation of hydrogen power. However, it had not yet obligated those funds as of March 2024.[396]

State Provided $255 Million to Support Financing for the World Bank Recovery Program in Ukraine

On April 3, State obligated $255 million for World Bank trust funds to support rebuilding in Ukraine.[397] Most of these funds ($230 million) went to the Ukraine Relief, Recovery, Reconstruction, and Reform Trust Fund (URTF), which helps the Ukrainian government sustain its administrative capacity, deliver services, and conduct relief efforts.[398] The fund will support Ukrainian transport and trade by providing loaders/unloaders and multi-functional equipment for cargo handling and transshipment at Ukraine's Danube ports of Reni and Izmail, as well as locomotives and rolling stock to strengthen railway logistics chains and support export of Ukraine's agricultural commodities.[399] The funding will also restore essential bridges and railways to link communities and improve westward transport linkages to mitigate impacts of Black Sea shipping disruptions.[400] Moreover, State said, this effort will support delivery of aid and essential services to communities directly affected by the war and will boost the economy and government revenues in Ukraine, by facilitating transport and trade, and help Ukraine transition from an economy focused on exports to Russia to an economy focused on exports heading west.[401]

On April 3, State obligated $255 million for World Bank trust funds to support rebuilding in Ukraine.

The remaining $25 million went to Multilateral Investment Guarantee Agency's (MIGA) Ukraine Reconstruction and Economy Trust Fund.[402] MIGA, a member of the World Bank Group, promotes cross-border investment in developing countries by providing political risk insurance and credit enhancements to investors and lenders.[403] MIGA uses the Support to Ukraine's Reconstruction and Economy Trust Fund to mitigate risks resulting from a "virtually non-existent" private sector reinsurance capacity in Ukraine.[404] State said the fund will support private sector investment in Ukraine by providing political risk insurance guarantees to support commercial banks in Ukraine, providing liquidity to small- and medium-sized enterprises, trade in essential goods, and foreign investment projects.[405]

HUMANITARIAN ASSISTANCE

The U.S. Government, primarily through USAID, supports the provision of assistance for civilians affected by the conflict in Ukraine. USAID organizes its activities according to the UN Humanitarian Response Plan for Ukraine.[406] (See Table 16.) USAID BHA has provided more than $2 billion in humanitarian funding, including more than $60 million through sub-awards to about 190 local and national NGOs in Ukraine that are working to provide food, medical supplies and basic health services, hygiene items, and other essential relief commodities across Ukraine, including conflict-affected and hard-to-reach areas.[407]

Additionally, BHA has provided approximately $55 million to pooled funds that support localization since February 2022.[408] USAID has emphasized its shift towards localization—by not just directing awards to local organizations, but through a shift in how local actors are perceived, valuing their knowledge, respecting their expertise, championing their agency, recognizing their commitment and integrity, and engaging them as partners rather than as just agents and beneficiaries.[409] USAID OIG currently has an ongoing audit of USAID BHA's localization approach in Ukraine. This audit aims to determine the extent to which USAID has developed objectives and metrics for the program(s) under review; determine progress towards achieving those objectives; and to determine how, and to what extent, USAID is monitoring implementer performance in accordance with USAID's standard policies and procedures.

In some respects, humanitarian needs are trending downward though the number of Ukrainians in need remain high, according to USAID. The UN Office for the Coordination of Humanitarian Affairs (OCHA) estimated that 14.6 million people will need humanitarian assistance in 2024, down from 17.6 million in 2023 and 17.7 million in 2022.[410] Similarly, the estimated number of internally displaced persons in Ukraine, 3.5 million, declined from 3.7 million in 2023.[411] The UN High Commissioner for Refugees (UNHCR) reported a slight increase in the number of Ukrainian refugees residing in other European countries: 5.9 million as of December 2023, compared to 5.7 million in 2022.[412]

Since February 2022, the conflict has resulted in more than 30,000 civilian casualties as of March 2024; displaced more than 6 million Ukrainian refugees; and damaged or destroyed critical infrastructure.[413] Civilian casualties resulting from Russia's attacks increased by 40 percent between November 2023 and January 2024, due to intensified Russia's missile and UAV attacks across the country, according to the UNHCR.[414] UN-confirmed civilian deaths resulting from the conflict to reached almost 11,000, with more than 20,000 injured.[415] Russia's increased aerial attacks since December 2023 continued to disrupt critical services, including electricity and heating, amid sub-freezing temperatures, the United Nations reported.[416]

> **Since February 2022, the conflict has resulted in more than 30,000 civilian casualties as of March 2024; displaced more than 6 million Ukrainian refugees; and damaged or destroyed critical infrastructure.**

Table 16.

UN Goals Related to Humanitarian Assistance

Humanitarian Response Plan
Provide principles and timely multisectoral lifesaving assistance to internally displaced people, non-displaced war affected people and returnees, ensuring their safety and dignity.
Enable access to basic services for internally displaced people, non-displaced war-affected people and returnees.

Source: UN OCHA, "Humanitarian Needs and Response Plan Ukraine," 1/3/2024.

Security Environment Challenges Assistance Delivery, Monitoring

Humanitarian actors, including U.S. Government partners, delivered critical multi-sector assistance to conflict-affected communities across the country and along the front line in early 2024, according to the United Nations.[417]

USAID's Bureau for Humanitarian Assistance (BHA) reported that it focused on NGO safety and security, and attacks impacting humanitarian implementers during the quarter.[418] The Ukraine Disaster Assistance Response Team (DART) and Response Management Team are tracking changes in the safety and security landscape that pose risk to implementing partners, including the proliferation of short-range improvised combat UAVs, which can either target humanitarian actors or incorrectly identify them as military-affiliated.[419] Recent incidents have led to the death or injury of NGO staff.[420] In response to such incidents, a USAID BHA-funded security organization released new guidance for NGO partners, with recommended operational precautions to increase safety and security.[421]

While the DART continued to conduct site visits to monitor program implementation, these visits were sporadic due to security concerns and restrictions, and generally limited to Kyiv city limits and immediate surroundings.[422] In September 2023, the DART significantly increased its footprint in Kyiv, with most of the DART members now residing in Kyiv instead of in Krakow.[423] This move increased DART members' ability to meet with partners in person, attend cluster and/or coordination meetings with other donors, and occasionally conduct site visits in and around Kyiv.[424] USAID BHA relies heavily on third-party monitoring reports, in conjunction with regular written and verbal program updates from partners.[425]

USAID Responds to Health Needs in Ukraine

There is a marked trend of Russia targeting health facilities in Ukraine.[426] Physicians for Human Rights have published an open source report with the numbers of attacks on healthcare infrastructure and personnel in Ukraine since the start of the full scale invasion through February 2024: more than 1,300 attacks on health care, about 700 attacks damaged or destroyed hospitals/clinics, more than 80 ambulances attacked, nearly 200 health workers killed, almost 140 health workers injured, almost 80 attacks affecting children's hospitals, more than 50 attacks affecting women's health facilities, and 60 attacks that damaged or destroyed a hospital's energy and/or water supply system or limited a hospital's ability to access these utilities.[427]

In particular, the nature of the HIV epidemic in Ukraine has shifted over the course of the conflict, due to population migration and emerging risk groups, including military service members and war veterans.[428] Preliminary data from a biobehavioral study conducted by the Ministry of Health/Center for Public Health among people who inject drugs, suggests changing demographics and relocations due to safety of those in this population living with HIV and increased HIV burden in some regions in Western Ukraine, as compared with pre-war findings.[429]

As of March 11, USAID has provided more than $11.7 million in direct funding to Ukrainian NGOs, recognizing their critical role in addressing the crisis and building local response capacity.

Since the full-scale invasion, USAID—as a PEPFAR partner—has provided nearly 300,000 HIV tests, and more than 9,200 people have been identified as HIV positive.[430] During the quarter, USAID delivered more than $2.7 million worth of public health commodities, including antiretroviral drugs for HIV treatment and prevention, rapid tests for HIV antibody detection, as well as test kits for Hepatitis B, Hepatitis C, and syphilis.[431] Every person identified as positive by a PEPFAR-funded USAID project is referred to life-saving treatment services.[432] USAID has scaled up self-testing to reach more individuals who may not be reached through traditional service delivery during war, providing self-test kits to roughly 157,000 people.[433] USAID OIG has an ongoing audit of USAID Ukraine's HIV/AIDs prevention activities. This audit aims to determine the mission's role in ensuring that IDPs living with HIV/AIDs have access to medical and social services, and medications during the war.

This quarter, USAID obligated approximately $44 million to support Ukraine's health sector.[434] USAID this quarter continued to prioritize restoration of essential services, reconnecting people to care by equipping the health workforce with critical clinical and managerial skills, providing minor repairs, and procuring and furnishing centers with basic medical and facilities.[435] More than 930 primary healthcare facilities affected by war have benefitted from USAID support for repairs or equipment.[436]

A Ukrainian government resolution in December 2023 reduced the maximum number of staff at the National Health Service of Ukraine from more than 1,000 to fewer than 350 and the Ministry of Health from about 330 to fewer than 240.[437] Based on WHO's calculations, this puts the Ukrainian government's ability to administer the state Program of Medical Guarantees at risk due to insufficient staff to ensure efficient, effective, and transparent use of government resources.[438]

The Ukrainian National Health Service is the agency that functions as the national insurer.[439] It is not the medical delivery system, so there is no direct impact on clinical services.[440] However, recruitment of qualified staff in various health technical sectors continues to be a challenge due to experts being internally displaced or having fled the country.[441]

USAID Supports Winterization Efforts

USAID BHA supported nine international non-governmental organizations partners and three UN partners with $184 million to provide multipurpose cash assistance, protection, shelter, and water, sanitation, and hygiene assistance to vulnerable populations during the 2023-2024 winter season.[442] USAID BHA also supported the delivery of generators to health and sanitation facilities and provided winter-related relief commodities, such as blankets, fuel, and mattresses.[443]

USAID partners during the quarter faced considerable operational challenges, including conflict-related threats to safety and security in frontline areas, and other natural hazards posed by the environment, especially in winter.[444] Persons residing in front-line areas are often elderly, especially vulnerable, or lacking means to relocate, meaning that there are specialized services needed to reach them.[445] USAID advised NGOs to limit activities in immediate frontline areas to only the most critical, such as medical support for populations in need.[446]

USAID BHA supported nine international non-governmental organizations partners and three UN partners with $184 million to provide multipurpose cash assistance, protection, shelter, and water, sanitation, and hygiene assistance to vulnerable populations during the 2023-2024 winter season.

U.S. Government Funds Cash Assistance and Other Support for Refugees and IDPs

State's Bureau of Population, Refugees, and Migration (PRM) acts as the U.S. Government's lead on the refugee response. USAID's Bureau for Humanitarian Assistance is the lead federal coordinator for the U.S. Government on the humanitarian response inside Ukraine and has primary responsibility for addressing the needs of internally displaced persons (IDP) in Ukraine.[447]

USAID noted that while IDPs are more likely to meet vulnerability criteria for humanitarian assistance due to conflict-related displacement, the assistance types are not specifically different than for individuals who are not displaced.[448] Qualifying IDPs may receive assistance in the form of multi-purpose cash assistance; food assistance; shelter assistance; water, sanitation and hygiene assistance; protection assistance; health assistance; and provision of emergency commodities and non-food items.[449] Local USAID implementers coordinate with relevant cluster coordination bodies, which coordinate humanitarian action when a national government requests international support to prevent duplication of support.[450]

As of March 2024, State PRM reported that it had expended approximately $3.2 billion, or 96 percent, of the $3.3 billion it received in the Ukraine supplemental appropriations.[451] Of the total $3.3 billion, more than $862 million was obligated to support the Ukraine response as of March 2024. As of March 2024, more than $7 million of the appropriated funds remained unallocated. The remainder of the appropriated funds were provided to crises other than the Ukraine response.[452]

State PRM funds public international organizations (PIO) for activities outlined in their appeals. Because PIOs have specialized mandates, this funding is not earmarked for specific sectors or activities to provide partners with flexibility to meet the most urgent needs for refugees, IDPs, and other vulnerable persons. State PRM contributed to PIO needs based on their respective specialized sectors within the Ukraine Regional Refugee Response Plan.[453] For example, as of mid-January 2024, the UNHCR, a State PRM partner, has helped to repair more than 27,500 homes across Ukraine since the full-scale invasion in February 2022. These repairs ensure that homes are inhabitable and can be kept warm during cold winter months.[454]

> **UNHCR support extended to Ukrainian refugees in nearby countries, including Bulgaria, Czechia, Estonia, Hungary, Latvia, Lithuania, Moldova, Poland, Romania, and Slovakia.**

State PRM also provided support to vulnerable families in Ukraine during the quarter.[455] According to provisional UNHCR financial information, between January 1 and the first week of March, the UNHCR provided a total of $35.7 million in cash assistance to nearly 95,000 individuals. This included multipurpose cash assistance, targeted cash assistance for shelter rehabilitation, rent, livelihood, and utilities.[456] For the remainder of March, the UNHCR in Ukraine aimed to deliver a total of $5.7 million to support more than 86,000 individuals, through multipurpose cash assistance and cash for utilities.[457]

UNHCR support extended to Ukrainian refugees in nearby countries, including Bulgaria, Czechia, Estonia, Hungary, Latvia, Lithuania, Moldova, Poland, Romania, and Slovakia.[458] In Moldova and Slovakia, the UNHCR provided a total of $15.3 million in cash assistance to more than 46,000 individuals from January to the first week of March. For the remainder of March, the UNHCR planned to support an additional 40,000 individuals in Bulgaria,

Moldova, and Slovakia with $6.7 million in cash assistance. The UNHCR has ceased its cash-based initiative operations in Poland and does not plan to deliver cash assistance in 2024 under the current budgetary allocations.[459] The UNHCR distributed a total of $223.8 million in Ukraine to benefit more than 840,000 individuals during 2023.[460]

During the quarter, State PRM monitored implementing partners' performance inside Ukraine and the region through multiple avenues, including programmatic desk monitoring, field monitoring, and financial desk monitoring.[461] State PRM also reviewed regular programmatic and operational updates from international partners, visited program sites, and met with partners on the ground in Ukraine.[462] During field visits to partner activity sites, State PRM often meets with populations of concern, interviews partner staff and their sub-grantees, and directly observes protection-related activities, registration, verification, distribution, and post-distribution monitoring exercises, State said. During the quarter, State PRM visited sites in Czechia, Moldova, Poland, Romania, as well as Kyiv city and oblast.[463]

State's CSO Bureau Promoted Reintegration of Ukraine Veterans and IDPs

During the quarter, State advanced reconciliation and reintegration along two lines of effort: veteran reintegration and IDP integration.[464] Since 2019, State's Bureau of Conflict and Stabilization Operations (CSO) has supported a Veteran Reintegration program.[465] The program developed the capacities of Ukraine's Ministry of Veterans Affairs, while supporting local veterans' associations and conducting research involving veterans of the fighting in Ukraine's Crimea and Donbas regions dating back to 2014.[466] With the onset of Russia's full-scale invasion, State CSO applied supplemental funding to complete the veteran e-registry to accelerate the modernization of veteran services to serve a larger population with more veterans suffering from disabilities such as amputated limbs.[467]

During the quarter, State CSO launched the Veterans Rehabilitation and Reintegration program to continue and expand these initiatives, with a particular focus on helping modernize policy in light of the full-scale invasion, State reported.[468] In parallel with State CSO's efforts, State's Bureau of Democracy, Human Rights, and Labor (DRL) has been supporting civil society to deliver critical support services, including physical and psychological rehabilitation, and to some of the most vulnerable veterans and their families in remote regions of Ukraine, State said.[469]

During the quarter, State CSO also continued programs aimed at promoting social cohesion between IDPs and host communities, according to State.[470] The first program, Cohesion through Youth-Led Action, filled a gap in support for IDP youth (ages 18 to 29) and allowed for the pilot of the IDP Council concept, adapted from Colombia. The United Voices in Action program, focused on children (below age 18) and adults (ages 30 and above), brought the IDP Council to scale.[471] A forthcoming program, called Voices in Action 2.0, will continue to develop the capacity of IDP Councils and promote regional coordination. Voices in Action has informed the development of Ukraine's 2025 IDP Strategy, which includes mandating the creation of IDP Councils across Ukraine, according to State.[472]

During the quarter, State advanced reconciliation and reintegration along two lines of effort: veteran reintegration and IDP integration.

Monitoring and Evaluation

U.S. EMBASSY KYIV IMPLEMENTED NEW MONITORING AND EVALUATION GUIDELINES

In December 2023, the U.S. Embassy in Kyiv approved strategic planning guidelines for the embassy's monitoring and evaluation missions.[473] The goal of the guidelines is to guide each agency and to provide specific directions and prioritization for off-site, in-person monitoring and evaluations missions outside of Kyiv.[474] The guidelines state that the embassy seeks to align current and future programs or projects with higher-level strategies or objectives; ensure that programs or projects have clear goals and objectives; assess effectiveness in the context of the ongoing conflict; and seek to identify any cases of misuse or misdirection of U.S. assistance.[475]

The embassy's Office of the Assistance Coordinator (ACOORD) is responsible for ensuring all implementing sections and agencies can perform in-person oversight and monitoring despite limited resources, such as drivers, vehicles, and protective details. ACOORD coordinates all requested monitoring site visits with the implementing section and the Regional Security Office, the General Services Office, and the embassy's Front Office.[476] ACOORD reviews all proposed monitoring travel requests and prioritizes them based on several factors, including cost; relative importance to wartime or reconstruction needs; monitoring that requires U.S. direct hire personnel, such as EUM; fraud or misdirection concerns across the breadth of U.S. assistance; the location of the assistance or distance from Kyiv where the assistance operates; and safety and life-saving assistance considerations.[477]

State and USAID said that oversight relies on a mix of in-person visits and virtual monitoring.[478] According to State, some State bureaus, as well as the DoD and USAID, hold regular, in-person meetings with partners in Kyiv and conduct program site visits in and outside of Kyiv to discuss ongoing programming, outcomes, and challenges.[479] USAID BHA reported that it focused on NGO safety and security, and attacks impacting humanitarian implementers during the quarter. USAID BHA relies heavily on third-party monitoring reports, in conjunction with regular written and verbal program updates from partners, to monitor programs.[480] State INL and State ISN's Export Control and Related Border Security programs (EXBS) conduct EUM that requires in-person verification of certain commodities provided to the Ukrainian government. Both State INL and the EXBS program use a risk-based approach to prioritize such inspections. Such monitoring is accomplished by locally employed staff and third-party support via the Department of Justice.[481]

Assistance implementers also make use of virtual consultations, regular telephone calls, and messenger apps to conduct oversight.[482] For example, the U.S. President's Emergency Plan for AIDS Relief (PEPFAR) in Kyiv uses virtual methodologies to collect, analyze, and triangulate program data each quarter. CSO uses virtual technologies to conduct monitoring and virtual training with participants throughout Ukraine. State said that it uses telephones, video-conferencing, and email to maintain oversight of assistance and advance programmatic goals.[483]

The embassy held its FY 2024 Q2 foreign assistance oversight review in February 2024.[484] The meeting focused on accountability of U.S. Government foreign assistance, including successes and challenges in conducting EUM of security assistance and the monitoring and evaluation

(continued on next page)

Monitoring and Evaluation *(continued from previous page)*

of humanitarian, economic, and development assistance in Ukraine. The U.S. Ambassador underscored the importance of appropriate oversight for the $75 billion of U.S. security, economic, and humanitarian assistance as one of the mission's top goals.[485]

State noted that in December 2023, the last full month before the guidelines were implemented, embassy personnel completed eight trips outside of Kyiv city to conduct oversight or as part of high-level meetings or visits.[486] From January to March 2024, embassy personnel completed 51 total trips outside Kyiv city, 25 of which were to implement programs or conduct oversight.[487] Data on embassy staff movements indicate DoD elements conducted site visits and oversight in Berdychiv, Bila Tservka, Brovary, Danylivka, Protsiv, and Zhytomyr.[488] Similarly, State INL conducted border guard inspections in Lviv for 3 days in January, and USAID traveled to Borodyanka, Hostomel, and Irpin to conduct site visits.[489] The EXBS program conducted EUM in Chernivtsi, Khmelnytskyy, and Lviv.[490] State PRM personnel traveled to Irpin, Borodyanka, Kukhari, and Olyva to conduct site visits.[491]

STATE BEGINS IMPLEMENTING THE MEASURE CONTRACT

State also said it had begun implementing the Monitoring, Evaluation, and Audit Services for Ukraine (MEASURE) contract, awarded in FY 2023 to support State's Office of the U.S. Assistance Coordinator for Europe, Eurasia, and Central Asia's monitoring and evaluation efforts for non-military assistance programs.[492] The contract's purpose is to monitor U.S. Government foreign assistance provided under the four (and any future) Ukraine supplemental appropriations to ensure the funds are directed toward the foreign policy and foreign assistance objectives for which they are intended.[493]

According to State, as of mid-March 2024, planning for the first round of MEASURE contract site visits was underway.[494] In addition, on March 1 the MEASURE contractor submitted the draft of its first quarterly report on assistance results to State. The report focuses on lessons learned from engagements with partners on outcome indicator compilations. State said the draft report also identified weaknesses and gaps in outcome indicators, which will be addressed in the next round of engagement with partners.[495] Finally, the U.S. Assistance Coordinator for Europe, Eurasia, and Central Asia's Ukraine assessments were underway during the quarter, the results of which will contribute to decisions on future site visit locations and become the basis for evaluation planning and scheduling.[496]

Aircraft from nearly 50 countries are parked at Ramstein Air Base, Germany, as delegates attend the 20th Ukraine Defense Contact Group, March 19, 2024. (U.S. Air Force photo)

PUBLIC DIPLOMACY, HUMAN RIGHTS, AND SANCTIONS

PUBLIC DIPLOMACY, HUMAN RIGHTS, AND SANCTIONS

PUBLIC DIPLOMACY AND COUNTERING DISINFORMATION

The U.S. Government has led and supported efforts in Ukraine to counter disinformation, thereby mitigating the negative impact of what State has called "the Kremlin's self-serving narratives" and "fake historical narratives" both inside Ukraine and beyond its borders.[497] In Russia-occupied parts of Ukraine especially, audiences have limited access to objective, independent, and reliable sources of information and news. Populations in these areas are therefore vulnerable to Russian propaganda and disinformation.[498]

The Public Diplomacy section at the U.S. Embassy in Kyiv funded the work of several Ukrainian media outlets during the quarter, using Ukraine supplemental funds.[499] (See Table 17.) Monitoring of progress and quality for Ukraine-based grants outside Kyiv remains constrained, State reported.[500] Administrators have adopted a set of desk monitoring methodologies allowing for long-distance quality controls and required grantees to submit interim reports on their progress.[501] Disbursement of grant funds takes place in installments, State said, based on alignment with the milestones and objectives outlined in the grant agreements.[502]

Table 17.

Grants Supported by the U.S. Public Diplomacy Section During the Quarter

Program	Activity During the Quarter
Media Development Fund Commission $1.96 million in grants since 2023 17 grants worth $1.63 million, remained active during the quarter	• Supported media outlets' operations during wartime to boost the resilience of the Ukrainian media space. • Supported a local media organization, which during the quarter produced five investigations, nine analytical reports, and held security training for nearly two dozen journalists from the southern cities of Kherson, Mykolaiv, and Odesa. • Supported two media organizations to produce reports, hold trainings on media law and reporting, and coverage of IDP issues.
Democracy Commission $2.31 million in grants since 2023 17 grants, worth $1.98 million, remained active during the quarter	• Supported demining trainings for school-aged children, legal consultations, workshops in employment in business development for IDPs, tactical medicine trainings, and war crimes documentation.

Source: State, response to State OIG request for information, 3/22/2024

The embassy's Public Diplomacy section also funded a public radio station. The station developed a multifaceted, comprehensive program for media literacy enhancement, meant to promote "info hygiene" and the dissemination of accurate information among Ukrainian audiences. The programming sought to counter disinformation, misinformation, and "malign narratives"—often through social- and traditional-media networks. The target groups for these malign narratives included Ukrainian youth, NGO representatives, librarians, teachers, and military service personnel, according to the embassy.[503]

In January 2024, the radio station published nine short videos featuring interviews of media experts and opinion leaders. These videos have earned more than 200,000 views on social media alone, while regional TV and radio disseminated elements of these reports further, reaching a total audience of more than 1 million people.[504]

U.S. AGENCY FOR GLOBAL MEDIA

The U.S. Agency for Global Media (USAGM) seeks to "inform, engage, and connect people around the world in support of freedom and democracy."[505] In Ukraine, USAGM provides news and related programming through several platforms, including Voice of America (VOA) and Radio Free Europe/Radio Liberty (RFE/RL). VOA's Russian- and Ukrainian-language services produce podcasts that have been available since the start of the war on Apple, Google, and YouTube platforms.[506] USAGM has supported public radio in Ukraine by enabling 17 million Ukrainians to receive trustworthy news during Russia's war of aggression.[507]

VOA's Ukrainian Satellite TV Channel, which began after the start of the war and broadcasts in Ukrainian and English, provides round-the-clock coverage in Ukraine and neighboring countries, where many displaced Ukrainians are now living. The channel is built upon VOA's programming in Ukrainian and English, supplemented by content from RFE/RL, as well as Deutsche Welle, Germany's public broadcast network.[508]

VOA, RFE/RL Expand Ranks, Coverage Amid Security Concerns

USAGM networks that support Ukraine coverage made a number of changes in personnel during the quarter.[509] VOA used supplemental funding to add 30 multimedia journalists to their robust coverage of the war as well as a broader network of stringers and freelancers across Eastern Europe who cover war-related stories, the agency said.[510] Inside Ukraine, VOA uses Ukraine Supplemental funding to hire security consultants to ensure the physical safety of the network's employees.[511] RFE/RL's technical and reporting teams during the quarter remained fully staffed given current funding levels.[512]

The expanded coverage requirements have necessitated hiring consultants to ensure standardized programming and branding across various RFE/RL channels. Pre-existing programs, including Votvot and Current Time, delivered additional coverage, requiring RFE/RL to invest in expanded digital storage capacity for production systems and databases. RFE/RL continued to review its spending to ensure that funds go toward the greatest needs.[513]

USAGM reported during the quarter that it needed to change its life insurance provider and protective personal equipment for personnel at RFE/RL. The previous provider of those goods and services had discontinued coverage in light of the ongoing war risk.[514] The new plan incurred a cost increase of more than $800,000.[515]

New stipulations under the current insurance plan include a requirement to provide the insurer with advance notice before each trip to high-risk areas, as well as a pre-departure security briefing. These measures add costs in time and labor. The change in insurance provider did not lead to the departure of any RFE/RL employee, USAGM said.[516]

Networks Focus on Growth

USAGM said that during the quarter, VOA focused on continuing to surge its programming, and enhancing digital content production and distribution, made possible by the Ukraine supplemental funding. In February, on and around the 2-year mark of Russia's full-scale invasion of Ukraine, VOA Language Services produced anniversary coverage of the war from Ukraine and Washington, digital explainers on where the battlefield conflict stands, and status updates on U.S. assistance.[517]

USAGM said VOA maintains a notable social media presence on Telegram and YouTube, channels that remain unblocked in Russia despite unprecedented domestic censorship. VOA content on these channels plays a critical role in public information in these target areas.[518]

RFE/RL also did not launch new platforms during the quarter but focused on growing its existing operations. RFE/RL is maintaining the journalism initiatives and enhancements in digital content production that were made possible by the Ukraine supplemental funding.[519]

VOA used supplemental funding to add 30 multimedia journalists to their robust coverage of the war as well as a broader network of stringers and freelancers across Eastern Europe who cover war-related stories, the agency said.

Coverage Targets Strategic Audiences

USAGM reported that VOA and RFE/RL services for Ukraine and Russia during the quarter received 60.7 million total web visits, 245 million video views (web and social media), and 3 million social media engagements (comments, reposts, etc.).[520] Since the start of the war, USAGM said, RFE/RL and VOA Ukrainian and Russian-language digital video content has received more than 10 billion total views, with a significant portion of traffic coming from Russia.[521]

RFE/RL likewise covered the Ukraine war in terms of its cost to Russia. RFE/RL's Russian Service's regional reporting project "Siberia.Realities" estimated the cost of unfinished infrastructure projects in Russian regions, delayed due to budget constraints resulting from Russia's invasion of Ukraine. For example, the construction of the Lena River bridge in Siberia, deemed unaffordable, equals just four days of Russian war expenses, the report said.[522]

A USAGM-commissioned survey in July 2023 found more than 20 percent of adults in Ukraine—nearly 6.5 million people—reported consuming RFE/RL or VOA content. A July 2022 survey showed that more than 11.5 million Russian adults consumed VOA and RFE/RL content at least once a week.

USAGM planned further market research to better understand Russian-language audiences throughout Europe and other countries where large numbers of Russians have migrated since the start of the war. The new projects follow a procurement of 12 research projects in November 2023, for a total of $1.05 million, for the same kinds of market research.[523] The projects' research methods include focus groups, media monitoring panels, and national surveys. Fieldwork for the first 12 projects will occur from March to May 2024, with results expected from late summer this year, USAGM reported.[524] In addition to continued market research on Russian and Ukrainian audiences, the research will examine the impact of Kremlin-backed disinformation in key regional markets outside Europe and Eurasia, particularly Africa and Latin America.[525]

Radio Free Asia (RFA) created an English-language hub page of the "Bear East" project, which went online at the start of December 2023.[526] Translated versions of selected content in Mandarin, Korean, Thai, Burmese, and Vietnamese languages were published in January and February 2024. The Office of Cuba Broadcasting published articles, in-depth reports, and videos in collaboration with the Center for Disinformation Studies at Odesa National University in Ukraine.[527] The main goal of the office's efforts is to counteract Russia's propaganda found in Cuban media outlets and unveil the narratives propagated by the Kremlin on the island.[528]

USAGM Continues Efforts to Counter Censorship

With assistance from USAGM's Open Technology Fund, the VOA Russian and Ukrainian services actively deployed circumvention tools, including mirror sites and VPN-enabled browsing, to provide access to their digital properties, including websites and mobile apps.[529] Both services offer content on unblocked platforms such as YouTube and Telegram. VOA's Press Freedom Teams and Language Services provide reporting on Russia's propaganda efforts and attacks, and repression of media, on a near-weekly basis.[530]

USAGM said its networks continued to report on the two American journalists detained in Russia: Evan Gershkovich and RFE/RL's Alsu Kurmasheva.[531] Mr. Gershkovich passed the 1-year mark of his Russian detention on March 29; Mrs. Kurmasheva, a dual Russian-American national detained since June 2023, received on April 1 an additional 2-month detention, pending investigation and trial for spreading false information and for failing to register as a foreign agent.[532]

The USAGM Open Technology Fund fully obligated its supplemental funding during the quarter.[533] The fund's purpose is to provide access to secure, open-source circumvention tools to audiences in Russia, enabling news consumers to bypass Russian government censorship and access the free and open internet. The fund currently supports 14.7 million monthly active users inside Russia, USAGM said.[534]

USAGM Networks Drive Transparency Globally

According USAGM, VOA divisions worldwide continued covering the war in Ukraine and its implications. VOA's Latin America Division sent two correspondents to Ukraine for coverage of the invasion's anniversary. The Swahili service sent a reporter to Poland to explore the experiences of African international students who relocated to Poland from Ukraine because of the war. VOA Persian commissioned a series of investigative TV documentaries exposing Iran's clandestine support of Moscow's war effort, war crimes, violence against Ukrainian women, and the toll of Tehran's pro-Russian foreign policy on Iran's faltering economy and society. The Africa division produced several radio and television stories on the extent of Russia's military, political and economic influence in several African countries. [535]

USAGM said RFE/RL produced similarly wide-ranging coverage during the quarter. The network aired a variety of milestone coverage to mark two years of Russian aggression, with interviews of Ukrainian soldiers, senior government leaders, and prominent cultural figures. The Ukrainian Service's Refugee Desk tracked where the millions of Ukrainians fleeing Russia's full-scale invasion have found refuge in the past two years, and how many refugees have since returned to Ukraine. A joint project from the Belarus Service and Ukrainian Service's "Schemes" investigative team uncovered exclusive documents revealing Belarus's role as a center for the "re-education" of Ukrainian children and their parents as pro-Russian citizens.[536]

Navalny Death Spurs Audience Growth and Use of VPNs to Access News

Russian political opposition leader Alexei Navalny, who opposed Russia's war in Ukraine, died in a Russian Arctic prison on February 16 under suspicious circumstances.[537] One expert noted that with Navalny's death, "there is no longer any alternative to the war and the repressive political order [Putin] has imposed, of which Navalny's elimination is a part."[538]

According to USAGM, RFE/RL's Ukrainian- and Russian-language audience sizes surged following Navalny's death and the network's coverage of Navalny's March 1 funeral, which the U.S. Ambassador to Russia attended.[539] According to USAGM, website traffic spiked by 38 percent over average levels in the first hours after the news broke. The largest gains in traffic occurred on RFE/RL's English language website, with a 61 percent jump in page views in the 24 hours following the announcement.[540]

USAGM said that on February 20, the Russian Ministry of Justice added RFE/RL to its list of "undesirable organizations."[541] The designation effectively banned RFE/RL from working inside Russia, as well as criminalizing cooperation with the network and distribution of its content.[542] By February 22—just prior to the February 24 anniversary of Russia's full-scale invasion of Ukraine—Kremlin internet regulators completely blocked the website domains of all five of RFE/RL's Central Asian services. The move brought to 19 the total number of RFE/RL domains that became inaccessible within Russia, except with the use of circumvention tools such as virtual private networks.[543]

Coverage of Navalny's death and March 1 funeral involved livestreams of original VOA content from Los Angeles, Munich, New York City, Tbilisi, and Washington, which garnered millions of views on social media platforms. USAGM stated that VOA's broadcast on the Current Time network included simultaneous translation of President Biden's address on Navalny's death, which was then re-streamed live by the official Navalny YouTube channel.[544] According to USAGM, about one-fifth of these page views immediately following Navalny's death came to RFE/RL websites through technologies like VPNs, suggesting that audiences were most likely visiting from Russia or other countries where RFE/RL websites were blocked.[545]

USAGM stated that VOA and RFE/RL during the quarter continued to report on U.S. and Western military aid to Ukraine. For VOA, the network's programming was broadcast on all major Ukrainian TV channels, including the national TV channel "United News Marathon." It received citations in dozens of online media outlets.[546] VOA's audiences in Eurasia received special TV broadcasts in Russian and Ukrainian, including comprehensive coverage of President Biden's March 7 State of the Union address, as well as the second anniversary of the full-scale war's beginning. USAGM reported the coverage of each event accumulated hundreds of thousands of views and interactions on social media, and the Eurasia Division's State of the Union coverage was distributed to more than 50 national and regional television channels regionwide.[547]

GLOBAL ENGAGEMENT CENTER

State's Global Engagement Center (GEC) is responsible for U.S. Government efforts to recognize, understand, expose, and counter foreign state and non-state propaganda and disinformation efforts aimed at undermining or influencing the policies, security, or stability of the United States, its allies, and partner nations.[548] According to State, in the lead-up to Russia's full-scale invasion of Ukraine, GEC scaled up its efforts to publicly expose and disrupt Russia's campaigns of information manipulation.[549] GEC has published more than 20 public reports and bulletins exposing Russia's tactics and techniques, discrediting Russia's purveyors of disinformation, and debunking Russia's persistent disinformation narratives targeting global public opinion.[550]

According to State, GEC continued its thematic and regional efforts against disinformation during the quarter. On January 25, GEC published a report detailing Russia's official use of antisemitism in public discourse for disinformation and propaganda purposes. Historic Russian antisemitism is a long-running phenomenon, State said, and has now been applied specifically to Russia's war in Ukraine. Russian leaders and propagandists seek to spread anti-Jewish conspiracy theories and use Jewish people as scapegoats to shift blame and distort world events.[551]

In February 2024, GEC exposed Russia's intelligence services for providing material support and guidance to "African Initiative," a new information agency focused on Africa-Russia relations that includes efforts to amplify Russia's disinformation narratives about the United States, our allies, and our partners supporting Ukraine.[552]

The GEC coordinates U.S. Government efforts to identify, analyze, and reveal foreign manipulation of information, including by Russia. The GEC unmasked the Kremlin's covert campaign to undermine support for Ukraine across the Western Hemisphere, Secretary of State Antony Blinken said, by "laundering Russian content through Latin American media to make it look like it was organic."[553]

On March 20, State announced U.S. sanctions against two individuals and two entities involved in spreading disinformation on behalf of the Russian government. The companies and their founders implemented a network of more than 60 websites that imitated genuine news organizations' websites in Europe, then used fake social media accounts to amplify the misleading content on the fictitious websites.[554] State said the sanctions reflect its work in continuing to counter the Kremlin's malign influence operations, and to further expose Russia's ongoing efforts to mislead audiences through state-directed deception campaigns.[555]

PRESERVING UKRAINE'S CULTURAL HERITAGE

State said the Bureau of Education and Cultural Affairs (ECA) supported during the quarter a variety of funds and programs intended to protect and preserve Ukrainian cultural heritage, which has come under attack from Russia's aggression. State ECA's partners during the quarter included UNESCO, to which ECA obligated $1.5 million to protect art by past and present Ukrainian female artists.[556] This funding supported the assessment, documentation, and conservation of paintings by folk artist Maria Prymachenko (1908-1997), the protection of other damaged objects from the Ivankiv Museum in Kyiv oblast, and the development of an inventory of Ukrainian women artists represented in Ukrainian collections.[557]

Through a $645,000 State ECA grant, the ALIPH Foundation seeks to protect at-risk archival collections in Ukraine. The foundation launched a pilot program in February to begin work at 20 regional archives in Ukraine.[558]

Finally, State ECA implemented the BridgeUSA program, which supports foreign scholars at universities, and research bodies.[559] State ECA provided $500,000 to the American Councils for International Education to run the Ukrainian Academic Fellows Program. An estimated 37 scholars will be selected for participation and likely travel later in 2024.[560]

In a second BridgeUSA project, the World Press Institute, a media organization based in St. Paul, Minnesota, will implement the Media Fellowship Program, a 3-year federal award program, by training three experienced journalists from Ukraine. The World Press Institute Ukraine journalism program's goals are to collaborate with American media experts, share best practices for reporting from conflict zones, and enhance broadcast and reporting quality at local media outlets. Past participants are Ukrainian journalists from across the spectrum of print, digital, and broadcast media, USAGM said.[561]

HUMAN RIGHTS

The Organization for Security and Cooperation in Europe (OSCE) has documented Russia's widespread violations of human rights in Ukraine. According to State, Russia has engaged in several practices that violate human rights to suppress Ukrainian resistance and enforce loyalty in the areas of Ukraine Russia controls.[562] Such practices include separating individuals, including children, from their families; transferring people to different locations; confinement and "re-education," and deporting people to Russia and elsewhere. State is working with Ukraine and international partners to hold Russia accountable for human rights violations.[563]

Russia Continues Patterns of Crimes Against Children

Russia has also been involved in the unlawful transfer, forcible deportation, confinement, or "re-education" of Ukrainian children, according to State.[564] These children have been taken to locations in Belarus, Russia, or Russia-occupied Crimea, for purposes of indoctrination, State said.[565] These activities amount to human rights abuses of Ukrainian civilian minors, State reported.[566]

The International Criminal Court, which has issued arrest warrants for Russian leaders, including President Putin, for oversight of children's transferal out of Ukraine, considers such actions proof of an "intention to permanently remove these children from their own country, State said."[567] State also noted that child deportations violate rules of the fourth Geneva Convention, a guiding international legal framework since its adoption in 1949. The removal of children from Ukraine marks a "grave breach" of Geneva Convention rules and constitutes an internationally recognized war crime, according to State.[568]

Table 18.

U.S. Goals Related to War Crimes and Human Rights

Integrated Country Strategy
Ukraine builds its capacity to document, investigate, and prosecute war crimes and enlists support from international partners to ensure perpetrators of war crimes are held to account.

Source: State, "Integrated Country Strategy-Ukraine," 8/29/2023.

RUSSIAN FILTRATION IN UKRAINE

Russian forces practice "filtration," or the forcible separation of individuals of all ages considered a potential threat to Russia's military interests in Ukraine. Filtration measures have been applied to men, women, and children, and have resulted in the separation of families. Between 900,000 and 1.6 million Ukrainian citizens have been filtered, according to State.

Russian forces bring Ukrainian citizens to filtration centers, where they are often photographed, fingerprinted, and strip-searched for any "nationalistic" tattoos expressing loyalty to Ukraine. The searches have also included passport confiscation and searches of detainees' cell phones. Russian authorities have at times also downloaded the digital contacts lists of Ukrainian detainees. Agents have also interrogated children without the agreement or presence of their parents.

In addition to detention or imprisonment, detainees are sometimes disappeared or detained in inhumane conditions.

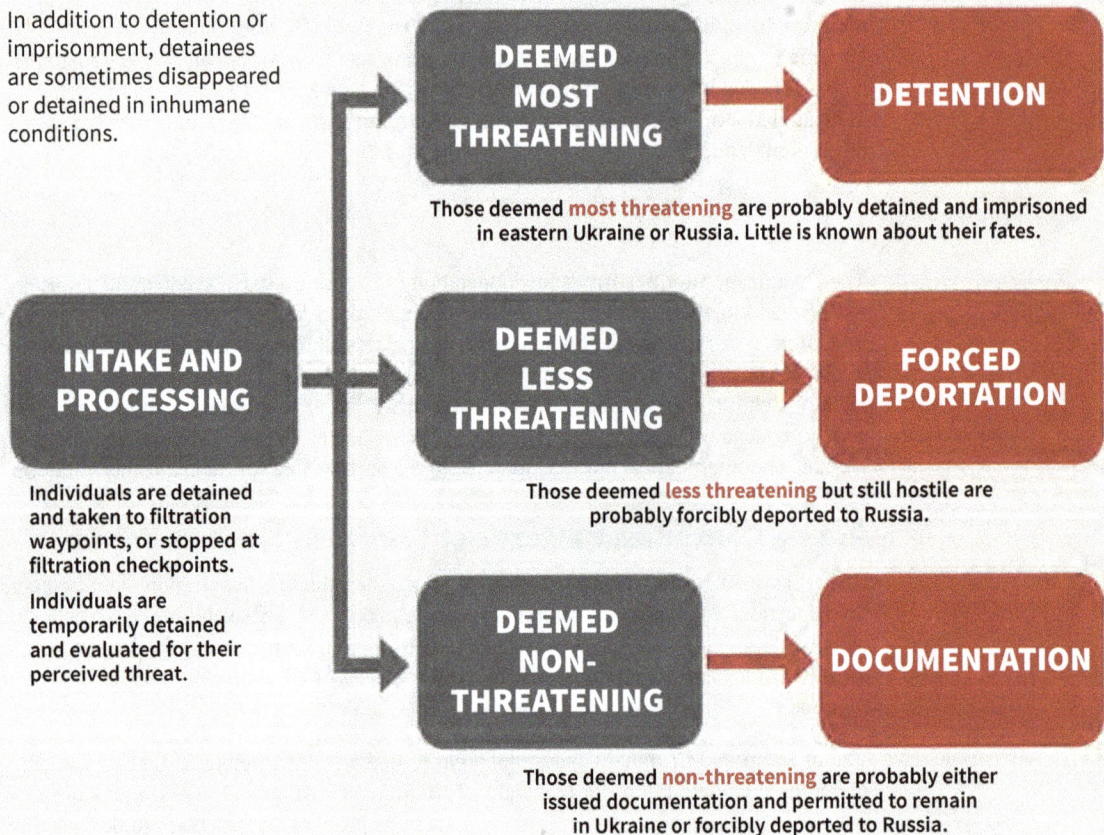

INTAKE AND PROCESSING

Individuals are detained and taken to filtration waypoints, or stopped at filtration checkpoints.

Individuals are temporarily detained and evaluated for their perceived threat.

DEEMED MOST THREATENING → **DETENTION**

Those deemed most threatening are probably detained and imprisoned in eastern Ukraine or Russia. Little is known about their fates.

DEEMED LESS THREATENING → **FORCED DEPORTATION**

Those deemed less threatening but still hostile are probably forcibly deported to Russia.

DEEMED NON-THREATENING → **DOCUMENTATION**

Those deemed non-threatening are probably either issued documentation and permitted to remain in Ukraine or forcibly deported to Russia.

" The goal [of filtration] is to change sentiments by force. To provide a fraudulent veneer of legitimacy for the Russian occupation and eventual, purported annexation of even more Ukrainian territory." –Linda Thomas-Greenfield, U.S. Ambassador to the United Nations

Sources: State, website, "Russia's Filtration Operations and Forced Relocations," undated; State, Global Engagement Center, press release, "The Kremlin's War Against Ukraine's Children," 8/24/2023; U.S. Mission to the United Nations, transcript, "Remarks by Ambassador Linda Thomas-Greenfield at a UN Security Council Meeting on Russia's Filtration Operations," 9/7/2022.

Evidence of illegal deportation of children continued to mount through the quarter. In March, media reported on a Ukrainian child deportee to Russia now living in Poland, who described how Russian authorities used him as a poster child, repeatedly putting him in front of Russian media, where he recited pro-Kremlin talking points.[569] Russian authorities castigated the child for complaining about his housing conditions and threatened him with physical abuse.[570]

In February 2023, Secretary Blinken issued an official State determination that Russia's removal of children from Ukraine constituted a crime against humanity.[571] Secretary Blinken called the pattern of deportation "part of the Kremlin's widespread and systematic attack against Ukraine's civilian population," and pledged that "the United States will pursue justice for the people of Ukraine as long as it takes."[572] On February 23, State announced sanctions for five Kremlin-backed individuals in Ukraine for their connection to the confinement and deportation of Ukrainian children.[573]

During the second quarter, State took actions to counter these crimes against children. On February 23, State announced new, broader sanctions on three Belarusian government and civil society individuals who had overseen the transfer of Ukrainian children out of Ukraine into Belarus.[574] In addition, on March 7, State announced that it had joined the International Coalition for the Return of Ukrainian Children, which "aims to identify the locations of young Ukrainians who have been illegally deported or forcibly displaced [and] reunite them with their families or place them in family-based care."[575] The United States will "support the safe return of all Ukrainian children who have been unlawfully deported or forcibly transferred by Russia," and will "ensure those responsible face consequences," State said.[576]

State Works to Hold War Criminals and Suspects Accountable

State has worked to hold Russia accountable for war crimes and atrocities through various channels of justice.[577] State said it coordinates justice for Ukraine across five pathways.[578] (See Table 19.)

On February 29, State, joining the diplomatic and other representations of 44 countries, invoked the OSCE's Moscow Mechanism to address reports of arbitrary detention of civilians and any other "arbitrary deprivation of liberty" in Russia-occupied Ukraine.[579] The Moscow Mechanism can be used to determine, in the context of Russia's current aggression toward Ukraine, whether the detentions and associated abuses "constitute war crimes or crimes against humanity" or violate international human rights law.[580]

The invocation of the Moscow Mechanism follows OSCE reports from April 2022, July 2022, and May 2023, each of which documented "widespread human rights abuses and violations of international humanitarian law" in Russia-occupied Ukraine.[581] These abuses included evidence of forcible transfer and deportation of Ukrainian children to Russia, State said.[582]

State's Office of Global Criminal Justice (GCJ), in coordination with INL, remains focused on working with Ukraine and the international community to hold accountable those responsible for Russia's war crimes committed in Ukraine.[583] The GCJ's Atrocity Crimes Advisory Group, which State helped launch in May 2022, is a US-UK-EU initiative that provides strategic advice and technical assistance to Ukraine's Office of the Prosecutor General through five implementing entities.[584]

In February 2023, Secretary Blinken issued an official State determination that Russia's removal of children from Ukraine constituted a crime against humanity.

Table 19.

State-Supported Programs to Hold Russia Accountable

Pathway	Activity
Support Ukraine's own justice system as it documents, investigates, and prosecutes war crimes	• The Atrocity Crimes Advisory Group for Ukraine (ACA), a joint US-UK-EU initiative, with implementers funded by GCJ and INL, advances this pathway by providing guidance and training to Ukraine's Office of the Prosecutor General (OPG). • INL also provides technical assistance, training and equipment to the National Police of Ukraine (NPU) as it investigates war crimes and atrocities.
Support international investigative efforts	• Supports the efforts of the International Criminal Court, the International Independent Commission of Inquiry, the Expert Missions under the OSCE's Moscow Mechanism; and the UN Special Representative of the Secretary General on Sexual Violence in Conflict, among others. • On February 29, State, joining the diplomatic and other representations of 44 countries, invoked the OSCE's Moscow Mechanism to address reports of arbitrary detention of civilians and any other "arbitrary deprivation of liberty" in Russia-occupied Ukraine.
Support justice work in national courts outside of Ukraine	• In Europe, State has supported the mass mobilization of prosecutorial and investigative authorities operating under the Eurojust umbrella to coordinate strategies, track potential defendants, and share evidence and other information. • In coordination with the Department of Justice (DoJ), State supported civil society by advancing documentation, case building, and possible strategic litigation related to the war. State's Office of Advanced Analytics manages the Conflict Observatory, a program for documenting, storing, and disseminating open-source evidence of potential human rights abuses.
Cases in U.S. courts	• State supported DoJ leadership on efforts to bring justice for war crimes in Ukraine, State said. In December 2023, DoJ announced it had charged four Russia-affiliated military personnel for war crimes, which spurred significant interest and has galvanized U.S. efforts to hold perpetrators of international war crimes responsible, State reported.
Hold Russia accountable for the crime of aggression	• State advanced plans during the quarter to provide a contribution to the International Center for the Prosecution of the Crime of Aggression (ICPA), an EU body, thereby advancing the work from across legal systems to investigate and prosecute those involved in Russia's war of aggression.

Sources: State, press release, "Invocation of the OSCE Moscow Mechanism to Examine Reports of the Russian Federation's Arbitrary Detention of Civilians in Ukraine," 2/29/2024; State, response to State OIG request for information, 3/22/2024; State, press release, "Launch of the Atrocity Crimes Advisory Group (ACA) for Ukraine," 3/25/2022.

During the quarter, the GCJ continued its leadership in promoting comprehensive justice for crimes committed against Ukraine and its people, including the International Centre for the Prosecution of the Crime of Aggression Against Ukraine, established at The Hague, Netherlands.[585]

Related efforts during the quarter included the Ukrainian government's creation of a Special Tribunal for the Crime of Aggression, which aims to bring justice to responsible parties and to establish a system of compensation that would also seek to use Russia's seized financial assets outside Russia, State said.[586]

During the quarter, State INL donated the final 12—of a total of 142—Renault Duster vehicles to the National Police Unit's (NPU) War Crimes Department.

Creating the tribunal would align with policy goals that President Zelenskyy discussed during the quarter. Russia's total assets abroad are estimated at $300 billion. State and its Ukrainian counterparts have discussed whether and how to spend the money toward Ukraine's reconstruction and recovery. "This is a historic opportunity to make the terrorist state pay for its terror," Zelenskyy said. "We firmly rely on G7 leadership on this matter."[587]

More broadly, during the quarter, State's Bureau of Democracy, Human Rights, and Labor (DRL) initiated a program aimed at preventing and mitigating the impact of transnational repression in Eurasia. State said the new program targets restrictions on and repression of civil society in authoritarian countries in Eurasia to advance human rights and fundamental freedoms. State said DRL obligated $2 million for the program, which will operate via a grant and is scheduled for completion in March 2026.[588]

INL Provides Training, Equipment to Enhance Ukraine's Capacity to Investigate War Crimes

State INL reported that it donated equipment to Ukrainian investigators and prosecutors to support the documentation and investigation of war crimes.[589] During the quarter, State INL donated the final 12—of a total of 142—Renault Duster vehicles to the National Police Unit's (NPU) War Crimes Department.[590] These vehicles will allow investigators to access alleged sites of war crimes closer to the front lines.[591] State INL also provided 30 additional vehicles, drones, rapid DNA analyzers, and 3D scanners to the NPU to support investigation of war crimes on the front lines.[592] The War Crimes Department of the Ukrainian Office of the Prosecutor General received six armored vehicles valued at $1.5 million, also from State INL.[593] The assistance is critical to holding Russia responsible for war crimes and enables investigators and prosecutors to collect evidence safely and efficiently, according to State INL.[594]

State INL stated that the NPU's capacity to investigate war crimes has increased through INL-funded Commission for International Justice and Accountability mentorship. The commission's work with NPU war crimes investigators has assisted them in adapting evidence collection and analysis techniques around identifying unit structures, chains of command, and movements, rather than individual perpetrators, to better prioritize among the more than 125,000 war crimes cases and to enable prosecutors to prove the responsibility of senior commanders and easily identify perpetrators by linking specific units to a location and time of known war crimes.[595]

Similarly, Department of Homeland Security's Human Rights Violators and War Crimes Center has provided support to investigations where atrocities are uncovered, and where the U.S. can apply jurisdiction. The Center supported the production of a human rights assessment on the activities of the Russian 64th Motorized Rifle Brigade and 76th Guards Airborne Assault Division. The Center created subject records on more than 170 suspected human rights violators connected to Russia. In Fall 2023, the Center deployed a criminal intelligence analyst to the U.S. European Command (USEUCOM) to support broader DoD efforts. The Center has not provided material or training directly to Ukrainian military, police, security services, or any other government entities.[596]

Atrocity Crimes Advisory Group Supports Ukrainian Prosecutors

In May 2022, the United States, the United Kingdom, and the European Union established the Atrocity Crimes Advisory Group for Ukraine (ACA) to provide coordinated, timely, multidisciplinary training, consultation, and strategic guidance to Ukraine's Office of the Prosecutor General (OPG) as well as regional prosecutors, State reported.[597] Based in Ukraine, with direction from its lead implementer Georgetown University, the ACA organizes joint efforts on all aspects of advancing accountability for atrocity crimes.[598] ACA helps the OPG pursue justice for victims of atrocity crimes as they continue to happen, according to State.[599] The ACA is composed of five implementing entities supported by the U.S., UK and EU.[600]

ACA activities and accomplishments have varied, both during the quarter and previously, State said.[601] The ACA advised OPG leadership on alignment of office and operations to better address atrocities, which shaped OPG's Strategic Plan for the Prosecution of International Crimes for 2023-2025.[602] The ACA has likewise encouraged strategies for longer-term success, such as building cases against higher levels of Russian military and political leadership, alignment with international best practices, and atrocity-related legislative reforms to the Ukrainian Criminal Code, State reported.[603] The ACA has sought to address war-time atrocities as they evolve, including environmental war crimes, attacks on cultural heritage, deportation of children, conflict-related sexual violence, and cybercrimes, according to State.[604]

As of March 2024, ACA experts had advised OPG personnel on more than 100 atrocity crimes cases, State said.[605] Ukrainian courts have achieved 80 convictions to date; however, all atrocity cases have been tried in absentia, State reported.[606] The ACA has conducted over 100 field missions across 15 regions in Ukraine, including hard-hit eastern and southern regions. The ACA guided OPG on victim-focused approaches to atrocity justice, leading to OPG's first-ever strategy on victim and witness support and establishment of a Victim Witness Coordination Center.[607] With ACA implementing entities based in Kyiv and elsewhere in Ukraine, personnel from the U.S. Embassy in Kyiv meet with ACA personnel and stakeholders on a regular basis, State said.[608]

The ACA measures the effectiveness of its atrocity justice work by monitoring progress and quality against donors' grant terms, including performance and financial reports, according to State.[609] The lead ACA implementer issues an operational update every two months. State INL likewise conducts biweekly calls with its implementers to measure progress, in addition to State INL's quarterly financial and performance reports, State said.[610]

As of March 2024, ACA experts had advised OPG personnel on more than 100 atrocity crimes cases, State said.

SANCTIONS

The United States, in coordination with the European Union and others, began applying sanctions against Russia following the 2014 invasion of Ukraine.[611] In response to Russia's full-scale invasion of Ukraine in February 2022, the United States greatly expanded its approach, initiating an unprecedented range of comprehensive financial and trade sanctions.[612]

Financial sector sanctions included freezing Russia's central bank's holdings of foreign exchange reserves, blocking Russia's banks from sending payments to other banks using the Society for Worldwide Interbank Financial Telecommunication (SWIFT) system, freezing Russia's banks' U.S.-held assets, and prohibiting U.S. financial institutions from processing Russia's government debt payments, among other measures.[613]

Trade sanctions included export controls on a wide variety of technologies used in Russia's manufacturing and service industries, including controlled electronics, computers, telecommunications, sensors, lasers, navigation, avionics, marine, aerospace, and propulsion technologies. In addition, the sanctions prohibited imports of Russia's oil, coal, and petroleum products; minerals, such as nickel, copper, and non-industrial diamonds; and consumables, such as seafood and alcoholic beverages.[614] The sanctions also capped the price of Russia's seaborne oil exports with the intent of limiting the amount of revenue Russia earned, while also continuing the supply of Russia's oil available on the global market.[615]

Export controls are comparable to, yet distinct from, sanctions. Export controls are often applied to otherwise legitimate technologies or goods, sometimes called dual-use goods, which can serve military and civilian purposes. The United States and its G7 partners have established numerous export control measures to restrict Russian access to these vital components.[616] For example, the Bureau of Industry and Security (BIS) at the Department of Commerce maintains a list, with a current total of 45 entries, of "Common High Priority Items" related to Russia's war against Ukraine.[617] These items are subject to U.S. export controls that require a BIS-issued license before their export or re-export to Russia or Belarus.[618]

Other areas of U.S. sanctions activity include export and import controls, visa restrictions, justice and accountability, and private-sector actions.[619]

U.S. Government Expands Sanctions Following Navalny Death

During the quarter, State said it took the following actions alongside allies and partners: applied powerful sanctions on Russia's largest financial institutions and its sovereign wealth fund; made it difficult for Russia to find funding for its war beyond its borders; choked off Russia's imports of key technologies; and targeted the financial networks and assets of Russian and Belarusian elites, including President Putin and members of his security council.[620] Treasury reported that it has imposed sanctions on more than 80 percent of Russia's banking system, preventing access to the global system. Treasury has also issued hundreds of designations, which aim to hinder Russia's efforts to evade sanctions in third countries.[621]

On February 23, State and Treasury added to U.S. sanctions lists more than 300 individuals and entities involved in Russia's aggression against Ukraine.[622] The announcement followed the February 16 death of Russian opposition politician Alexei Navalny.[623] The newly sanctioned individuals and entities include three Russian government officials with connections to Navalny's death.[624]

The sanctions also include more than 90 companies in Russia's energy, metals, military-industrial, and mining sectors, and more than two-dozen third-country "sanctions evaders" worldwide.[625] In particular, the sanctions target the Mir National Payment System, a digital payments platform set up by the Bank of Russia, which Treasury called a "major cog in Russia's financial infrastructure."[626]

Treasury noted that the expansion of sanctions "is the largest number of sanctions imposed since Russia's full-scale invasion of Ukraine."[627] More than 4,000 Russian individuals and entities with a connection to Russia's war in Ukraine are now subject to sanctions.[628]

In addition, State's Bureau for International Security and Nonproliferation (ISN) completed a series of consultations with the senior compliance officials of major financial firms in the British Virgin Islands, Germany, India, Malaysia, the Seychelles, South Korea, Spain, and Türkiye, among others, to highlight amendments to U.S. sanctions on Russia. State ISN emphasized the increased reputational, financial, and sanctions risks on financial firms that conduct significant transactions of high-priority items with Russia or its agents. State ISN also engaged with public and private sector stakeholders in the United Kingdom and East Asia on sanctions enforcement to prevent Russian access to critical defense technologies, and on Russian use of cryptocurrency to evade sanctions.[629]

Sanctioning Individuals

Beyond controlling the flow of goods valuable for Russia's war against Ukraine, State is also involved in monitoring foreign persons who may act as intermediaries for Russia while holding or applying for travel visas or other legal-entry documentation from the United States. These actions, conducted while present in the United States, constitute visa fraud or technology transfer violations, or both.[630]

In addition to direct sanctions on individuals and entities involved with Russia's war against Ukraine, the United States during the quarter also took steps to make cross-border business and trade more difficult for Russia's partners. State, in partnership with U.S. Government agencies and international partners, has sanctioned or otherwise limited the export of foreign-made technology and equipment—in particular, technology used in weapons systems—to Russia.[631]

These sanctions focus on entities in third countries, including in China, Iran, Kazakhstan, Türkiye, and the United Arab Emirates.[632] Press reports during the quarter also found that entities in Taiwan have shipped equipment, like high-precision machine tools commonly used to manufacture military materiel, to Russia.[633] Certain actors in these countries "abet Russia's war of aggression in Ukraine by providing Russia with technology and equipment," State said.[634] Actors involved in procurement for the Russian military often engage in strategies of "transshipment," or actions as third-party intermediaries, for the purpose of

On February 23, State and Treasury added to U.S. sanctions lists more than 300 individuals and entities involved in Russia's aggression against Ukraine.

obscuring the true identities of Russian end-users.[635] Similar evasion tactics are used for electronic chips and other dual-use items, which, despite export bans, are smuggled into Russia via indirect paths through Central Asia, China, Türkiye, and other trade hubs.[636]

State said that its Visa and Passport Analysis Branch cross-referenced U.S. export restrictions lists, international trade records, and U.S. visa application data to uncover insights on individuals potentially linked to Russia's networks for military procurement, according to a press report.[637] The Visa Passport and Analysis Branch identified 70 individuals employed at companies exporting "Common High Priority Items" to Russia, who applied for U.S. visas. Of these applicants, 36 percent had third-country ties "consistent with known transshipment activity."[638]

During and prior to this quarter, the loss of Western financing, companies, and workers limited Russia's access to technology, knowledge, and services, State said.[639] Russia's seizures of departing firms' assets will weaken Russia's international business reputation for years, State reported.[640] Because of U.S. Government actions, Russia has had to pursue a costly realignment of its supply chains, State said, to import lower-quality substitutes for high-tech military components from Iran, the People's Republic of China, and North Korea.[641]

More than $500 Million in Russian Assets Seized

Ukraine, with U.S. assistance, is working to enforce domestic and international sanctions and export controls.[642] U.S. assistance supports elevating the practices and capabilities of Ukraine's police and border guards to international standards, building capacity for sanctions enforcement, and control exports in order to disrupt the flow of weapons into Ukraine by malign networks.[643]

Task Force KleptoCapture is a Department of Justice (DoJ)-led interagency task force dedicated to enforcing the sweeping economic sanctions, export restrictions, and economic countermeasures that the United States imposed in response to Russia's further invasion of Ukraine in 2022. The task force investigates and prosecutes individuals and entities that support Russia's unlawful war in Ukraine, while additionally working toward seizing and ultimately forfeiting assets that can be transferred to Ukraine. To date, Task Force KleptoCapture has criminally charged over 70 individuals and entities with violating U.S. law, worked with foreign law enforcement partners to arrest multiple individuals, and seized, forfeited, or otherwise restrained more than $500 million in assets belonging to Russian oligarchs and others who unlawfully supported the Russian regime and evaded U.S. economic countermeasures.[644]

The Disruptive Technology Strike Force is an interagency enforcement effort co-led by the DoJ National Security Division and the Department of Commerce's BIS. The Strike Force is focused on pursuing criminal prosecutions and other types of enforcement actions against those who engage in the illicit transfer of emerging technologies in violation of U.S. laws. Since it was announced in February 2023, the Strike Force has launched 16 criminal cases, including the prosecutions of individuals and entities accused of illicitly providing microelectronics and other advanced technologies to companies affiliated with the Russian government and military.[645]

Sanctions Hurt Russia's Economy but Not Its Ability to Continue the War

State said that current sanctions against Russia and its partners, along with export controls, have damaged Russia's economy and limited the country's access to the goods and finances necessary for its war against Ukraine.[646] In addition, State said current sanctions and export controls have contributed to a depreciated ruble, increased inflation, and Russia's reduced ability to maintain its war machine, especially with advanced-technology components.[647] State acknowledged that more remained to be done in enforcing sanctions.[648]

ECONOMY

In total, sanctions and other restrictions imposed on Russia since February 2022 have cost Russia more than $400 billion, State said, citing one estimate.[649] The World Bank and others reported that Russia's 2022 gross domestic product dropped by 2.1 percent.[650] Some Russian policymakers, including its Finance Minister, have conceded that western sanctions have posed major challenges, State said, which could force a contraction in Russia's economic growth.[651]

Despite these positive outputs, economic sanctions have not caused the Russian government to alter its Ukraine policy, nor have sanctions significantly inhibited Russia's capacity to continue the war. President Putin has publicly touted the robustness of the Russian economy, which continues to earn billions of dollars from oil and diamond exports, despite a comprehensive international sanctions regime targeting 15,000 Russian entities and individuals. Russia's military factories continue to support the war effort, and many Russian banks have found ways of maintaining access the international financial system. According to media reporting, the Russian economy is 1 percent larger than it was on the eve of the full-scale invasion. While inflation is high—about 7 percent—unemployment is less than 3 percent.[652]

There are other indications that the Russian economy is weathering the sanctions. For instance, Russian tourists made 7 million foreign trips in the first nine months of 2023, an increase of 50 percent from the same period in 2022, albeit to countries like Türkiye, Egypt, and Thailand, rather than the United States or Europe. However, one Russian airline reported that about 20 percent of its aircraft were grounded because their U.S.-made engines could not be repaired. Luxury goods stores in Moscow continue to sell Western products, many of which are now imported from third countries like Kazakhstan.[653] Russian copycat versions of Western consumer brands are helping fill sanctions-related trade gaps, media reported.[654]

A Treasury task force reported that sanctions evasion tactics included: using family and close associates to maintain access to frozen accounts; buying real estate to park wealth or launder proceeds derived from sanctions evasion; creating shell companies to avoid detection; and using third-party individuals and jurisdictions to open bank accounts, create corporate structures, and falsify trade information to facilitate the shipment of sensitive goods to Russia.[655] Additionally, according to the Biden Administration, Russia has created "cutouts" and front companies to circumvent restrictions, often involving "witting and unwitting" financial intermediaries.[656]

State said that dual-use goods continue to make their way into Russia, via intermediary countries including Kazakhstan, Kyrgyzstan, Türkiye, and the United Arab Emirates. In 2023, over $650 million in priority dual-use goods transited these and other countries, State said. State engages diplomatic and other counterparts to raise concerns over the dangers that dual-use goods can pose, and requests specific actions to disrupt and deter dual-use trade flows into Russia.[657] Modest gains on this front took place during the quarter, State said, for example through the March decisions by Japan, Taiwan, and South Korea to implement more comprehensive export and re-export restrictions for machine tools. Discussions on dual-use trade restrictions in Taiwan and Türkiye are expected to continue, State said.[658] Internationally, G7 leaders have committed to increasing restrictions on Russia's use of the global financial system, to stop the country from expanding its military-industrial base amid its continuing war on Ukraine, State said.[659]

MILITARY

Russian forces are employing satellite imagery provided by private U.S. companies to direct their cruise missile strikes against Ukrainian targets, media reported. These companies offer on demand, high-resolution satellite images at costs in the low thousands of dollars.[660] Many of the companies offer a backlist of archived images, including dates and coordinates, requested by clients. Independent media reporting found a strong correlation between Ukrainian targets struck by Russian missiles and locations imaged by these companies shortly before and after the strikes. These companies are prohibited from dealing with the Russian government, which likely purchased the satellite images through third-party intermediaries, a common tactic for evading sanctions.[661]

> **Russia's economy has benefited from a massive fiscal stimulus from the war effort, increasing spending by $30 billion in 2024 without widening its budget deficit due to oil revenues, according to the European Council.**

Russia's economy has benefited from a massive fiscal stimulus from the war effort, increasing spending by $30 billion in 2024 without widening its budget deficit due to oil revenues, according to the European Council.[662] One Russian state-owned defense company increased the production of armored vehicles nearly fivefold in 2023, and other firms have seen similarly large increases in the production of munitions and UAVs.[663] Former Ukrainian General Valeriy Zaluzhnyy during the quarter commented on the "weakness of the international sanctions' regime" allowing Russia to maintain its robust military-industrial complex.[664]

Russia imported more than $900 million worth of battlefield and dual-use technology per month in the first half of 2023, according to media reporting. While much of this materiel comes from friendly countries like the PRC—which accounts for roughly half of all Russian imports—the UK National Crime Agency recently reported that the Russian government was attempting to procure UK sanctioned goods through intermediary countries, using complex supply chains and alternative supply routes. The U.S. Treasury has sanctioned several PRC, Turkish, and UAE companies attempting to obtain equipment from U.S. firms on behalf of Russia.[665]

Russia's long-term economic prospects may not be as healthy, given that the war is diverting a significant share of the country's resources from non-military purposes. The Russian government will devote 40 percent of its budget to the military in 2024, withholding resources from other sectors like education and healthcare.[666]

Oil Price Cap Limits Russian Oil Sector Revenues

The United States has worked with allies to establish the Price Cap Coalition, a group of countries that, short of refusing further purchases of Russian crude oil, will commit instead to buy oil at a maximum price of $60 per barrel when delivered as a maritime import.[667] Global crude prices averaged above $80 per barrel during the quarter.[668] The price cap will serve to limit Russia's oil profits amid a higher price environment, which State has termed a "wartime premium" on Russia's oil sales. [669]

In February, Treasury stated that increased enforcement of the price cap on Russian oil had forced Russia to sell at a steep discount, resulting in reduced oil tax revenue in the first nine months of 2023.[670]

Russia's oil export revenue in December 2023 fell by $2.6 billion compared to November 2022, before implementation of the Coalition's import bans and price cap policy, State said. Russia's oil tax revenue declined by 36 percent in January through October 2023 relative to the same period in 2022, State reported.[671] According to a January 2024 report published by Russia's Finance Ministry, Russia's annual oil and natural gas revenues fell to just over $99 billion in 2023, a 24 percent decrease, after the start of Russia's war in Ukraine in February 2022, according to State.[672] In addition, hydrocarbon-generated revenues in 2023 amounted to their the lowest since 2020, when the COVID-19 pandemic pushed oil demand and prices sharply lower, State reported.[673] This has significant implications for Russia, considering that Russia in 2021 relied on oil and gas revenues for 45 percent of its federal budget, State said.[674]

Nonetheless, global demand for oil and other commodities—keystones of the Russian economy—remain high, and most Asian countries have not agreed to participate in sanctions against Russia. The PRC and India's collective purchases of Russian oil and gas have increased 13-fold since February 2022 and now account for about 90 percent of Russia's energy exports, media reported.[675] Russia has also found ways to circumvent sanctions, such as developing a network of shipping companies from nations outside the sanctions regime, to keep its oil flowing. According to media reporting, 71 percent of Russia's oil exports are now moving on ships whose ownership and registration details are camouflaged.[676]

Russian individuals and entities continued to evade restrictions during the quarter, while the Kremlin continued to circumvent efforts to cap oil revenues through the use of "ghost" fleets and mid-ocean transfers that obscure the oil's origin, or by routing invoices through intermediary companies.[677] Similar evasion tactics are used for electronic chips and other dual-use items, which, despite export bans, are smuggled into Russia via indirect paths through Central Asia or China.[678]

Russia's oil export revenue in December 2023 fell by $2.6 billion compared to November 2022, before implementation of the Coalition's import bans and price cap policy, State said.

The Department of the Treasury's Office of Foreign Assets Control (OFAC) imposed sanctions on five entities and identified 19 vessels as blocked property as part of the United States' price cap enforcement actions this quarter.

U.S. Applies Additional Energy Sector Sanctions

The United States during the quarter continued its efforts to take actions against those who violate or evade the oil price cap. The Department of the Treasury's Office of Foreign Assets Control (OFAC) imposed sanctions on five entities and identified 19 vessels as blocked property as part of the United States' price cap enforcement actions this quarter. State cited the example of the shipping company Hennesea Holdings Limited, the owner of the vessel HS Atlantica, which has shipped Russian crude priced above $60 per barrel while using the Price Cap Coalition's services.[679] OFAC took further steps during the quarter to responsibly reduce Russia's revenue from oil sales, including designating Sovcomflot, Russia's state-owned shipping company and fleet operator, on February 24, 2024.[680]

The United States continued during the quarter its efforts to sanction entities involved in the expansion of Russia's energy production and export capacities.[681] This included designations during the quarter of major entities involved in the financing and construction of highly specialized liquefied natural gas tankers specifically for LLC Arctic LNG 2, the operator of Russia's Arctic LNG 2 project, as well as several other entities involved in the development of Arctic LNG 2 and other future energy projects in Russia. These actions followed the U.S. Department of State's designation of LLC Arctic LNG 2 in November 2023 and multiple other sanctions designations targeting the Arctic LNG 2 project. These designations have resulted in Arctic LNG 2 project delays, including the project's suspension of production as it has been unable to begin commercial deliveries.[682]

COUNTERNARCOTICS

Prior to February 2022, Ukraine served as a transit country for non-domestically produced drugs such as cocaine and heroin, which were most frequently bound for consumer markets in the European Union and Russia. Ukraine's southern ports on the Black Sea, notably Odesa and Pivdennyy, served as the primary inject points for the transit of illicit drugs. This trafficking model was dramatically disrupted following Russia's full-scale invasion of Ukraine, which severely diminished ship traffic in and out of Ukraine's Black Sea ports.[683]

The Drug Enforcement Agency (DEA) said that the disruption of transit through northern, eastern, and southeastern Ukraine has created an unacceptable risk for international illicit trafficking activities. Further, while Ukraine is under martial law, numerous security checkpoints throughout the country apply greater scrutiny to the movement of overland cargo. In response, transnational criminal organizations have shifted illicit trafficking activities through nearby countries.[684]

While displacement due to the conflict has curtailed production and distribution for domestically produced illicit drugs, clandestine laboratory activity quickly resumed to meet domestic demand. The DEA reported that these operations are increasingly numerous, although smaller in scale, with distribution activities supported by internet-based sales and delivery through the Ukrainian postal system, taxi services, or "dead drops." Illicit trafficking activities are further supported by a network of call centers which operate throughout Ukraine and Eastern Europe to manage and support the internet-based drug marketplace.[685]

The DEA reported that the United States enjoys strong bilateral cooperation with the Ukrainian State Border Guard Service Investigative Activities Department and the National Police Unit Counternarcotics Department. The DEA said that while it has had bilateral investigative and operational successes in recent years, widespread corruption in Ukraine's justice system continues to impede investigations into the most prolific drug trafficking organizations operating in the country.[686]

ADMINISTRATION OF FOREIGN AFFAIRS

Table 21.

Use of Ukraine Supplemental Funds Appropriated to Administration of Foreign Affairs Accounts

Account	Activity
Capital Investment Fund	• The fund is used to procure and enhance information technology and other related capital investments, and to ensure efficient management, coordination, operation, and utilization of such assets. As of this quarter, State had obligated $38 million and expended $27 million in Ukraine supplemental funds for such information technology and related capital investments.
Diplomatic Programs	• The Diplomatic Programs funds State's overseas and domestic administrative operations. As of March 31, 2024, State had obligated $237 million and expended $152.5 million of the Diplomatic Programs funds appropriated under the Ukraine supplemental appropriations.
Emergencies in the Diplomatic and Consular Service	• The fund is used to meet unforeseen emergency requirements in the conduct of foreign affairs, including evacuations of U.S. Government personnel and their families overseas, and, in certain circumstances, private U.S. citizens and third-country nationals, as well as other authorized activities that further the realization of U.S. foreign policy objectives. • To date, State has allocated $5 million for EDCS, but no requests have been made to use the funds.
Bureau of Overseas Buildings Operations Embassy Security, Construction, and Maintenance account	• State received $110 million in Ukraine supplemental appropriations for the Embassy Security, Construction, and Maintenance account. As of March 31, 2024, State had obligated approximately $15 million and expended $14 million. In January 2024, State completed construction of improvements to Embassy Kyiv's fourth floor.

Sources: State, "Congressional Budget Justification: Department of State, Foreign Operations, and Related Programs, Fiscal Year 2022," 5/28/2021; State, responses to State OIG request for information, 3/22/2024 and 4/22/2024.

A Norwegian F-35 Lightning II maneuvers into position to receive fuel from a KC-135 Stratotanker during the Nordic Response 24 exercise. (DoD photo)

APPENDIXES

APPENDIX A
Classified Appendix to this Report

A classified appendix to this report provides additional information on Operation Atlantic Resolve (OAR) and the U.S. Government's response to Russia's invasion of Ukraine. The appendix will be delivered to relevant agencies and congressional committees.

APPENDIX B
About the Special Inspector General for OAR

The Inspector General Act of 1978, as amended (5 U.S.C. Section 419, previously found at 5 U.S.C. App, Section 8L) established the Lead Inspector General (Lead IG) framework for oversight of overseas contingency operations. The primary Lead IG agencies are the Offices of Inspector General (OIG) of the Department of Defense (DoD), the Department of State (State), and the U.S. Agency for International Development (USAID).

Section 419 requires the Council of the Inspectors General on Integrity and Efficiency (CIGIE) to appoint a Lead Inspector General from among the inspectors general of the primary Lead IG agencies upon the commencement or designation of a military operation that exceeds 60 days as an overseas contingency operation; or receipt of notification thereof.

On August 18, 2023, the DoD designated OAR as an overseas contingency operation. The CIGIE Chair selected the DoD IG to be the Lead IG for OAR, and the State IG was selected to be the Associate Lead IG for OAR, effective October 18, 2023.

Section 1250B of the National Defense Authorization Act of 2024 redesignated Lead IG for OAR the Special Inspector General for OAR. The law specifies that the redesignation does not limit the DoD OIG and its partner agencies from exercising their responsibilities under the Lead IG framework.

Both the Special IG and Lead IG oversight of the operation "sunsets" at the end of the first fiscal year after commencement or designation in which the total amount appropriated for the operation is less than $100,000,000.

The Lead IG agencies collectively carry out the Lead IG statutory responsibilities to:

- Submit to Congress on a quarterly basis a report on the contingency operation and to make that report available to the public. The National Defense Authorization Act of 2024 specifies that the quarterly report for OAR be submitted to Congress no later than 45 days after the end of each quarter.
- Develop a joint strategic plan to conduct comprehensive oversight of the operation.
- Ensure independent and effective oversight of programs and operations of the U.S. Government in support of the operation through either joint or individual audits, inspections, investigations, and evaluations.

APPENDIX C
Methodology for Preparing this Special IG Quarterly Report

This report complies with Section 1250B of the National Defense Authorization Act of 2024 and the Inspector General Act of 1978, as amended (5 U.S.C. Section 419). The Inspector General Act requires that the DoD IG--as the previously designated Lead IG for OAR and now the Special IG for OAR--must provide a quarterly report, available to the public, on each overseas contingency operation. This requirement is consistent with the requirement that the Lead IG publish a biannual report on the activities of the Inspectors General with respect to that overseas contingency operation.

This report covers the period from January 1 through March 31, 2024. The DoD OIG, State OIG, USAID OIG, and partner oversight agencies contributed to the content of this report.

To fulfill the congressional mandate to report on OAR, the DoD, State, and USAID OIGs gather data and information from Federal agencies and open sources. The sources of information contained in this report are listed in endnotes or notes to tables and figures. Except in the case of audits, inspections, investigations, and evaluations referenced in this report, the OIGs have not verified or audited the information collected through open-source research or from Federal agencies, and the information provided represents the view of the source cited in each instance.

INFORMATION COLLECTION FROM AGENCIES AND OPEN SOURCES

Each quarter, the DoD, State, and USAID OIGs gather information about their programs and operations related to OAR from Federal government agencies. This report also draws on current, publicly available information from reputable sources. Sources used in this report may include the following:

- U.S. Government statements, press conferences, and reports
- Reports issued by international organizations, nongovernmental organizations, and think tanks
- Media reports

The Lead IG agencies use open-source information to assess information obtained through their agency information collection process and provide additional detail about the operation.

REPORT PRODUCTION

The DoD IG, as the Special IG (and previously designated Lead IG) for OAR, is responsible for assembling and producing this report. The DoD, State, and USAID OIGs draft the sections of the report related to the activities of their agencies and then participate in editing the entire report. Once assembled, each OIG coordinates a two-phase review of the report within its own agency. During the first review, the Lead IG agencies ask relevant offices within their agencies to comment, correct inaccuracies, and provide additional documentation. The three OIGs incorporate agency comments, where appropriate, and send the report back to the agencies for a second review prior to publication. The final report reflects the editorial view of the DoD, State, and USAID OIGs as independent oversight agencies.

APPENDIX D
U.S. Weapons, Equipment, and Ammunition Committed to Ukraine

Air Defense

- One Patriot air defense battery and munitions
- 12 National Advanced Surface-to-Air Missile Systems (NASAMS) and munitions
- HAWK air defense systems and munitions
- AIM-7, RIM-7, and AIM-9M missiles for air defense
- More than 2,000 Stinger anti-aircraft missiles
- Avenger air defense systems
- VAMPIRE counter-Unmanned Aerial Systems (c-UAS) and munitions
- c-UAS gun trucks and ammunition
- Mobile c-UAS laser-guided rocket systems
- Other c-UAS equipment
- Anti-aircraft guns and ammunition
- Air defense systems components
- Equipment to integrate Western launchers, missiles, and radars with Ukraine's systems
- Equipment to support and sustain Ukraine's existing air defense capabilities
- Equipment to protect critical national infrastructure
- 21 air surveillance radars

Ground Maneuver

- 31 Abrams tanks
- 45 T-72B tanks
- 186 Bradley Infantry Fighting Vehicles
- Four Bradley Fire Support Team vehicles
- 189 Stryker Armored Personnel Carriers
- 300 M113 Armored Personnel Carriers
- 250 M1117 Armored Security Vehicles
- More than 500 Mine Resistant Ambush Protected Vehicles (MRAPs)

- More than 2,000 High Mobility Multipurpose Wheeled Vehicles (HMMWVs)
- More than 200 light tactical vehicles
- 300 armored medical treatment vehicles
- 80 trucks and 124 trailers to transport heavy equipment
- More than 800 tactical vehicles to tow and haul equipment
- 131 tactical vehicles to recover equipment
- 10 command post vehicles
- 30 ammunition support vehicles
- 18 armored bridging systems
- Eight logistics support vehicles and equipment
- 239 fuel tankers and 105 fuel trailers
- 58 water trailers
- Six armored utility trucks
- 125mm, 120mm, and 105mm tank ammunition
- More than 1,800,000 rounds of 25mm ammunition
- Mine clearing equipment.

Fires

- 39 High Mobility Artillery Rocket Systems and ammunition
- Ground-Launched Small Diameter Bomb launchers and guided rockets
- 198 155mm Howitzers and more than 2,000,000 155mm artillery rounds
- More than 7,000 precision-guided 155mm artillery rounds
- More than 40,000 155mm rounds of Remote Anti-Armor Mine (RAAM) Systems
- 72 105mm Howitzers and more than 800,000 105mm artillery rounds
- 10,000 203mm artillery rounds
- More than 200,000 152mm artillery rounds
- Approximately 40,000 130mm artillery rounds

- 40,000 122mm artillery rounds
- 60,000 122mm GRAD rockets
- 47 120mm mortar systems
- 10 82mm mortar systems
- 112 81mm mortar systems
- 58 60mm mortar systems
- More than 400,000 mortar rounds
- More than 70 counter-artillery and counter-mortar radars
- 20 multi-mission radars

Aircraft and Unmanned Aerial Systems

- 20 Mi-17 helicopters
- Switchblade Unmanned Aerial Systems (UAS)
- Phoenix Ghost UAS
- CyberLux K8 UAS
- Altius-600 UAS
- Jump-20 UAS
- Hornet UAS
- Puma UAS
- Scan Eagle UAS
- Penguin UAS
- Two radars for UAS
- High-speed Anti-radiation missiles (HARMs)
- Precision aerial munitions
- More than 6,000 Zuni aircraft rockets
- More than 20,000 Hydra-70 aircraft rockets
- Munitions for UAS

Anti-armor and Small Arms

- More than 10,000 Javelin anti-armor systems
- More than 90,000 other anti-armor systems and munitions
- More than 9,000 Tube-Launched, Optically-Tracked, Wire-Guided (TOW) missiles
- More than 35,000 grenade launchers and small arms
- More than 400,000,000 rounds of small arms ammunition and grenades

- Laser-guided rocket systems and munitions
- Rocket launchers and ammunition
- Anti-tank mines

Maritime

- Two Harpoon coastal defense systems and anti-ship missiles
- 62 coastal and riverine patrol boats
- Unmanned Coastal Defense Vessels
- Port and harbor security equipment

Other Capabilities

- M18A1 Claymore anti-personnel munitions
- C-4 explosives, demolition munitions, and demolition equipment for obstacle clearing
- Obstacle emplacement equipment
- Counter air defense capability
- More than 100,000 sets of body armor and helmets
- Tactical secure communications systems and support equipment
- Four satellite communications (SATCOM) antennas
- SATCOM terminals and services
- Electronic warfare (EW) and counter-EW equipment
- Commercial satellite imagery services
- Night vision devices, surveillance and thermal imagery systems, optics, and rangefinders
- Explosive ordnance disposal equipment and protective gear
- Chemical, Biological, Radiological, Nuclear protective equipment
- Medical supplies, including first aid kits, bandages, monitors, and other equipment
- Field equipment, cold weather gear, generators, and spare parts
- Support for training, maintenance, and sustainment activities

Source: DoD, fact sheet, "Fact Sheet on U.S. Security Assistance to Ukraine," 3/12/2024.

APPENDIX E
DoD Funding for Ukraine Assistance

Table 22.

DoD Execution of First Ukraine Supplemental (P.L. 117-103), in $ Thousands

Department	Category	Period of Availability	Available Funds Apportioned	Cumulative Obligations	Cumulative Disbursements
Direct Military & Other Support					
Army	Military Personnel, Army	2022	130,377	124,255	123,662
	Operation & Maintenance	2022	1,113,234	1,108,110	1,042,011
Army Total			**1,243,611**	**1,232,365**	**1,165,673**
Navy	Military Personnel, Marine Corps	2022	3,079	1,026	1,026
	Operation & Maintenance, Marine Corps	2022	21,440	21,440	13,156
	Research, Development, Test & Evaluation, Navy	2022/2023	31,100	31,100	31,100
	Military Personnel, Navy	2022/2023	11,645	967	967
	Operation & Maintenance, Navy	2022/2023	202,797	202,797	202,797
Navy Total			**270,061**	**257,330**	**249,046**
Air Force	Other Procurement, Air Force	2022/2024	213,693	206,537	186,464
	Operation & Maintenance, Air Force	2022	418,442	418,442	418,442
	Operation & Maintenance, Space Force	2022	800	800	800
	Military Personnel, Air Force	2022	50,396	40,226	40,226
	Research, Development, Test, & Evaluation, Air Force	2022/2023	47,500	47,500	45,287
Air Force Total			**730,831**	**713,505**	**691,218**
Defense-Wide	Operation & Maintenance, Defense-Wide	2022	316,583	316,583	221,129
	Procurement, Defense-Wide	2022/2024	6,259	6,259	4,407
	Research, Development, Test, & Evaluation, Defense-Wide	2022/2023	51,745	51,745	39,935
	Defense Working Capital Fund	2022	409,000	408,482	408,482
Defense-Wide Total			**783,587**	**783,069**	**673,953**
DIRECT MILITARY & OTHER SUPPORT TOTAL			**3,028,090**	**2,986,269**	**2,779,891**

Department	Category	Period of Availability	Available Funds Apportioned	Cumulative Obligations	Cumulative Disbursements
DoD Stocks Replenishment					
Army	Operation & Maintenance, Army	2022	351,367	350,014	128,600
	Operation & Maintenance, Army	2022/2023	48,799	48,799	27,562
	Missile Procurement, Army	2022/2024	1,298,497	1,296,791	280,051
	Procurement Of Weapons & Tracked Combat Vehicles, Army	2022/2024	933	920	914
	Procurement Of Weapons & Tracked Combat Vehicles, Army	2022/2025	278,400	271,771	0
	Procurement Of Ammunition, Army	2022/2024	563,226	545,603	140,563
	Other Procurement, Army	2022/2024	77,615	70,105	18,364
Army Total			**2,618,837**	**2,584,002**	**596,053**
Navy	Operation & Maintenance, Marine Corps.	2022	23,437	23,437	23,437
	Procurement, Marine Corps	2022/2024	686,657	683,423	57,741
	Procurement of Ammunition, Navy and Marine Corps	2022/2024	32,902	32,896	3,435
	Operation & Maintenance, Navy	2022	7,638	7,638	7,638
Navy Total			**750,634**	**747,394**	**92,251**
Air Force	Operation & Maintenance, Air Force	2022/2023	60,803	60,803	24,725
Air Force Total			**60,803**	**60,803**	**24,725**
Defense-Wide	Operation & Maintenance, Defense-Wide (PDA Replenishment)	2022/2023	69,726	0	0
Defense-Wide Total			**69,726**	**0**	**0**
DoD STOCKS REPLENISHMENT TOTAL			**3,500,000**	**3,392,200**	**713,029**
P.L. 117-103 TOTAL			**6,528,090**	**6,378,469**	**3,492,919**

Source: OUSD(C), response to DoD OIG request for information, 24.2 OAR 003, 4/3/2024.

Table 23.

DoD Execution of Second Ukraine Supplemental (P.L. 117-128), in $ Thousands

Department	Category	Period of Availability	Available Funds Apportioned	Cumulative Obligations	Cumulative Disbursements
Direct Military & Other Support					
Army	Military Personnel, Army	2022	12,750	12,750	12,750
	Operation & Maintenance, Army	2022	1,495,459	1,491,068	1,410,212
	Missile Procurement, Army	2022/2024	660,682	630,807	95,782
	Procurement Of Weapons & Tracked Combat Vehicles, Army	2022/2024	255	102	95
	Procurement Of Ammunition, Army	2022/2024	45	45	45
	Other Procurement, Army	2022/2024	113,440	84,259	30,041
	Research, Development, Test, & Evaluation, Army	2022/2023	128,700	128,700	124,866
Army Total			**2,411,331**	**2,347,731**	**1,673,791**
Navy	Military Personnel, Marine Corps	2022	675	0	0
	Research, Development, Test & Evaluation, Navy	2022/2023	43,000	43,000	26,076
	Military Personnel, Navy	2022	38	0	0
	Weapons Procurement, Navy	2022/2024	74,264	74,264	30,317
	Operation & Maintenance, Navy	2022	939,779	939,779	939,779
	Other Procurement, Navy	2022/2024	1,250	1,250	1,001
Navy Total			**1,059,006**	**1,058,293**	**997,173**
Air Force	Aircraft Procurement, Air Force	2022/2024	28,500	28,500	10,221
	Missile Procurement, Air Force	2022/2024	114,097	111,730	47,777
	Other Procurement, Air Force	2022/2024	155,382	135,614	76,504
	Operation & Maintenance, Air Force	2022	195,262	195,262	195,262
	Operation & Maintenance, Space Force	2022	800	800	800
	Military Personnel, Air Force	2022	1,590	1,545	1,545
	Research, Development, Test, & Evaluation, Air Force	2022/2023	119,815	119,789	54,836
Air Force Total			**615,446**	**593,241**	**386,945**

Department	Category	Period of Availability	Available Funds Apportioned	Cumulative Obligations	Cumulative Disbursements
Defense-Wide	Operation & Maintenance, Defense-Wide	2022	206,824	206,824	206,824
	Defense Health Program	2022	13,900	686	686
	Procurement, Defense-Wide	2022/2024	24,218	15,895	11,496
	Defense Production Act Purchases, Defense	2022 until expended	600,000	358,299	29,814
	Research, Development, Test & Evaluation, Defense-Wide	2022/2023	122,103	120,562	44,499
	Defense Working Capital Fund	2022	965	904	902
Defense-Wide Total			**968,010**	**703,170**	**294,221**
DIRECT MILITARY & OTHER SUPPORT TOTAL			**5,053,793**	**4,702,435**	**3,352,130**
DoD Stocks Replenishment					
Army	Operation & Maintenance, Army	2022	2,750	2,633	1,759
	Operation & Maintenance, Army	2023/2023	414,795	414,795	287,771
	Missile Procurement, Army	2022/2024	1,191,544	1,191,540	182,959
	Missile Procurement, Army	2023/2025	489,790	488,862	33,491
	Procurement Of Weapons & Tracked Combat Vehicles, Army	2022/2024	961,707	935,294	56,308
	Procurement Of Weapons & Tracked Combat Vehicles, Army	2023/2025	457,020	349,143	14,755
	Procurement Of Ammunition, Army	2022/2024	1,016,077	1,006,711	407,361
	Procurement Of Ammunition, Army	2023/2025	2,076,062	2,045,917	56,873
	Other Procurement, Army	2022/2024	291,901	275,946	21,028
	Other Procurement, Army	2023/2025	567,186	471,325	44,685
Army Total			**7,468,832**	**7,182,167**	**1,106,990**
Navy	Operation & Maintenance, Marine Corps	2022	38,446	38,446	32,234
	Operation & Maintenance, Marine Corps	2023/2023	11,011	11,011	10,502
	Procurement, Marine Corps	2022/2024	51,074	50,990	14,779
	Weapons Procurement, Navy	2022/2024	106,108	105,415	4,837
	Weapons Procurement, Navy	2023/2025	14,410	14,410	5,364
	Procurement of Ammunition, Navy and Marine Corps	2022/2024	124,390	124,390	1,747

(continued on next page)

Department	Category	Period of Availability	Available Funds Apportioned	Cumulative Obligations	Cumulative Disbursements
	Procurement of Ammunition, Navy and Marine Corps	2023/2025	24,875	24,873	16
	Operation & Maintenance, Navy	2022	205,465	195,967	2,372
	Operation & Maintenance, Navy	2023/2023	55,795	53,950	25,946
	Other Procurement, Navy	2022/2024	98,220	98,220	98,220
Navy Total			**807,302**	**795,117**	**218,524**
Air Force	Missile Procurement, Air Force	2023/2025	144,624	144,608	7,223
	Operation & Maintenance, Air Force	2022	265,043	265,043	265,043
	Operation & Maintenance, Air Force	2023/2023	187,824	187,824	187,824
	Procurement of Ammunition, Air Force	2023/2025	1,016	1,012	85
Air Force Total			**598,507**	**598,487**	**460,175**
Defense-Wide	Operation & Maintenance, Defense-Wide	2023/2023	15,935	15,282	830
	Operation & Maintenance, Defense-Wide [PDA Replenishment]	2022/2023	0	0	0
	Procurement, Defense-Wide	2023/2025	13,424	13,424	13,416
	Defense Production Act Purchases, Defense	2022 until expended	146,000	0	0
Defense-Wide Total			**175,359**	**28,706**	**14,246**
DoD STOCKS REPLENISHMENT TOTAL			**9,050,000**	**8,604,477**	**1,799,935**
Ukraine Security Assistance Initiative (USAI) Defense-Wide					
USAI Defense-Wide	Operation & Maintenance, Defense-Wide [USAI]	2022/2023	6,000,000	5,987,367	5,984,086
USAI DEFENSE-WIDE TOTAL			**6,000,000**	**5,987,367**	**5,984,086**
P.L. 117-128 TOTAL			**20,103,793**	**19,294,279**	**11,136,151**

Source: OUSD(C), response to DoD OIG request for information, 24.2 OAR 003, 4/3/2024.

Table 24.

DoD Execution of Third Ukraine Supplemental (P.L. 117-180), in $ Thousands

Department	Category	Period of Availability	Available Funds Apportioned	Cumulative Obligations	Cumulative Disbursements
Direct Military & Other Support					
Army	Military Personnel, Army	2023/2023	110,107	110,107	110,107
	Operation & Maintenance, Army	2023/2023	654,696	654,696	517,647
	Missile Procurement, Army	2023/2025	450,000	450,000	65,133
	Procurement Of Ammunition, Army	2023/2025	540,000	459,424	25,352
	Other Procurement, Army	2023/2025	3,890	3,890	2,206
	Research, Development, Test & Evaluation, Army	2023/2024	3,300	3,300	2,254
Army Total			**1,761,993**	**1,681,417**	**722,698**
Navy	Military Personnel, Marine Corps	2023/2023	600	600	600
	Operation & Maintenance, Marine Corps	2023/2023	34,984	34,984	24,559
	Research, Development, Test & Evaluation, Navy	2023/2024	2,077	2,077	2,077
	Military Personnel, Navy	2023/2023	462	462	462
	Operation & Maintenance, Navy	2023/2023	433,035	433,035	363,522
	Other Procurement, Navy	2023/2025	2,170	2,170	661
Navy Total			**473,328**	**473,328**	**391,881**
Air Force	Other Procurement, Air Force	2023/2025	437,991	396,343	215,817
	Operation & Maintenance, Air Force	2023/2023	267,084	267,084	196,957
	Operation & Maintenance, Space Force	2023/2023	1,771	1,771	1,313
	Military Personnel, Air Force	2023/2023	11,582	11,582	11,582
	Research, Development, Test, & Evaluation, Air Force	2023/2024	99,704	88,251	46,283
Air Force Total			**818,132**	**765,031**	**471,953**

(continued on next page)

Department	Category	Period of Availability	Available Funds Apportioned	Cumulative Obligations	Cumulative Disbursements
Defense-Wide	Operation & Maintenance, Defense-Wide	2023/2023	213,544	213,544	151,432
	Office of the Inspector General	2023/2023	9,770	8,701	1,837
	Procurement, Defense-Wide	2023/2025	31,230	27,900	27,723
	Research, Development, Test, & Evaluation, Defense-Wide	2023/2024	2,000	2,000	2,000
Defense-Wide Total			**256,544**	**252,145**	**182,992**
DIRECT MILITARY & OTHER SUPPORT TOTAL			**3,309,997**	**3,171,921**	**1,769,523**
DoD Stocks Replenishment					
Army	Missile Procurement, Army	2023/2025	606,701	252,255	14,867
	Procurement Of Weapons & Tracked Combat Vehicles, Army	2023/2025	800,658	12,913	0
	Procurement Of Ammunition, Army	2023/2025	92,565	56,974	2,185
Army Total			**1,499,924**	**322,141**	**17,053**
Navy	Procurement of Ammunition, Navy and Marine Corps	2023/2025	36	0	0
Navy Total			**36**	**0**	**0**
Defense-Wide	Operation & Maintenance, Defense-Wide [USAI]	2023/2024	40	0	0
Defense-Wide Total			**40**	**0**	**0**
DoD STOCKS REPLENISHMENT TOTAL			**1,500,000**	**322,141**	**17,053**
USAI Defense-Wide					
Defense-Wide	Operation & Maintenance, Defense-Wide [USAI]	2023/2024	3,000,000	2,866,777	2,821,373
USAI DEFENSE-WIDE TOTAL			**3,000,000**	**2,866,777**	**2,821,373**
P.L. 117-180 TOTAL			**7,809,997**	**6,360,839**	**4,607,949**

Source: OUSD(C), response to DoD OIG request for information, 24.2 OAR 003, 4/3/2024.

Table 25.

DoD Execution of Fourth Ukraine Supplemental (P.L. 117-328), in $ Thousands

Department	Category	Period of Availability	Available Funds Apportioned	Cumulative Obligations	Cumulative Disbursements
Direct Military & Other Support					
Army	Military Personnel, Army	2023/2023	54,252	54,252	54,252
	Operation & Maintenance, Army	2023/2023	3,020,741	3,020,741	2,324,805
	Missile Procurement, Army	2023/2025	354,000	224,109	6,887
	Procurement Of Ammunition, Army	2023/2025	687,000	542,268	266,119
	Other Procurement, Army	2023/2025	6,000	6,000	1,398
	Research, Development, Test, & Evaluation, Army	2023/2024	5,800	5,800	466
Army Total			**4,127,793**	**3,853,170**	**2,653,926**
Navy	Military Personnel, Marine Corps	2023/2023	1,400	674	674
	Operation & Maintenance, Marine Corps	2023/2023	14,620	14,620	11,527
	Research, Development, Test, & Evaluation, Navy	2023/2024	38,500	38,500	38,500
	Military Personnel, Navy	2023/2023	1,386	1,386	1,386
	Operation & Maintenance, Navy	2023/2023	871,410	871,410	604,024
Navy Total			**927,316**	**926,590**	**656,110**
Air Force	Other Procurement, Air Force	2023/2025	730,045	591,236	256,239
	Operation & Maintenance, Air Force	2023/2023	580,266	580,266	343,887
	Operation & Maintenance, Space Force	2023/2023	8,742	8,698	4,602
	Military Personnel, Air Force	2023/2023	31,028	28,253	9,445
	Military Personnel, Space Force	2023/2023	185,142	150,668	92,506
	Research, Development, Test, & Evaluation, Air Force	2023/2024	3,663	3,663	3,663
Air Force Total			**1,538,886**	**1,362,784**	**710,341**

(continued on next page)

Department	Category	Period of Availability	Available Funds Apportioned	Cumulative Obligations	Cumulative Disbursements
Defense-Wide	Operation & Maintenance, Defense-Wide	2023/2023	280,737	280,737	68,077
	Office of the Inspector General	2023/2023	14,100	644	644
	Defense Health Program	2023/2023	3,326	2,202	487
	Procurement, Defense-Wide	2023/2025	89,515	83,586	37,762
	Research, Development, Test, & Evaluation, Defense-Wide	2023/2024	6,000	6,000	5,511
Defense-Wide Total			**393,678**	**373,169**	**112,481**
DIRECT MILITARY & OTHER SUPPORT TOTAL			**6,987,673**	**6,515,713**	**4,132,858**
DoD Stocks Replenishment					
Army	Operation & Maintenance, Army	2023/2023	6,064	6,064	3,679
	Operation & Maintenance, Army	2024/2024	12,685	12,317	6,629
	Missile Procurement, Army	2023/2025	3,165,231	1,955,830	190,722
	Missile Procurement, Army	2024/2026	634,950	0	0
	Procurement Of Weapons & Tracked Combat Vehicles, Army	2023/2025	2,142,508	986,090	16,297
	Procurement Of Ammunition, Army	2023/2025	3,308,802	1,182,577	127,741
	Procurement Of Ammunition, Army	2024/2026	209,512	43	3
	Other Procurement, Army	2023/2025	348,975	272,278	48,841
	Aircraft Procurement, Army	2023/2025	545	0	0
Army Total			**9,829,272**	**4,415,200**	**393,912**
Navy	Operation & Maintenance, Marine Corps	2023/2023	598,735	257,091	8,478
	Procurement, Marine Corps	2023/2025	94,509	60,140	477
	Weapons Procurement, Navy	2023/2025	129,344	0	0
	Weapons Procurement, Navy	2024/2026	717,840	650,951	1,402
	Procurement of Ammunition, Navy and Marine Corps	2023/2025	124,639	124,639	124,639
	Operation & Maintenance, Navy	2023/2023	28,266	27,970	23,716
	Other Procurement, Navy	2023/2025	3,071	2,276	1,519
Navy Total			**1,696,404**	**1,123,067**	**160,231**

Department	Category	Period of Availability	Available Funds Apportioned	Cumulative Obligations	Cumulative Disbursements
Air Force	Missile Procurement, Air Force	2023/2025	266,640	157,930	380
	Operation & Maintenance, Air Force	2023/2023	4,267	4,267	0
	Operation & Maintenance, Air Force	2024/2024	29,091	2,054	968
	Procurement of Ammunition, Air Force	2024/2026	10,212	0	0
Air Force Total			**310,210**	**164,251**	**1,348**
Defense-Wide	Operation & Maintenance, Defense-Wide	2024/2024	100	0	0
	Operation & Maintenance, Defense-Wide [PDA Replenishment]	2023/2024	3,016	0	0
	Procurement, Defense-Wide	2023/2025	24,041	24,041	93
	Procurement, Defense-Wide	2024/2026	16,957	16,693	0
Defense-Wide Total			**44,114**	**40,734**	**93**
DoD STOCKS REPLENISHMENT TOTAL			**11,880,000**	**5,743,252**	**555,583**
USAI Defense-Wide					
Defense-Wide	Operation & Maintenance, Defense-Wide [USAI]	2023/2024	9,000,000	8,426,358	8,413,275
USAI DEFENSE-WIDE TOTAL			**9,000,000**	**8,426,358**	**8,413,275**
P.L. 117-328 TOTAL			**27,867,673**	**20,685,323**	**13,101,716**

Source: OUSD(C), response to DoD OIG request for information, 24.2 OAR 003, 4/3/2024.

Table 26.

DoD Execution of Base Budget to Support Ukraine, in $ Thousands

Category	Period of Availability	Available Funds Apportioned	Cumulative Obligations	Cumulative Disbursement
ARMY				
Military Personnel, Army	2023/2023	0	381	381
Operation & Maintenance, Army	2022	0	93,653	81,945
Operation & Maintenance, Army	2023/2023	0	165,268	0
Operation & Maintenance, Army	2024/2024	0	616,019	221,111
Missile Procurement, Army	2022/2024	0	0	0
Missile Procurement, Army	2023/2025	0	0	0
Procurement Of Weapons & Tracked Combat Vehicles, Army	2022/2024	0	0	0
Procurement Of Weapons & Tracked Combat Vehicles, Army	2023/2025	0	0	0
Procurement Of Ammunition, Army	2022/2024	0	0	0
Army Total		**0**	**875,322**	**303,438**
NAVY				
Operation & Maintenance, Marine Corps	2022	0	2,660	0
Operation & Maintenance, Marine Corps	2023/2023	0	14,940	0
Procurement, Marine Corps	2022/2024	0	0	0
Procurement, Marine Corps	2023/2025	0	0	0
Research, Development, Test & Evaluation, Navy	2022/2023	0	88,928	0
Research, Development, Test & Evaluation, Navy	2023/2024	0	39,146	29,139
Military Personnel, Navy	2023/2023	0	686	686
Operation & Maintenance, Navy	2023/2023	0	11,529	0
Operation & Maintenance, Navy	2024/2024	0	187,552	149,273
Navy Total		**0**	**345,440**	**179,098**

Category	Period of Availability	Available Funds Apportioned	Cumulative Obligations	Cumulative Disbursement
AIR FORCE				
Operation & Maintenance, Air Force	2022	0	82,871	46,617
Operation & Maintenance, Air Force	2023/2023	0	547	0
Operation & Maintenance, Air Force	2024/2024	0	85,541	45,662
Operation & Maintenance, Space Force	2022	0	720	663
Operation & Maintenance, Space Force	2024/2024	0	151	146
Military Personnel, Space Force	2024/2024	0	0	0
Air Force Total		**0**	**169,831**	**93,088**
DEFENSE-WIDE				
Office of the Inspector General	2023/2023	0	13	0
Defense Working Capital Fund	2024/2024	0	551	521
Operation & Maintenance, Defense-Wide	2022	0	33,589	31,852
Operation & Maintenance, Defense-Wide	2024/2024	0	7,413	4,200
Defense Health Program	2024/2024	0	277	146
Cooperative Threat Reduction Account	2020/2022	0	11,100	11,100
Cooperative Threat Reduction Account	2021/2023	0	46,623	46,569
Cooperative Threat Reduction Account	2022/2024	0	28,600	23,649
Cooperative Threat Reduction Account	2023/2025	0	3,300	2,702
Defense Production Act Purchases, Defense	2022 until expended	0	0	0
Defense Wide Total		**0**	**131,466**	**120,740**
BASE EXECUTION TOTAL		**0**	**1,522,059**	**696,364**
USAI				
Operation & Maintenance, Defense-Wide [USAI]	2022/2023	300,000	299,267	299,140
Operation & Maintenance, Defense-Wide [USAI]	2023/2024	300,000	299,873	299,873
Operation & Maintenance, Defense-Wide [USAI]	2024/2025	300,000	300,000	0
USAI TOTAL		**900,000**	**899,140**	**599,013**
TOTAL BASE EXECUTION		**900,000**	**2,421,199**	**1,295,377**

Source: OUSD(C), response to DoD OIG request for information, 24.2 OAR 003, 4/3/2024.

Table 27.

DoD Execution of European Deterrence Initiative (EDI) Funding, FY 2022–present, in $ Thousands

Category	FY 2022		FY 2023		FY 2024	
	Enacted	Cumulative Obligations	Enacted	Cumulative Obligations	Enacted	Cumulative Obligations
ARMY						
Military Personnel, Army	173,241	277,621	310,131	258,379	295,671	105,119
Operation and Maintenance, Army	1,580,906	1,569,050	1,635,631	1,691,987	1,762,790	1,064,042
Aircraft Procurement, Army	6,087	0	8,309	7,398	4,567	1,567
Missile Procurement Army	266,420	0	412,086	383,892	394,569	0
Procurement of Weapons and Tracked Combat Vehicles, Army	28,224	0	96,019	31,530	17,956	933
Procurement of Ammunition, Army	24,664	0	37,546	3,905	6,365	
Other Procurement, Army	184,894	0	118,310	77,099	90,019	1,254
Research, Development, Test and Evaluation, Army	3,290	0	0	0	0	0
Military Construction, Army	121,285	0	224,292	0	1,638	
National Guard Personnel, Army	11,794	0	12,128	11,629	11,152	2,816
Operation and Maintenance, Army National Guard	0	0	0	746	0	74
Reserve Personnel, Army	10,630	0	10,784	10,413	9,452	1,138
Working Capital Fund, Army	7,071	0	0	0	0	0
Army Total	**2,418,506**	**1,846,671**	**2,865,236**	**2,476,978**	**2,594,179**	**1,176,943**
NAVY						
Military Construction, Navy and Marine Corps	131,375	0	112,181	0	77,072	0
Research, Development, Test, and Evaluation, Navy	0	0	0	0	0	0
Military Personnel, Navy		6,713	4,620	12,360	6,210	10,207
Weapons Procurement, Navy	6,500	0	6,500	6,500	6,630	489
Operation and Maintenance, Navy	13,222	0	82,136	72,527	18,448	590
Other Procurement, Navy	86,335	0	54,995	0	0	0
Military Personnel, Marine Corps	0	0	0	0	430	0
Operation and Maintenance, Marine Corps	37,686	36,388	38,511	38,515	20,139	31,267
Navy Total	**275,118**	**43,101**	**298,943**	**129,902**	**128,929**	**42,552**

Category	FY 2022		FY 2023		FY 2024	
	Enacted	**Cumulative Obligations**	**Enacted**	**Cumulative Obligations**	**Enacted**	**Cumulative Obligations**
AIR FORCE						
Aircraft Procurement	0	0	0	0	0	0
Missile Procurement	0	0	0	0	0	0
Other Procurement	171,697	132,139	34,727	28,543	130,120	0
Military Construction	162,404	8,084	244,922	52,618	225,648	0
Operation and Maintenance	338,364	393,655	367,273	391,462	378,562	127,395
Military Personnel	31,271	31,141	35,273	34,260	60,081	13,832
Research, Development, Test and Evaluation	0	0	0	0	0	0
Operation and Maintenance, Space Force	0	0	0	0	0	193
Air Force Total	**703,736**	**565,019**	**682,195**	**506,883**	**794,411**	**141,420**
DEFENSE-WIDE						
Operation and Maintenance, Defense-Wide	411,176	72,586	410,092	45,363	109,170	9,646
Procurement, Defense-Wide	3,092	0	10,903	0	3,040	0
Military Construction, Defense-Wide	0	0	0	0	0	0
Defense-Wide Total	**414,268**	**72,586**	**420,995**	**45,363**	**112,210**	**9,646**
GRAND TOTAL	**3,811,628**	**2,527,377**	**4,267,369**	**3,159,126**	**3,629,729**	**1,370,561**

Source: OUSD(C), response to DoD OIG request for information, 24.2 OAR 003, 4/3/2024.

APPENDIX F
State Funding for the Ukraine Response

Table 28.

Ukraine Supplemental Appropriations Available to the Department of State and U.S. Agency for Global Media: April 2024, in $ Millions

Purpose/Account	Amount of Appropriations					
	USAA 2022	AUSAA 2022	USAA 2023	AUSAA 2023	USSAA 2024	TOTAL
Funds Appropriated to the Department of State	1,559	1,164	0	2,168	468	**5,359**
Capital Investment Fund	0	10	0	0	0	**10**
Diplomatic Programs	125	190	0	147	60	**522**
Embassy Security Construction and Maintenance	0	110	0	0	0	**110**
Emergencies in Diplomatic Services	0	0	0	0	0	**0**
International Narcotics Control and Law Enforcement	30	400	0	375	300	**1,105**
Migration and Refugee Assistance	1,400	350	0	1,535	0	**3,285**
Nonproliferation, Anti-terrorism, Demining, and Related Programs	0	100	0	105	100	**305**
Office of Inspector General	4	4	0	6	8	**22**
Funds Appropriated to the President	5,187	17,114	4,500	14,385	11,099	**52,185**
Assistance for Europe, Eurasia, and Central Asia	1,120	0	0	350	1,575	**3,045**
Economic Support Funds	647	8,766	4,500	12,967	7,899	**34,799**
Foreign Military Financing	650	4,000	0	80	1,600	**6,330**
International Disaster Assistance	2,650	4,348	0	938	0	**7,836**
Transition Initiatives	120	0	0	50	25	**195**
Funds Appropriated to the U.S. Agency for Global Media	25	0	0	0	0	**25**
International Broadcasting Operations	25	0	0	0	0	**25**
GRAND TOTAL	**6,771**	**18,1788**	**4,500**	**16,552**	**11,567**	**57,568**

Sources: Consolidated Appropriations Act, 2022, P.L. 117-103, Div. N, 3/15/2022; Additional Ukraine Supplemental Appropriations Act, 2022, P.L. 117-128, 5/21/2022; Ukraine Supplemental Appropriations Act, 2023, P.L. 117-180, Div. B, 9/30/2022; Additional Ukraine Supplemental Appropriations Act, 2023, P.L. 117-328, Div. M, 12/29/2022; Ukraine Security Supplemental Appropriations Act, 2024, P.L. 118-150, Div B, 4/24/2024.

Table 29.

Application of State Ukraine Supplemental Assistance Funds by Funding Account, as of March 31, 2024, in $ Thousands

Account	Cumulative Funding, as of March 31, 2024			Funds Used January 1 to March 31, 2024	
	Allocations	Obligations	Expenditures	Obligations	Expenditures
Assistance for Europe, Eurasia, and Central Asia (AEECA)	295,465	236,308	62,594	7,119	4,799
Economic Support Fund (ESF)	534,703	200,157	49,595	23,412	300
Foreign Military Financing	4,730,000	4,260,000	1,396,000	60,000	400,194
International Narcotics Control and Law Enforcement (INCLE)	804,996	756,940	116,329	231	1,173
Migration and Refugee Assistance (MRA)	3,285,048	3,274,591	3,163,007	0	21,138
Nonproliferation, Anti-terrorism, Demining, and Related Programs (NADR)	211,200	184,389	79,961	1,952	2,156
GRAND TOTAL	**9,861,414**	**8,912,386**	**4,867,486**	**92,713**	**429,760**

Notes: Includes Ukraine supplemental funds directly appropriated to State, as well as funds appropriated to the President and subsequently allocated to State. MRA includes funds "for additional support for other vulnerable populations and communities," as authorized by the Ukraine Supplemental Appropriations Act, 2022 and the Additional Ukraine Supplemental Appropriations Act, 2023.

Sources: State, responses to State OIG request for information, 4/3/2024 and 4/28/2024; Consolidated Appropriations Act, 2022, P.L. 117-103, Div. N, 3/15/2022; and Additional Ukraine Supplemental Appropriations Act, 2023, P.L. 117-328, Div. M, 12/29/2022.

Table 30.

Application of State Ukraine Supplemental Assistance Funds by Type of Assistance, as of March 31, 2024, in $ Thousands

Type of Assistance	Cumulative Funding, as of March 31, 2024			Funds Used January 1 to March 31, 2024	
	Allocations	Obligations	Expenditures	Obligations	Expenditures
Development and Economic	**743,538**	**363,899**	**78,599**	**26,788**	**2,998**
Agriculture	1,310	1,310	82	0	82
Democracy Assistance	240,515	165,114	28,474	7,038	2,850
Economic Assistance	282,599	12,982	640	0	17
Energy Assistance	51,271	27,500	349	19,750	48
Global Food Security	145,000	145,000	47,738	0	0
Health Assistance	9,250	5,100	0	0	0
Other	13,593	6,893	1,316	0	0

(continued on next page)

Type of Assistance	Cumulative Funding, as of March 31, 2024			Funds Used January 1 to March 31, 2024	
	Allocations	Obligations	Expenditures	Obligations	Expenditures
Humanitarian Assistance	**3,285,048**	**3,274,591**	**3,163,007**	**0**	**21,138**
Inside Ukraine	323,700	323,700	323,700	0	10,700
Ukraine Regional Response	538,466	538,466	470,417	0	10,438
Other	2,422,882	2,412,425	2,368,890	0	0
Security Sector Assistance	**5,828,826**	**5,270,029**	**1,624,171**	**65,925**	**405,600**
Civilian Security Assistance	893,276	830,243	153,217	5,925	5,406
Cyber Assistance	28,550	17,158	185	0	0
Demining Assistance	167,000	152,629	74,769	0	0
Military Assistance	4,740,000	4,270,000	1,396,000	60,000	400,194
GRAND TOTAL	**9,857,412**	**8,908,520**	**4,865,778**	**92,713**	**429,735**

Notes: Includes Ukraine supplemental funds directly appropriated to State, as well as funds appropriated to the President and subsequently allocated to State. MRA "Other" includes funds allocated, obligated, and authorized "for additional support for other vulnerable populations and communities," as authorized under the Ukraine Supplemental Appropriations Act, 2022 and the Additional Ukraine Supplemental Appropriations Act, 2023.

Sources: State, response to State OIG request for information, 4/3/2024; Consolidated Appropriations Act, 2022, P.L. 117-103, Div. N, 3/15/2022; and Additional Ukraine Supplemental Appropriations Act, 2023, P.L. 117-328, Div. M, 12/29/2022.

Table 31.

Application of State Ukraine Supplemental Assistance Funds by Standardized Programs Structure and Definitions (SPSD) Category, as of March 31, 2024, in $ Thousands

SPSD Category	Cumulative Funding, as of March 31, 2024			Funds Used January 1 to March 31, 2024	
	Allocations	Obligations	Expenditures	Obligations	Expenditures
Democracy, Human Rights and Governance	244,265	165,214	28,474	7,038	2,850
Economic Growth	480,180	186,792	48,810	19,750	147
Education and Social Services	12,343	6,342	1,147	0	0
Humanitarian Assistance	3,285,048	3,274,591	3,163,007	0	21,138
Health Assistance	5,500	5,000	0	0	0
Peace and Security	5,830,076	5,270,580	1,624,341	65,925	405,600
GRAND TOTAL	**9,857,412**	**8,848,520**	**4,451,910**	**92,713**	**429,735**

Notes: Includes Ukraine supplemental funds directly appropriated to State, as well as funds appropriated to the President and subsequently allocated to State. SPSD is an inventory of broadly agreed-upon definitions for foreign assistance programs, providing a common language to describe programs. MRA includes funds "for other vulnerable populations and communities," as authorized under the Ukraine Supplemental Appropriations Act, 2022 and the Additional Ukraine Supplemental Appropriations Act, 2023.

Sources: State, response to State OIG request for information, 4/3/2024; State, website, "Standardized Program Structure and Definitions," undated; ; Consolidated Appropriations Act, 2022, P.L. 117-103, Div. N, 3/15/2022; and Additional Ukraine Supplemental Appropriations Act, 2023, P.L. 117-328, Div. M, 12/29/2022.

Table 32.

Application of State Administration of Foreign Affairs Ukraine Supplemental Appropriations, by Account, as of March 31, 2024, in $ Thousands

Account	Cumulative Funding, as of March 31, 2024			Funds Used January 1 to March 31, 2024	
	Allocations	Obligations	Expenditures	Obligations	Expenditures
Capital Investment Fund	44,170	37,590	27,380	110	1,550
Diplomatic Programs	349,090	237,190	152,490	44,570	13,670
Transfers to Emergencies in Diplomatic and Consular Services	5,000	0	0	0	0
Transfers to Education and Cultural Exchanges	12,738	7,780	670	1,040	210
Embassy Security, Contraction, and Maintenance	110,000	14,640	14,350	100	860
Office of Inspector General	13,500	6,710	6,050	230	260
GRAND TOTAL	**534,498**	**303,910**	**200,940**	**46,050**	**16,550**

Source: State, response to State OIG request for information, 4/22/2024.

Table 33.

Application of USAGM Ukraine Supplemental Funding by Program and Activity, as of March 31, 2024, in $ Thousands

Program/Activity	Cumulative Funding, as of March 31, 2024			Funds Used January 1 to March 31, 2024	
	Allocations	Obligations	Expenditures	Obligations	Expenditures
Radio Free Europe/Radio Liberty	**9,013**	**9,013**	**6,748**	**4,468**	**2,202**
Mobile Equipment	698	909	787	303	180
Travel, Emergency Relocation, and Realignment of Operations	801	401	401	0	0
New Capabilities and Programs	3,993	5,266	3,491	3,358	1,582
Marketing and Program Support	300	243	220	93	70
Kyiv and Regional Bureau Initiative	3,142	2,063	1,752	662	350
Baltic Waves Radio	78	130	97	52	19
Technology, Services, and Innovation	**2,688**	**2,660**	**1,530**	**750**	**457**
Astra 4A Satellite	849	848	520	0	110
Astra 19.2 Satellite	1,500	1,500	750	750	250
MW Transmissions–Armenia and Estonia	339	311	259	0	98
Voice of America	**9,174**	**5,533**	**4,160**	**1,926**	**1,697**
Ukraine Regional Reporting	2,015	2,343	1,334	871	515
Content for New Ukrainian TV Channel	3,640	1,664	1,473	499	538
Expanded VOA Washington Coverage	1,994	877	837	352	323
Expanded Polygraph: Fighting Misinformation	1,525	649	516	205	321
Office of Policy and Research	**2,429**	**1,052**	**15**	**0**	**0**
Open Technology Fund	1,320	1,320	1,320	0	0
Rapid Response Fund	0	0	0	0	0
Providing Ukraine/Russia Coverage in Regional Markets to Counter Disinformation	**375**	**345**	**345**	**75**	**89**
Middle East Broadcasting	125	125	125	0	0
Networks	**125**	**125**	**125**	**0**	**0**
Radio Free Asia				0	30
Office of Cuba Broadcasting	125	125	125	30	27
GRAND TOTAL	**25,000**	**19,923**	**14,117**	**7,218**	**4,445**

Source: USAGM, response to State OIG request for information, 4/4/2024.

APPENDIX G
USAID Funding for the Ukraine Response

Table 34.

USAID Development Funding Related to Ukraine, FY 2022-FY 2024, in $ Thousands

Account	FY 2022		FY 2023		FY 2024 Q1–Q2		
	Enacted (Disbursements)	**Obligations**	**Enacted** (Disbursements)	**Obligations**	**Enacted** (Disbursements)	**Obligations**	**Unobligated (pipeline) Funding**
Assistance for Europe, Eurasia, and Central Asia (AEECA)-Global Food Systems Institute (GFSI)	186	7,000	6,814	0	0	0	0
Assistance for Europe, Eurasia, and Central Asia (AEECA)-Global Food Systems Institute (GFSI)-Ukraine Supplemental Appropriations Act (USAA)	0	46,000	38,967	3,000	8,190	0	0
Assistance for Europe, Eurasia, and Central Asia (AEECA)-Overseas Contingency Operations (OCO)	2,490	837	5,221	2,103	2,326	2,230	0
Assistance for Europe, Eurasia, and Central Asia (AEECA)-SFOAA	188,231	164,405	175,277	45,914	21,948	4,557	0
Assistance for Europe, Eurasia, and Central Asia (AEECA)-Ukraine Supplemental Appropriations Act (USAA)	495	53,339	152,867	219,993	88,204	104,398	0
Development Assistance (DV)	1,721	2,050	1,996	650	21	0	0
Economic Support Funds (ESF)	101	90	0	0	0	0	0
Economic Support Funds (ESF)-Population Planning (DP)	49	0	0	0	0	0	0
Economic Support Funds (ESF)-APRA	1,804	5,234	4,406	0	342	0	0
Economic Support Funds (ESF)—Additional Ukraine Supplemental Appropriations (AUSAA)	0	0	70,535	708,956	199,453	714,453	0
Economic Support Funds (ESF)-Overseas Contingency Operations (OCO)	88	88	259	179	0	0	0
Gift Funds	3,263	1,676	4,166	3,997	78	15,715	0
Global AIDs Initiative (GAI)	15	0	0	13	4	0	0
Global Health (GH-H)	15,734	14,987	12,711	13,179	5,179	4,244	4,604
Global Health COVID (GH-C-CV)	152	0	32	0	17	0	0

(continued on next page)

Account	FY 2022		FY 2023		FY 2024 Q1–Q2		
	Enacted (Disbursements)	Obligations	Enacted (Disbursements)	Obligations	Enacted (Disbursements)	Obligations	Unobligated (pipeline) Funding
Global Health Advocacy Incubator (GH-C-AI)	0	1,700	1,328	0	372	4,636	0
Global Health-TB	5,875	8,793	9,359	8,054	3,285	446	0
Office of Transition Initiatives							
TI-X-UKR (Supp 1)	68,489	77,477	5,903	5,903	3	0	0
TI-X23-UKR (Supp 4)	0	0	6,986	39,700	8,190	0	0
AEECA (EC 21/22)	10,000	10,000	0	0	0	0	0
TOTAL	**298,692**	**393,496**	**496,829**	**1,051,640**	**337,612**	**850,680**	**4,604**

Sources: USAID Ukraine, response to USAID OIG request for information, 3/25/2024; USAID OTI, response to USAID OIG request for information, 3/25/2024.

Table 35.

USAID BHA Humanitarian Assistance Funding related to Ukraine, FY 2022-FY 2024, in $ Thousands

Category	FY 2022		FY 2023		FY 2024 Q1–Q2	
	Enacted (Disbursements)	Obligations	Enacted (Disbursements)	Obligations	Enacted (Disbursements)	Obligations
International Disaster Assistance (IDA)	1,038,115	1,038,115	954,473	954,473	23,807	23,807

Source: USAID BHA, response to USAID OIG financial request for information, 3/25/2024

Table 36.

USAID Development Funding, by Sector, FY 2024 (Q1 and Q2) Obligations, in $

Sector	FY 2024 Q1-Q2 Obligations
Peace and Security	29,238,053
Democracy, Human Rights and Governance	246,009,603
Health	44,062,214
Education and Social Services	8,500,000
Economic Growth	509,983,206
Program Development and Oversight	12,886,469
USAID SUBTOTAL	**850,679,545**

Source: USAID Ukraine, response to USAID OIG request for information, 3/25/2024.

APPENDIX H
Completed Oversight Projects

FY 2024 Joint Strategic Oversight Plan for Operation Atlantic Resolve, including U.S. Government Activities Related to Ukraine

As of March 31, 2024, the DoD, State, and USAID OIGs had issued 11 oversight reports, including 3 management advisories, related to OAR and the Ukraine response, as detailed below. Completed reports by DoD, State, and USAID OIGs are available on their respective web pages.

A complete list of related projects since Russia's full-scale invasion, including those prior to the designation of OAR as an overseas contingency operation, can be found in the *FY 2024 Joint Strategic Oversight Plan for Operation Atlantic Resolve, including U.S. Government Activities Related to Ukraine*.

FINAL REPORTS BY LEAD IG AGENCIES

DEPARTMENT OF DEFENSE OFFICE OF INSPECTOR GENERAL

Management Advisory: The Navy's Execution of Funds to Assist Ukraine

DODIG-2024-069; March 26, 2024

The DoD OIG issued this management advisory as part of its audit to determine whether the DoD used the Ukraine supplemental funds in accordance with Federal laws and DoD policies. The scope includes transactions reported through Advana between January 1 and December 31, 2022. While the audit is ongoing, this management advisory focuses specifically on the Navy's execution of these funds.

Through public laws, the Navy was appropriated $1.7 billion in Ukraine supplemental funds that are in the scope of the audit. The DoD OIG determined that due to the lack of automated controls in Navy Standard Accounting, Budgeting, and Reporting System and the lack of effective manual controls, the Navy over executed its funding on three occasions. While the Navy had funds available to reverse the over execution on these occasions, such funds may not be available in the future, which could result in a potential Antideficiency Act violation. Until the Navy fully implements a system that has automated controls in place or implements effective manual preventive internal controls, there is a risk this condition will continue. The DoD OIG made three recommendations to the Assistant Secretary of the Navy (Financial Management & Comptroller) to take appropriate actions to ensure the appropriate use of Ukraine supplemental funds. Management agreed with the recommendations, which will remain open until the DoD OIG receives documentation that all agreed upon actions have been completed.

Evaluation of the DoD's Sustainment Plan for Bradley, Stryker, and Abrams Armored Weapon Systems Transferred to the Ukrainian Armed Forces

DODIG-2024-057; February 15, 2024

The DoD OIG conducted this evaluation to determine whether Security Assistance Group-Ukraine developed and implemented sustainment strategies to support selected U.S. weapons systems transferred to Ukraine.

Specifically, the evaluation reviewed the extent to which the DoD developed and implemented sustainment plans to support Bradley, Stryker, and Abrams armored weapon systems transferred to the UAF. In response to Ukrainian requests for security assistance, the DoD transferred Bradleys, Strykers, and Abrams to the UAF. The U.S. Army is responsible for developing and updating life-cycle sustainment plans for these weapon systems, specifically for supply, maintenance, training, and facilities.

The evaluation found that as of January 2024, the DoD had not developed or implemented a plan for sustaining the Bradleys, Strykers, and Abrams provided to the UAF. The DoD provided supply packages containing consumables and spare parts, as well as personnel and facilities to conduct field-level maintenance through the end of FY 2024. However, the existing efforts did not constitute a sustainment plan beyond the end of FY 2024.

The lack of sustainment planning occurred because current fiscal authorities used to provide Bradleys, Strykers, and Abrams to the UAF did not include a sustainment requirement. Providing weapon systems without a plan to ensure sustainment creates risks. Specifically, the UAF may not be able to independently sustain U.S.-provided Bradleys, Strykers, and Abrams in the future. Additionally, the DoD cannot accurately predict sustainment costs or assess long-term readiness impacts to other U.S. missions.

The DoD OIG issued multiple recommendations addressing the need for the DoD to develop and implement a sustainment plan for each of the weapon systems. The recommendations remain open until the DoD OIG receives documentation that all agreed upon actions have been completed.

Evaluation of Sustainment Strategies for the PATRIOT Air Defense Systems Transferred to the Ukrainian Armed Forces

DODIG-2024-056; February 15, 2024

The DoD OIG conducted this evaluation to determine the extent to which the DoD developed and implemented sustainment strategies in support of Phased Array Tracking Radar to Intercept on Target (PATRIOT) air defense systems transferred to the Ukrainian Armed Forces, in accordance with each system's operational requirements.

The DoD OIG determined that the DoD had not developed a sustainment strategy for the PATRIOT systems transferred to the Ukrainian Armed Forces. DoD officials provided basic operation and maintenance training courses for the Ukrainian Armed Forces on the PATRIOT systems, as well as initial parts and supplies. However, the DoD did not establish advanced training to address life cycle maintenance tasks, a process to anticipate sustainment needs, a supply system for providing replacement parts, or facilities necessary to perform life cycle sustainment activities.

DoD officials did not develop a strategy for the life-cycle sustainment of the PATRIOT air defense systems because the Presidential Drawdown Authority used to transfer the systems does not include requirements for ongoing sustainment. Further, the DoD did not issue specific guidance to establish the scope and time frame for sustainment for the systems provided to Ukraine. Finally, the DoD did not identify requirements for facilities and processes to provide life-cycle support for the PATRIOT systems.

Providing PATRIOT air defense systems to the Ukrainian Armed Forces without a strategy for sustainment increases risk that Ukraine may not be able to independently sustain the systems. To address the issues identified in the report, the DoD OIG issued multiple recommendations addressing the need for the DoD to develop and implement a sustainment plan for PATRIOT air defense systems transferred to the Ukrainian Armed Forces.

The DoD OIG made several recommendations to the Under Secretary of Defense for Policy, the Under Secretary of Defense for Acquisition and Sustainment, and the Commander of the U.S. European Command to take steps to implement and support a sustainment strategy for PATRIOT air defense systems transferred to the UAF. The recommendations remain resolved and open until the DoD OIG receives documentation that all agreed upon actions have been completed.

Evaluation of the U.S. European Command's Planning and Execution of Ground Transportation of Equipment to Support Ukraine from Port to Transfer Locations

DODIG-2024-053; February 8, 2024

The DoD OIG conducted this evaluation to determine whether, in support of Ukraine, the U.S. European Command and U.S. Army Europe and Africa implemented security and accountability controls during the planning and execution of ground transportation of equipment from European ports to transfer and storage locations.

Specifically, the evaluation reviewed the DoD's implementation of security and accountability controls for transportation of equipment bound for Ukraine, from European seaport to ground transportation. This evaluation highlights DoD tracking procedures for equipment traveling through the U.S. European Command area of responsibility.

DoD policy establishes security requirements for equipment transportation based on equipment classes. For sensitive items, DoD policy requires the equipment to be protected by armed escorts at all times. For less sensitive items, U.S. Army Europe and Africa policy states that tracking devices should be used while transporting equipment through Europe.

The DoD OIG determined that DoD personnel did not have an English translation of German rail service requirements, and therefore relied on local national employees to manage those requirements.

The DoD OIG recommended that the DoD develop and implement a plan to ensure near real-time visibility of equipment bound for Ukraine traveling by ground and that they ensure copies of all agreements are available in English. The responsible units concurred and have either implemented or are taking steps to implement the recommendations. The recommendations remain resolved and open until the DoD OIG receives documentation that all agreed upon actions have been completed.

Management Advisory: Leahy Vetting of DoD-Trained Ukrainian Armed Forces

DODIG-2024-046; January 17, 2024

The DoD OIG issued this management advisory as part of it audit to determine the extent to which the DoD trained the Ukrainian Armed Forces (UAF) to operate and maintain U.S.-provided defense articles.

The management advisory highlights limitations in the DoD's ability to demonstrate compliance with the Leahy Laws, which prohibit the United States from providing assistance to a unit of a foreign security force if credible information indicates that the unit committed a gross violation of human rights. Examples of gross violations of human rights include torture, extrajudicial killing, enforced disappearance, and rape.

The DoD's Leahy vetting process must ensure that security assistance, such as DoD training, is not provided to foreign military units suspected of war crimes. However, the DoD OIG found that the DoD's vetting process lacked the necessary data to ensure full compliance, which increased the risk that foreign troops may have been or may be allowed to attend DoD training who were prohibited from doing so. For example, officials in the Office of Defense Cooperation-Kyiv (ODC-Kyiv) and the Security Assistance Group-Ukraine (SAG-U) were unable to verify which UAF units had been vetted and authorized to send personnel to specific training events. SAG-U officials were also unable to fully verify whether UAF personnel arriving for training belonged to a Leahy-vetted unit.

The ODC-Kyiv took corrective measures by immediately changing how it documented units that received Leahy vetting and were approved to send personnel to training. Nevertheless, the DoD OIG made three recommendations to the Commander of the U.S. European Command to further improve compliance. Among them, the DoD OIG recommended that ODC-Kyiv officials update their standard operating procedures to reflect the implemented procedural improvements. The DoD OIG also recommended that DoD officials should collect and maintain the necessary information to verify that UAF personnel receiving training belong to a Leahy-vetted unit. One recommendation was closed, and two recommendations remain resolved and open until the DoD OIG receives documentation that all agreed upon actions have been completed.

Evaluation of the DoD's Enhanced End-Use Monitoring of Defense Articles Provided to Ukraine

DoDIG-2024-043; January 10, 2024

The DoD OIG conducted this evaluation to determine the extent to which the Security Assistance Group-Ukraine is managing, tracking, and coordinating the movement of U.S. defense articles throughout the U.S. European Command area of responsibility.

The DoD OIG determined that, while the DoD has improved its execution of enhanced end-use monitoring (EEUM) since the full-scale invasion of Ukraine in February 2022, it did not fully comply with the requirements. Multiple factors contributed to the reporting gaps, including the limited number of U.S. personnel at logistics hubs in a partner nation and in Ukraine, the absence of procedures for conducting EEUM in a hostile environment until December 2022, the movement restrictions for EEUM personnel within Ukraine, and a lack of internal controls for validating data in the database. While there has been significant improvement in the delinquency rate for inventorying sensitive equipment, the gaps identified may correlate with an inability to maintain complete accountability for this critical U.S. security assistance.

The evaluation made several recommendations for corrective action. These include improving the inventory procedures for EEUM-designated defense articles; coordinating with the Department of State to improve visibility of third-party transfers of EEUM-designated defense articles prior to transfer; establishing and implementing procedures sufficient to meet the requirement for serialized delivery records in advance of transferring EEUM articles to a hostile environment; and developing internal controls and updating the Defense Security Cooperation Agency's Security Assistance Management Manual to improve the accuracy and timeliness of the inventory entries within the designated database. The DoD has taken steps to implement some of these recommendations. However, the recommendations will remain open until the DoD OIG receives documentation that all agreed upon actions have been completed.

Management Advisory: Audit of Remote Maintenance and Distribution Cell-Ukraine Restructuring Contract Award

DODIG-2024-041; January 5, 2024

The DoD OIG issued this management advisory as part of an ongoing audit to determine whether Army contracting personnel awarded and monitored the U.S. Army Tank and Automotive and Armaments Command contract for the maintenance of equipment provided to Ukraine in accordance with Federal and DoD policies.

Specifically, the audit reviewed the extent to which Army contracting personnel followed federal and DoD policies to: properly award a contract for maintenance of equipment at the Remote Maintenance and Distribution Cell–Ukraine; appropriately plan for and establish controls for conducting surveillance of contractor performance; and effectively monitor contractor performance.

The DoD OIG determined that Army contracting personnel adequately planned the task order and properly supported the award decision. Overall, the Army contracting personnel complied with the procedures designed to ensure the selection of the most qualified contractor to repair and return critical equipment to the Ukrainian Armed Forces as they defend against the Russian full-scale invasion.

The DoD OIG continues to examine the execution of the contract and payments made under the task order and will provide interim results on findings to the Army as warranted. While this management advisory did not contain recommendations, the DoD OIG's forthcoming reporting may include additional findings and recommendations.

DEPARTMENT OF STATE OFFICE OF INSPECTOR GENERAL

Audit of the Bureau of International Security and Nonproliferation Administration of Assistance to Ukraine

AUD-GEER-24-14, March 26, 2024

State OIG conducted this audit to determine whether State's Bureau of International Security and Nonproliferation (ISN) administered its assistance programs and efforts in Ukraine in accordance with Federal law and State requirements.

From February through December 2022, ISN administered more than $82 million in grants, cooperative agreements, contracts, and interagency agreements to support Ukraine and neighboring countries affected by Russia's invasion of Ukraine. Among other things, the funding has been obligated for border security; advisory services; and critical equipment and training across the chemical, biological, radiological, nuclear, and explosive spectrum.

State OIG found that in ISN's administering its Ukrainian assistance programs, it generally complied with applicable requirements by performing required vetting and other due diligence, assessing and accepting risks, and using alternative methods for monitoring its assistance where in-person monitoring was not feasible. However, State OIG noted ways in which ISN's administration of its assistance to Ukraine in two areas—risk assessment and monitoring—could be improved. Regarding risk assessment, State OIG noted that to the extent ISN continues to provide support for Ukraine, it should reassess risks to safeguard against overreliance on subjective considerations and to account for changes to the risk environment. Regarding monitoring, given non-permissive conditions and staffing limitations at Embassy Kyiv, ISN employed alternative methods for monitoring its assistance to Ukraine by, for example, requiring end users to certify receipt of equipment and report on the use and status of that equipment. However, ISN was unable to travel to visit end users in-person to verify the accuracy of information report by the recipients. Further regarding monitoring, State OIG observed that ISN relied on the review of award recipients' progress reports to support its program monitoring efforts. However, because those reports lacked comparison of accomplishments to program objectives, ISN could improve monitoring efforts by requiring and enforcing terms and conditions for performance reports that include comparative information to facilitate and assessment of progress against program objectives.

State OIG made four recommendations to ISN to improve risk assessments and monitoring of its assistance to Ukraine. ISN concurred with all four recommendations and, at the time the report was issued, State OIG considered all four recommendations resolved, pending further action. The recommendations will remain open until State OIG receives documentation that all agreed upon actions have been completed.

Inspection of the U.S. Mission to the Organization for Security and Cooperation in Europe

ISP-I-24-05, January 3, 2024

State OIG inspected the executive direction, policy and program implementation, and information management operations of the U.S. Mission to the Organization for Security and Cooperation in Europe (USOSCE).

State OIG found that the Ambassador and Deputy Chief of Mission led USOSCE in a professional and collaborative manner; the work of USOSCE's sections was aligned with its Integrated Mission Strategy, including the goal of maintaining support for Ukraine's sovereignty and territorial integrity; and the Public Diplomacy section focused heavily on media engagement and arranged a large number of relevant and timely interviews for the Ambassador.

State OIG made two recommendations to USOSCE. USOSCE concurred with both recommendations and, at the time the report was issued, State OIG considered both recommendations resolved, pending further action. The recommendations will remain open until State OIG receives documentation that all agreed upon actions have been completed.

U.S. AGENCY FOR INTERNATIONAL DEVELOPMENT OFFICE OF INSPECTOR GENERAL

Information Brief: USAID's Assistance to Address Global Food Security Impacted by Russia's War Against Ukraine

9-000-24-001-A; February 2, 2024

USAID OIG issued this information brief to describe USAID's Bureau for Resilience and Food Security's respond to world-wide food security concerns resulting from the Ukrainian crises.

Russia's full-scale invasion of Ukraine has impacted the global food system and contributed to worldwide increases in agricultural commodity prices. As a result, countries far beyond Ukraine's borders have experienced increased food insecurity. Through supplemental appropriations, the U.S. government has devoted more than $1 billion of food security funding for development assistance to Ukraine and other countries experiencing an elevated risk of food insecurity. The information brief summarized USAID's assistance efforts to address global food security.

Direct Budget Support: USAID Ensured That the Government of Ukraine Adhered to Required Controls, but Did Not Verify the Accuracy of Salary Expenditures

8-121-24-001-M; February 13, 2024

USAID OIG conducted this evaluation to determine to what extent direct budget support safeguards and controls are operating effectively.

In February, USAID OIG completed an evaluation of USAID's management of the Single Donor Trust Fund contribution to Ukraine, "Direct Budget Support: OIG found that USAID Ensured That the Government of Ukraine Adhered to Required Controls, but Did Not Verify the Accuracy of Salary Expenditures." The objective of the evaluation was to determine to which extent the Single Donnor Trust Fund direct budget support safeguards and controls were operating effectively.

USAID ensured that USAID ensured that the Ukrainian government adhered to required controls, but did not verify the accuracy of healthcare worker salaries in expenditure reports. USAID verified that the Government of Ukraine met reporting requirements and contracted for monitoring activities of the Single Donnor Trust Fund. For example, the Agency ensured that the Government of Ukraine submitted monthly healthcare worker salary expenditure reports and corresponding bank statements in accordance with the bilateral agreement. However, Deloitte found discrepancies in the reported data and could not easily trace the information the Ukraine government used to calculate salary expenditures to source documents.

Despite these identified data quality concerns, USAID did not take additional action to confirm whether the reports were accurate and supported by valid documentation. This occurred because neither the bilateral agreement between USAID and the Ukraine government nor Agency policies required that USAID take corrective steps when oversight measures it put in place identified data quality issues.

Without accurate data and verified expenditures for healthcare worker salaries, USAID cannot fully implement the safeguards designed to ensure the integrity of direct budget support funding to support Ukraine's healthcare services during the war. USAID OIG recommended that USAID implement an action plan to verify the accuracy of salary expenditure reports and remediate any identified deficiencies, as appropriate. USAID agreed with the recommendation. The recommendation will remain open until USAID OIG receives documentation that all agreed upon actions have been completed.

FINAL REPORTS BY LEAD IG PARTNER AGENCIES

ARMY AUDIT AGENCY

Replenishment of Missiles Provided to Ukraine

A-2024-0022-AXZ; February 8, 2024

The Army Audit Agency conducted this audit to determine if the Army relied on well-supported planning assumptions (costs and timelines) to replenish and replace missiles.

The Army generally relied on supported planning assumptions to replenish the 8,430 Javelin and 468 Stinger missiles provided to Ukraine. It established a contract for Stinger replenishment and expanded capacity on a contract for Javelin missiles issued in 2023. Despite the expanded Javelin capacity, the Army could not replenish 1,316 missiles (about 16 percent) provided through Presidential Drawdown 35 because other requirements used the remaining capacity on the 2023 contract. The Army planned to put these missiles on contract when it exercised the option period for 2024. As a result, the Army planned to replenish, by October 2025 and June 2028, respectively, Stinger and Javelin missiles on contract that were provided to Ukraine through Presidential Drawdown 35. These actions should also ensure the Army can replace these missiles provided in later presidential drawdowns and into the future.

GOVERNMENT ACCOUNTABILITY OFFICE

Ukraine: DOD Should Improve Data for Both Defense Article Delivery and End-Use Monitoring

GAO-24-106289; March 13, 2024

The GAO conducted this review to evaluate the processes the U.S. Government has used to approve, track delivery, and monitor U.S.-origin defense articles provided to Ukraine through the Presidential Drawdown Authority (PDA) and Ukraine Security Assistance Initiative (USAI).

Since Russia's full-scale invasion began in February 2022, the United States has provided more than $42 billion in security assistance, including defense articles, training, and services, to the government of Ukraine. The DoD has established new entities to deliver an unprecedented volume of defense articles to Ukraine in condensed time frames using PDA and USAI. However, the DoD has not fully documented the roles and responsibilities of these new entities.

The GAO determined that the DoD does not have quality data to track delivery of defense articles to Ukraine. As a result, DoD officials sometimes record defense articles as delivered while they are in transit, weeks before they arrive in Ukraine. By taking steps to ensure the accuracy and completeness of its data, the DoD will better ensure that it has the quality data needed to inform strategic decisions.

The DoD has a program to monitor the end-use of all defense articles provided to Ukraine but has had to alter some traditional end-use monitoring procedures in response to the ongoing conflict. Proper monitoring will help the DoD better understand whether defense articles are used for the purposes for which they were provided.

The GAO made eight recommendations to the DoD, including that the DoD improve the accuracy of defense article delivery data and evaluate its end-use monitoring approach in Ukraine. DoD agreed with five recommendations and partially agreed with two. The DoD disagreed with a recommendation to clarify guidance for documenting alleged end-use violations. The GAO maintains that additional guidance is necessary to ensure that the DoD properly records allegations.

Ukraine: Status of Foreign Assistance

GAO-24-106884; March 28, 2024

Division M of the Consolidated Appropriations Act, 2023, included a provision for GAO to conduct oversight of the assistance provided in the Ukraine supplemental appropriation acts. This report is part of a series of reviews that GAO has underway evaluating the types of U.S. assistance, including security, development, and humanitarian assistance, being provided in response to the crisis in Ukraine.

Russia's February 2022 invasion of Ukraine had devastating consequences: causing tremendous loss of life, creating a humanitarian crisis, threatening democracy, and exacerbating global challenges such as food insecurity. In responses, Congress appropriated more than $113 billion under 4 Ukraine supplemental appropriation acts. From those appropriations, the Departments of State, the Treasury, and Agriculture (USDA), and the U.S. Agency for International Development (USAID) identified $43 billion in foreign assistance as allocated specifically in response to the crisis in Ukraine. In addition to the supplemental funding, State, Treasury, USDA, and USAID identified about $1.1 billion in other funding in response to the crisis in Ukraine. The combined $44.1 billion in foreign assistance was allocated largely for economic and humanitarian assistance.

GAO found that State was not using a systematic approach to categorize and separately track the status of foreign assistance specifically in response to the crisis in Ukraine. Consequently, State faced challenges in providing the status of this foreign assistance. Without such separate tracking, State cannot provide timely information on the status of foreign assistance related to the Ukraine crisis that can be used to understand the status of assistance and to inform decisions about future funding.

GAO is recommending that State implement improvements to financial systems to separately, more systematically, and comprehensively track the allocation, obligation, and disbursement of foreign assistance funding provided in response to the crisis in Ukraine. State agreed with the recommendation.

DEPARTMENT OF THE TREASURY OFFICE OF INSPECTOR GENERAL

Anti-Money Laundering/Terrorist Financing: TFI's Ukraine-/Russia-related Sanctions Program Complied With Requirements But Designation Decision Records Were Not Consistently Complete and Closed Timely

OIG-24-025; March 6, 2024

Treasury OIG conducted this audit to determine whether the Treasury Office of Terrorism and Financial Intelligence's Ukraine-/Russia-related sanctions program complies with applicable laws and regulations, including but not limited to the Countering America's Adversaries Through Sanctions Act (CAATSA); and decisions and deliberations were properly documented and approved by appropriate Office of Foreign Assets Control officials.

Treasury OIG determined that Treasury's Office of Terrorism and Financial Intelligence's (TFI) Ukraine-/Russia-related sanctions program complied with applicable laws and regulations, including CAATSA, and that sanctions decisions and deliberations were properly approved, but not always properly documented.

Treasury OIG made two recommendations to the Director of the Office of Foreign Assets Control develop and implement procedures to properly manage case files to ensure they are complete and closed timely. Management agreed with the recommendations, which will remain open until appropriate actions are taken.

APPENDIX I
Ongoing Oversight Projects

Tables 37 and 38 list the titles and objectives for the Special IG and partner agencies' ongoing oversight projects related to OAR and Ukraine.

Table 37.

Ongoing Oversight Projects Related to OAR and Ukraine by the DoD, State, and USAID OIGs, as of March 31, 2024

DEPARTMENT OF DEFENSE OFFICE OF INSPECTOR GENERAL

Evaluation of Combatant Command Military Deception Planning
To determine whether the combatant commands effectively conducted military deception operational planning in accordance with DoD policy.

Evaluation of the DoD's Replenishment and Management of 155mm High Explosive Ammunition
To determine whether the DoD developed a coordinated plan to meet total munition requirements for 155mm high explosive ammunition and an effective strategy to balance requirements for war reserve, training, operations, and testing.

Audit of U.S. European Command Force Protection Measures at Installations in Poland that Support Operation Atlantic Resolve
To determine whether the DoD implemented force protection measures at U.S. European Command installations in Poland in support of Operation Atlantic Resolve in accordance with DoD policy.

Evaluation of Classified Project
Please contact the DoD OIG for the objective.

Evaluation of Accountability Controls for Seaports of Debarkation in the U.S. European Command Area of Responsibility
To determine whether the U.S. European Command is effectively scaling, stocking, staffing, and preparing select seaports for movement of equipment provided to foreign partners.

Audit of the DoD's Management of European Deterrence Initiative Investments
To determine the extent to which DoD officials effectively prioritized and funded military construction and other investments under the European Deterrence Initiative to support the associated lines of effort.

Audit of the DoD's Execution of Funds Provided for Assistance to Ukraine
To determine whether the DoD used the Ukraine assistance funds in accordance with Federal laws and DoD policies. The President signed the Ukraine Supplemental Appropriations Acts with the purpose of responding to the situation in Ukraine. This audit will determine whether the appropriated funds meet that purpose.

Audit of the DoD's Controls for Validating and Responding to Ukraine's Requests for Military Equipment and Assistance
To determine the extent to which DoD implemented controls for validating Ukraine's requests for military equipment and assistance, coordinating requests with partner nations, and identifying DoD sources to support the requests.

Audit of the DoD Award and Administration of Noncompetitively Awarded Contracts in Support of Ukraine–Army Award
To determine whether, in support of the Ukraine response, DoD contracting officials properly awarded and administered noncompetitively awarded contracts in accordance with Federal regulations and DoD guidance.

Audit of DoD Maintenance Operations for Military Equipment Provided to Ukraine
To determine whether the DoD is efficiently and effectively providing maintenance support for U.S. weapon systems and equipment provided for Ukraine operations.

Audit of DoD Training of Ukrainian Armed Forces–Collective & Patriot
To determine the extent to which the DoD is training the Ukrainian Armed Forces to operate and maintain U.S.-provided defense articles.

Audit of the Army's Management of Undefinitized Contract Actions Awarded to Provide Ukraine Assistance
To determine whether Army contracting officials properly managed undefinitized contract actions awarded to assist Ukraine by obligating funds and definitizing actions within the required limits and adjusting profit for costs incurred, or properly waiving the requirements in accordance with Federal and DoD policies.

Evaluation of the Accountability of Ukraine-Bound Equipment to Sea Ports of Embarkation in the Continental United States
To determine whether DoD Components effectively implemented policies and procedures to account for Ukraine-bound defense articles from their points of origin to seaports of embarkation within the continental United States.

Evaluation of the DoD's Accountability of Lost or Destroyed Defense Articles Provided to Ukraine Requiring Enhanced End-Use Monitoring
To determine whether the U.S. European Command's Office of Defense Cooperation-Ukraine effectively obtained complete and timely loss reports for enhanced end-use monitoring (EEUM)-designated defense articles provided to the Ukrainian Armed Forces.

Audit of the Estimates Used in Valuing Assets Provided Under Presidential Drawdown Authority to Ukraine
To determine the extent and impact of the March 2023 estimation change for valuing assets provided under Presidential Drawdown Authority (PDA), determine whether DoD Components followed the current policy when updating the value of items provided to Ukraine through PDA, and assess whether the current PDA valuation policy complies with Federal laws and regulations.

Evaluation of the DoD's Efforts to Protect U.S. Personnel and Operations Supporting the Ukrainian Conflict
To determine whether the DoD is effectively and efficiently protecting U.S. personnel and operations, to include executing counterintelligence activities, within the U.S. European Command in accordance with DoD policy.

Evaluation of Security and Accountability Controls for Defense Items Transferred to Ukraine through Romania
To determine the effectiveness and efficiency of the DoD's security and accountability controls for U.S. defense items transferred to the Ukrainian Armed Forces through the Logistics Enabling Node in Romania.

Audit of Security and Accountability Controls for Defense Items Transferred to Ukraine through Slovakia
To determine the effectiveness and efficiency of the DoD's security and accountability controls for U.S. defense items transferred to the Ukrainian Armed Forces through the Logistics Enabling Node in Slovakia.

Follow-Up Evaluation of Enhanced End-Use Monitoring of Defense Articles Provided to Ukraine
To determine the extent to which the DoD conducted EEUM of designated defense articles provided to Ukraine in accordance with DoD policy during the period after June 2, 2023. This evaluation is a follow-up to DODIG-2024-043, "Evaluation of the DoD's Enhanced End-Use Monitoring of Defense Articles Provided to Ukraine," released on January 10, 2024.

Management Advisory: Audit of Remote Maintenance and Distribution Cell–Ukraine Restructuring Contract Invoice Oversight
To determine whether Army contracting personnel awarded and monitored the U.S. Army Tank-automotive and Armaments Command contract for the maintenance of equipment provided to Ukraine in accordance with Federal and DoD policies.

Audit of Remote Maintenance and Distribution Cell - Ukraine Restructuring Contract Surveillance and Oversight
To determine whether Army contracting personnel awarded and monitored the U.S. Army Tank-automotive and Armaments Command contract for the maintenance of equipment provided to Ukraine in accordance with Federal and DoD policies.

Summary of Oversight Reports on DoD Security Assistance to Ukraine to Inform Possible DoD Efforts to Support Israel and Other Future Foreign Assistance Efforts
To summarize systemic challenges and recommendations to address them identified in oversight reports related to DoD security assistance to Ukraine, to inform possible DoD efforts to support Israel and other future foreign assistance efforts.

Evaluation of the Accountability of PDA Defense Equipment Deliveries to Ukraine (Property Book II)
To determine whether the Defense Security Cooperation Agency (DSCA) and the Military Services are effectively and efficiently accounting for the delivery of Presidential Drawdown Authority defense equipment to Ukraine in accordance with DoD property book and DSCA security assistance policy.

Follow-up Evaluation of Management Advisory: The Protection of Sensitive Mission Data by the Security Assistance Group-Ukraine and Its Subordinate Commands (Report No. DODIG-2024-002)
To assess the extent to which the Security Assistance Group-Ukraine and Its subordinate commands, in coordination with the U.S. Army Europe and Africa, have fully implemented plans and issued guidance to improve compliance with DoD information security policies.

Follow-up Evaluation of Management Advisory: Sufficiency of Staffing at Logistics Hubs in Poland for Conducting Inventories of Items Requiring Enhanced End-Use Monitoring (Report No. DODIG-2023-090)
To assess the actions taken by the DoD to ensure that the Office of Defense Cooperation-Ukraine has sufficient capacity to effectively and efficiently conduct all required enhanced end-use monitoring inventories of designated defense articles prior to transfers into Ukraine.

Audit of the DoD Administration of Noncompetitively Awarded Contracts in Support of Ukraine–Administration
To determine whether, in support of the Ukraine response, DoD contracting officials properly administered noncompetitively awarded contracts in accordance with Federal regulations and DoD guidance.

Evaluation of DoD Efforts to Collect and Integrate Observations, Insights, and Lessons Learned from the Russia/Ukraine Conflict
To determine the effectiveness of the DoD's collection and use of observations, insights, and lessons learned from Russia's full-scale invasion of Ukraine and the DoD's support to Ukraine, to inform DoD doctrine, planning, training, and equipping.

Management Advisory: Security Concerns at Crane Army Ammunition Activity Identified While Evaluating DoD Accounting for Ammunition Being Provided to Ukraine
To determine whether DoD Components effectively implemented policies and procedures to account for Ukraine-bound defense articles from their points of origin to seaports of embarkation within the continental United States.

Management Advisory of Evaluation of Security and Accountability Controls for Defense Items Transferred to Ukraine through Romania
To determine the effectiveness and efficiency of the DoD's security and accountability controls for U.S. defense items transferred to the Ukrainian Armed Forces through the Logistics Enabling Node in Romania.

DEPARTMENT OF STATE OFFICE OF INSPECTOR GENERAL

Inspection of Embassy Warsaw and Constituent Post, Poland
To inspect the executive direction, policy and program implementation, resource management, and information management operations of the U.S. Embassy in Warsaw and the Consulate General in Krakow, Poland.

Review of Implementation of the Interagency Strategy to Counter Illicit Diversion of Advanced Conventional Weapons in Eastern Europe
To determine whether the Department of State's Bureau of Political-Military Affairs is implementing the interagency strategy to counter illicit diversion consistent with leading practices for interagency coordination; the implementation plan includes measurable, outcome-based metrics; and implementation of the plan is consistent with strategic planning and program design guidance.

Inspection of Embassy Bucharest, Romania
To inspect the executive direction, policy and program implementation, resource management, and information management operations of the U.S. Embassy in Bucharest, Romania.

Classified Inspection of the Bureau of Political-Military Affairs

To determine whether: 1) the Department of State's Bureau of Political-Military Affairs' leadership is following the Department leadership and management principles; 2) the bureau is carrying out its program and policy implementation responsibilities in accordance with applicable standards; 3) the bureau is meeting requirements to plan and execute bureau outreach and messaging to key audiences and stakeholders; 4) the bureau manages its resources in accordance with Department standards; and 5) the bureau manages its information technology operations in compliance with applicable information security and management standards.

Inspection of the Bureau of Political-Military Affairs

To determine whether: 1) the Department of State's Bureau of Political-Military Affairs' leadership is following the Department leadership and management principles; 2) the bureau is carrying out its program and policy implementation responsibilities in accordance with applicable standards; 3) the bureau is meeting requirements to plan and execute bureau outreach and messaging to key audiences and stakeholders; 4) the bureau manages its resources in accordance with Department standards; and 5) the bureau manages its information technology operations in compliance with applicable information security and management standards.

Classified Inspection of Embassy Bucharest, Romania

To inspect the executive direction, policy and program implementation, resource management, and information management operations of the U.S. Embassy in Bucharest, Romania.

Audit of Department of State Anti-Corruption Programs and Activities in Eastern Europe

To determine whether the Department of State implemented and monitored anti-corruption assistance programs and activities in Eastern European countries in accordance with federal and State requirements.

Audit of Department of State Anti-Corruption Programs and Activities in Eastern Europe

To determine whether the Department of State implemented and monitored anti-corruption assistance programs and activities in Eastern European countries in accordance with federal and State requirements.

Audit of Humanitarian Assistance to Ukraine

To determine whether the Department of State implemented humanitarian assistance in response to the situation in Ukraine in accordance with State policies, guidance, and award terms and conditions to ensure funds, and whether intended objectives were achieved.

Audit of the Disposition of Defensive Equipment and Armored Vehicles in Advance of Evacuations at U.S. Embassies Kabul and Kyiv

To determine whether Embassies Kabul and Kyiv managed, safeguarded, and disposed of sensitive security assets in advance of the evacuation and suspension of operations at each post in accordance with Department of State guidance and what challenges were encountered upon reopening Embassy Kyiv.

Review of the Kyiv Transit Platform

To describe the current operating status of the Kyiv Transit Platform and remote operations that support Embassy Kyiv; to examine the platform's operational effectiveness, assess accountability, and security issues; and review the coordination between the Ukraine and Poland missions as outlined in the 2023 memorandum of understanding covering the roles and responsibilities of the Kyiv Transit Platform.

Audit of the Worldwide Protective Services III Initial Training Consolidation Initiative

To determine whether the Bureau of Diplomatic Security's efforts to consolidate initial Worldwide Protective Services III training have improved training quality, enhanced oversight, and achieved the envisioned cost savings.

Management Assistance Report: Applying Lessons Learned from Previous Evacuations

To determine the extent to which the Department of State has aggregated lessons learned from past evacuations and included such lessons learned in formal guidance and instructions to aid in safeguarding, managing, or disposing of defensive equipment and armored vehicles at overseas posts.

Audit of the Bureau for Europe and Eurasia's Programming to Counter Disinformation
To determine the 1) extent to which USAID has developed objectives and metrics for the program(s) under review, 2) determine progress toward achieving those objectives, and 3) determine how, and to what extent, USAID is monitoring implementer performance in accordance with USAID's standard policies and procedures.

Audit of the E&E Bureau's Programming to Reduce Energy Vulnerabilities
To determine the 1) extent to which USAID has developed objectives and metrics for the program(s) under review, 2) determine progress toward achieving those objectives, and 3) determine how, and to what extent, USAID is monitoring implementer performance across the Europe and Eurasia region in accordance with USAID's standard policies and procedures.

Follow-up on USAID's Oversight of Public International Organizations
To follow up on the issues identified in our 2018 audit to determine if the efforts undertaken by USAID have improved its oversight of Public International Organizations to minimize risks of fraud, waste, and abuse.

Evaluation of USAID's Due Diligence Over Funding to Public International Organizations
To determine to what extent USAID performed expected due diligence over funding to selected public international organizations.

Audit of USAID Energy Activities in Ukraine
To assess USAID/Ukraine's oversight of the implementation of the Energy Security Project procurement process and determine whether USAID/Ukraine verified that the Energy Security Project delivered selected equipment and materials to recipients as intended.

Audit of USAID's Bureau for Humanitarian Assistance Localization Approach in Ukraine
To determine 1) the extent to which USAID has developed objectives and metrics for the program(s) under review, 2) determine progress toward achieving those objectives, and 3) determine how, and to what extent, USAID is monitoring implementer performance in accordance with USAID's standard policies and procedures.

Audit of the USAID's Office of Transition Initiatives Engagement of Local Partners in Ukraine to Contribute to Development Goals
To determine 1) the extent to which USAID has developed objectives and metrics for the program(s) under review, 2) determine progress toward achieving those objectives, and 3) determine how, and to what extent, USAID is monitoring implementer performance in accordance with USAID's standard policies and procedures.

Inspection of USAID Partner Controls to Prevent and Respond to Sexual Exploitation and Abuse in Ukraine
To verify whether USAID held partners responding to the Ukrainian crisis to required sexual exploitation and abuse measures prior to executing awards and will review the internal controls reported by partners.

Audit of Bureau for Resilience and Food Security Response to the Humanitarian Crisis Caused by Russia's War Against Ukraine
To examine steps taken by USAID's Bureau for Resilience and Food Security to respond to world-wide food security concerns resulting from the Ukrainian crises.

Audit of USAID/Ukraine's HIV/AIDS Prevention Activities
To determine the mission's role in ensuring that internally displaced persons living with HIV/AIDS have access to medical and social services, and medications during the war.

Review of USAID's Ukraine Staffing
To 1) describe USAID's current and pre-invasion staffing footprint, and changes in USAID-managed programming in Ukraine; and 2) identify challenges associated with—and actions taken in response to—changes to the staffing footprint and programming for Ukraine.

Incurred Cost Audits of USAID Resources
To 1) describe USAID's current and pre-invasion staffing footprint, and changes in USAID-managed programming in Ukraine, and 2) identify challenges associated with—and actions taken in response to—changes to the staffing footprint and programming for Ukraine.

Ukraine Investigations Dashboard for FY 2024
To summarize investigative oversight activities in FY 2024 related to USAID's Ukraine Response.

Incurred Cost Audits of USAID Resources
To determine whether costs claimed by 12 recipients of Ukraine awards and sub-awards for the period January 1, 2018, to December 31, 2022, are allowable, allocable, and reasonable in accordance with audit standards, award terms, and federal regulations.

Table 38.

Ongoing Oversight Projects Related to OAR and Ukraine by Partner Agencies, as of March 31, 2024

DEPARTMENT OF COMMERCE OFFICE OF INSPECTOR GENERAL

Audit of the Bureau of Industry and Security's Enforcement of Russia and Belarus Export Controls
To assess the actions taken by the Bureau of Industry and Security to detect and prosecute violations of Russia and Belarus export controls.

GOVERNMENT ACCOUNTABILITY OFFICE

Cyber Operations with Allies and Partners
To identify DoD cyber operations and activities in Europe since January 2022 and the mitigation of challenges in undertaking those actions.

DoD and NATO Logistics in Europe
To review the DoD and NATO capacity to transport personnel and materiel within Europe and consideration of related lessons learned from the effort to support Ukraine.

DoD Logistics in the European Theater
To review how DoD has identified the early deploying sustainment forces needed to meet early wartime missions and the extent to which these forces have the necessary equipment, personnel, and training to meet mission requirements performed early in a conflict.

Evaluation of USAID Risk Mitigation in Conflict Zones
To evaluate USAID's processes for assessing and mitigating risks to delivering assistance in conflict zones and its sharing of related lessons learned, in particular for the case study countries of Nigeria, Somalia, and Ukraine.

USAID and State's Use of Implementing Partners in Ukraine Assistance
To describe USAID's and the Department of State's implementing partners and sub-partners and how they were selected to provide certain non-security assistance in response to the war in Ukraine, including evaluating the extent to which the agencies reviewed potential partners' past performance.

Review of DoD Ukraine Weapon Replenishment Efforts
To evaluate the DoD's efforts to use $25.9 billion provided by Congress to replace weapons sent to Ukraine and actions the DoD is taking to address defense industrial base challenges that could delay replacement efforts.

DoD Funding in Support of Ukraine
To determine how the DoD has used and tracked funding in support of Ukraine and evaluated the Ukraine Security Assistance Initiative.

Ukraine Security Assistance Donor Coordination
To review foreign donations of defense articles to Ukraine, the U.S. role in coordinating those donations, and U.S. agency efforts to monitor certain defense articles.

DoD Efforts to Train Ukraine Forces
To examine the DoD's approaches to training Ukraine's armed forces, determine how the DoD assesses that training and collects lessons learned, and identify effects on U.S. military forces and training facilities in Europe.

Ukraine Asset Valuation
To assess whether the methodologies the DoD is using to value assets provided to Ukraine under Presidential Drawdown Authority are consistent with relevant guidance, given the $6.2 billion misvaluation DoD reported in 2023.

U.S. Direct Budget Support to Ukraine
To evaluate the transparency and accountability of the direct budget support USAID has provided to the Government of Ukraine through the World Bank's Public Expenditures for Administrative Capacity Endurance (PEACE) project, and other related matters.

U.S. Government Ukraine Recovery Planning
To assess the Department of State's and USAID's planning for recovery, the extent to which ongoing efforts align with U.S. priorities, and the coordination of these efforts with other donor nations and the Ukrainian government.

Readiness Implications of U.S. Military Assistance to Ukraine
To assess the impact of the DoD's provision of military equipment to Ukraine on the Geographic Combatant Commands' readiness to prepare for and conduct operations, the military Services' training and equipping capabilities, and the Army's efforts to sustain its weapons systems.

Russia/Ukraine Sanctions and Export Controls
To examine the objectives of sanctions and export controls related to the war in Ukraine and progress towards those objectives; changes in key Russian economic indicators since sanctions and export controls were imposed; and the amounts and uses of resources that agencies have received to implement and enforce those sanctions and export controls.

U.S. Support for Nuclear Security and Safety in Ukraine
To evaluate how the Department of Energy and other agencies have used supplemental appropriations to address nuclear and radiological security and safety risks in Ukraine.

Ukraine Security Training Coordination
To assess the extent that the DoD coordinates with the Ukrainian Government and partner nations on military training for Ukraine.

Status of Ukraine Supplemental Appropriations
To assess the status of the funds provided in the Ukraine supplemental appropriations acts and describe the types of activities agencies have funded with these appropriations.

Management of Presidential Drawdown Authority
To assess agency implementation of the Presidential Drawdown Authority, including processes for managing drawdowns and potentially replacing defense articles provided to partners.

Combatting Human Trafficking during Armed Conflicts, Including Ukraine
To assess the implementation of Department of State and USAID programs and projects to counter human trafficking in Ukraine and compare them with similar efforts in other countries experiencing armed conflict.

Reconstruction Lessons Learned Snapshot
To compile lessons learned from GAO's work assessing past U.S. experiences with reconstruction that could strengthen planning for Ukraine's recovery.

Ukraine Refugee and Internally Displaced Persons Assistance
To examine U.S. Government assistance to Ukrainian refugees and internally displaced persons, including efforts to coordinate internally as well as with international partners on a comprehensive strategy for addressing the crises and migration challenges.

APPENDIX J
Planned Oversight Projects

Table 39 lists the titles and objectives for Special IG and partner agencies' planned oversight projects related to OAR and Ukraine.

Table 39.

Planned Oversight Projects Related to OAR and Ukraine by the DoD, State, and USAID OIGs, as of March 31, 2024

DEPARTMENT OF DEFENSE OFFICE OF INSPECTOR GENERAL

Evaluation of DoD Contracting Officer Actions to Negotiate Fair and Reasonable Prices with Contractors for Ukraine Security Assistance
To determine whether DoD contracting officers complied with Federal, DoD, and Component policies in response to Defense Contract Audit Agency audit findings on pricing proposals related to Ukraine Security Assistance.

DoD and Department of State Joint Audit of U.S. Assistance Provided to Ukraine Through the Foreign Military Financing Program
To determine whether the DoD and the Department of State, as part of U.S. efforts to provide security assistance to Ukraine, implemented the Foreign Military Financing program in accordance with Federal and DoD policies.

DEPARTMENT OF STATE OFFICE OF INSPECTOR GENERAL

Inspection of Embassy Moscow, Russia
To evaluate the programs and operations of the U.S. Embassy in Moscow, Russia.

Classified Inspection of Embassy Moscow, Russia
To evaluate the programs and operations of the U.S. Embassy in Moscow, Russia.

Audit of the Global Threat Reduction Program in Eastern Europe
To determine whether the Department of State's Bureau of International Security and Nonproliferation planned, monitored, and evaluated Global Threat Reduction programs in Eastern Europe in accordance with State policies, and whether Global Threat Reduction programs in Eastern Europe achieved their objectives.

Joint Audit of the DoD and Department of State Oversight of the U.S. Assistance to Ukraine Through the Foreign Military Financing Program
To determine whether the Departments of Defense and State implemented effective oversight over foreign military financing provided to Ukraine for the acquisition of U.S. defense equipment, services, and training.

Audit of Emergency Action Planning at Selected U.S. Embassies in the Baltic States
To determine whether selected U.S. embassies in the Baltic States are prepared to respond and recover from emergencies.

Audit of Department of State Programs to Support Democracy and Human Rights in Europe and Eurasia
To determine whether 1) the Department of State's Bureau of Democracy, Human Rights, and Labor planned, implemented, monitored, and evaluated the use of foreign assistance funds that were provided in support of democracy and human rights programs in Europe and Eurasia in accordance with Federal requirements and State policies, and 2) the funded democracy and human rights programs achieved their desired outcomes.

Audit of Embassy Kyiv Records Retention for Electronic Messaging
To determine whether Embassy Kyiv has implemented measures to ensure Federal records created using electronic messaging applications are preserved.

U.S. AGENCY FOR INTERNATIONAL DEVELOPMENT OFFICE OF INSPECTOR GENERAL

Information Brief of USAID's Progress in Implementing the Countering Malign Kremlin Influence Framework
To describe the Europe and Eurasia Bureau's progress in implementing the Countering Malign Kremlin Influence Framework by outlining associated metrics and monitoring tools for missions in the region.

Evaluation of USAID's Policies and Practices Following Ordered Departures
To assess the policies and practices of USAID for the relocation of staff and oversight of programming after ordered departures of missions.

Audit of USAID's Bureau for Europe and Eurasia's Programming to Reduce Economic Vulnerabilities
To determine the 1) extent to which USAID has developed objectives and metrics for the program(s) under review, 2) determine progress toward achieving those objectives, and 3) determine how, and to what extent, USAID is monitoring implementer performance in accordance with USAID's standard policies and procedures.

Audit of Bureau for Europe and Eurasia's Programming to Counter Democratic Backsliding
To determine the 1) extent to which USAID has developed objectives and metrics for the program(s) under review, 2) determine progress toward achieving those objectives, and 3) determine how, and to what extent, USAID is monitoring implementer performance in accordance with USAID's standard policies and procedures.

Audit of USAID's Direct Budget Support to the Public Expenditures for Administrative Capacity Endurance Fund
To determine how USAID oversees its contributions to the Public Expenditures for Administrative Capacity Endurance (PEACE) Fund and assess the extent to which USAID's contributions to the PEACE fund supported eligible internally displaced persons.

Inspection of USAID's Disaster Assistance Response Team Response to the Humanitarian Crisis Resulting from Russia's War Against Ukraine
To assess internal controls to mitigate fraud risks and ensure quality of goods in the procurement of commodities supplied through Bureau for Humanitarian Assistance funding in Ukraine.

Audit of USAID's Interagency Coordination Process for Assistance to Ukraine
To examine the processes and procedures USAID has established for interagency coordination on its Ukrainian response.

Audit of USAID/Ukraine's Activities to Ensure Access to Critical Health Services
To determine the 1) extent to which USAID has developed objectives and metrics for the program(s) under review, 2) determine progress toward achieving those objectives, and 3) determine how, and to what extent, USAID is monitoring implementer performance in accordance with USAID's standard policies and procedures.

Audit of USAID/Ukraine's Modified Activities Two Years On
To determine the 1) extent to which USAID has developed objectives and metrics for the program(s) under review, 2) determine progress toward achieving those objectives, and 3) determine how, and to what extent, USAID is monitoring implementer performance in accordance with USAID's standard policies and procedures.

Audit of USAID's Agriculture Resilience Initiative for Ukraine
To determine how AGRI-Ukraine targets Ukraine's agricultural production and export challenges through 2023.

APPENDIX K
Investigations and Hotline Activity

HOTLINE ACTIVITY

The DoD, State, and USAID OIGs each maintain their own hotline to receive complaints specific to their agency. The hotlines provide a confidential, reliable means for individuals to report suspected violations of law, rule, or regulation; mismanagement; gross waste of funds; or abuse of authority. Each OIG Hotline office evaluates complaints received through the hotlines and forwards them to the respective investigative entity for review and investigation.

During the quarter, the DoD OIG Hotline investigator received 20 allegations related to OAR and referred 17 cases for further criminal investigation. State OIG received 19 allegations and the USAID OIG received 24 allegations. In some instances, a case may contain multiple subjects and allegations. (See Table 40.)

INVESTIGATIONS

Law enforcement personnel from the DoD, State, and USAID OIGs investigate allegations of misconduct that might compromise U.S. Government programming. Additionally, investigators identify, coordinate, and de-conflict fraud and corruption investigations; share best practices and investigative techniques; and coordinate proactive measures to detect and deter the criminals who would exploit U.S. Government assistance to Ukraine.

The Special Inspector General and the Lead Inspector General agencies coordinate OAR investigations with their partners in the Fraud and Corruption Investigative Working Group (FCIWG) and other forums. The FCIWG consists of representatives from: the Defense Criminal Investigative Service (DCIS, the DoD OIG's criminal investigative component), the DoS OIG, USAID OIG, the U.S. Army Criminal Investigation Division, the Naval Criminal Investigative Service, the Air Force Office of Special Investigations, the Federal Bureau of Investigation, and Homeland Security Investigations.

Table 40.

Hotline Allegations During the Quarter

DoD OIG		State OIG	USAID OIG	
20 Allegations		**19 Allegations**	**24 Allegations**	
Personal Misconduct/Ethical Violations		Contract Fraud	Corruption	Program Fraud
Procurement/Contract Administration		Other	Employee Misconduct	Theft
Personnel Matters			Contract Fraud	Other
Pay and Benefits			Ethics Violations	
Retaliation			Conspiracy	
Security			Conflict of Interest	

DoD, State, and USAID OIGs have positioned criminal investigators in Ukraine, Poland, and Germany to detect and deter criminal exploitation of U.S. funds appropriated for the purposes of economic, humanitarian, or security assistance to Ukraine. These investigators collaborate with other U.S. and host-nation law enforcement and prosecutorial personnel to protect U.S. programs, operations, assistance, and contracting from fraud, waste, and abuse, and to refer suspected crimes to appropriate authorities.

During the quarter, Lead IG agencies coordinating in the FCIWG reported 12 investigations initiated and 2 investigations closed. As of March 31, 2024, FCIWG agencies reported a total 62 open investigations. The open investigations involve grant and procurement fraud, corruption, theft, program irregularities, and counter-proliferation of technology of weapons systems components. Also during the quarter, FCIWG agencies conducted 35 fraud awareness briefings for 129 participants. (See Figure 6.)

Figure 6.

Investigations Activity Related to OAR, January 1–March 31, 2024

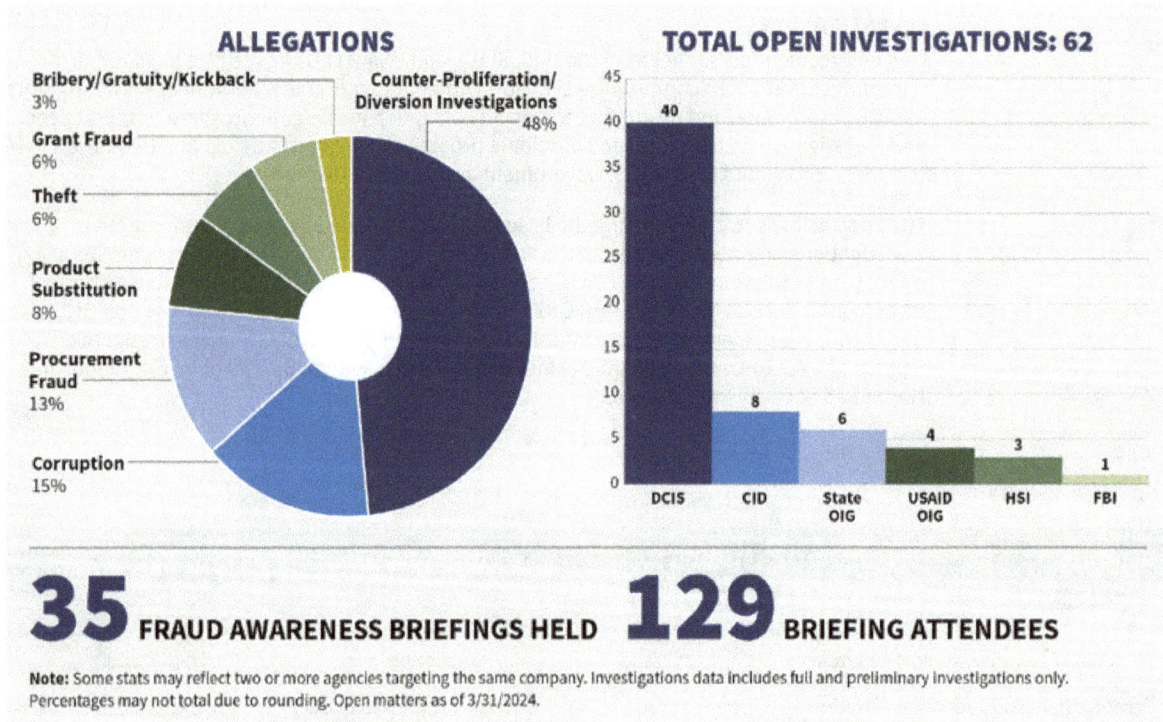

Note: Some stats may reflect two or more agencies targeting the same company. Investigations data includes full and preliminary investigations only. Percentages may not total due to rounding. Open matters as of 3/31/2024.

ACRONYMS

Acronym	
ACA	Atrocity Crimes Advisory Group for Ukraine
ACLED	Armed Conflict Location and Event Data Project
ACOORD	Office of the Assistance Coordinator
AEECA	Assistance to Europe, Eurasia, and Central Asia
BHA	USAID Bureau for Humanitarian Assistance
BIS	Commerce Bureau of Industry and Security
CBRN	chemical, biological, radiological, and nuclear
CSO	State Bureau of Conflict and Stabilization Operations
DART	Disaster Assistance Response Team
DEA	Drug Enforcement Agency
DIA	Defense Intelligence Agency
DoJ	Department of Justice
DRL	State Bureau of Democracy, Human Rights, and Labor
DSCA	Defense Security Cooperation Agency
ECA	State Bureau of Education and Cultural Affairs
EDI	European Deterrence Initiative
EEUM	enhanced end-use monitoring
ENR	State Bureau of Energy Resources
EOD	explosive ordnance disposal
EU	European Union
EUM	end-use monitoring
EXBS	Export Control and Related Border Security
FBI	Federal Bureau of Investigation
FCIWG	Fraud and Corruption Investigative Working Group
FMF	Foreign Military Financing
FMS	Foreign Military Sales
GAO	Government Accountability Office
GCJ	State Office of Global Criminal Justice
HACC	High Anti-Corruption Court

Acronym	
HCQJ	High Qualification Commission of Judges in Ukraine
HCJ	High Council of Justice
IDCC	International Donor Coordination Center
IDP	internally displaced person
INL	State Bureau of International Narcotics and Law Enforcement Affairs
IO	State Bureau of International Organization Affairs
MEASURE	Monitoring, Evaluation, and Audit Services for Ukraine contract
MDTF	Multi-donor Trust Fund
MIGA	Multilateral Investment Guarantee Agency
NABU	National Anti-Corruption Bureau of Ukraine
NGO	nongovernmental organization
NPU	National Police of Ukraine
OAR	Operation Atlantic Resolve
ODC-Kyiv	Office of Defense Cooperation-Kyiv
OECD	Organization for Economic Cooperation and Development
OFAC	Treasury Office of Foreign Assets Control
OPG	Office of the Prosecutor General
OUSD(P)	Office of the Undersecretary of Defense for Policy
PATRIOT	Phased Array Tracking Radar to Intercept on Target
PEACE	World Bank Public Expenditures for Administrative Capacity Endurance
PEPFAR	U.S. President's Emergency Plan for AIDS Relief
PIO	public international organization
PDA	Presidential Drawdown Authority
PRM	State Bureau of Population, Refugees, and Migration
PM/WRA	State Bureau of Political-Military Affairs Office of Weapons Removal and Abatement
RFE/RL	Radio Free Europe/Radio Liberty
SAG-U	Security Assistance Group-Ukraine

Acronym	
SAPO	Specialized Anti-Corruption Prosecutor's Office
SDTF	Single Donor Trust Fund
SMR	safe small modular reactor
UAF	Ukrainian Armed Forces
UAV	unmanned aerial vehicle
UDCG	Ukraine Defense Contact Group
UNHCR	UN High Commissioner for Refugees
URTF	Ukraine Relief, Recovery, Reconstruction and Reform Trust Fund

Acronym	
USAGM	U.S. Agency for Global Media
USAI	Ukraine Security Assistance Initiative
USAREUR-AF	U.S. Army Europe and Africa
USEUCOM	U.S. European Command
USOSCE	U.S. Mission to the Organization for Security and Cooperation in Europe
USTRANSCOM	U.S. Transportation Command
VOA	Voice of America

A Stryker armored fighting vehicle participates in during a training exercise held at Vilseck, Germany. (U.S. Army Reserve photo)

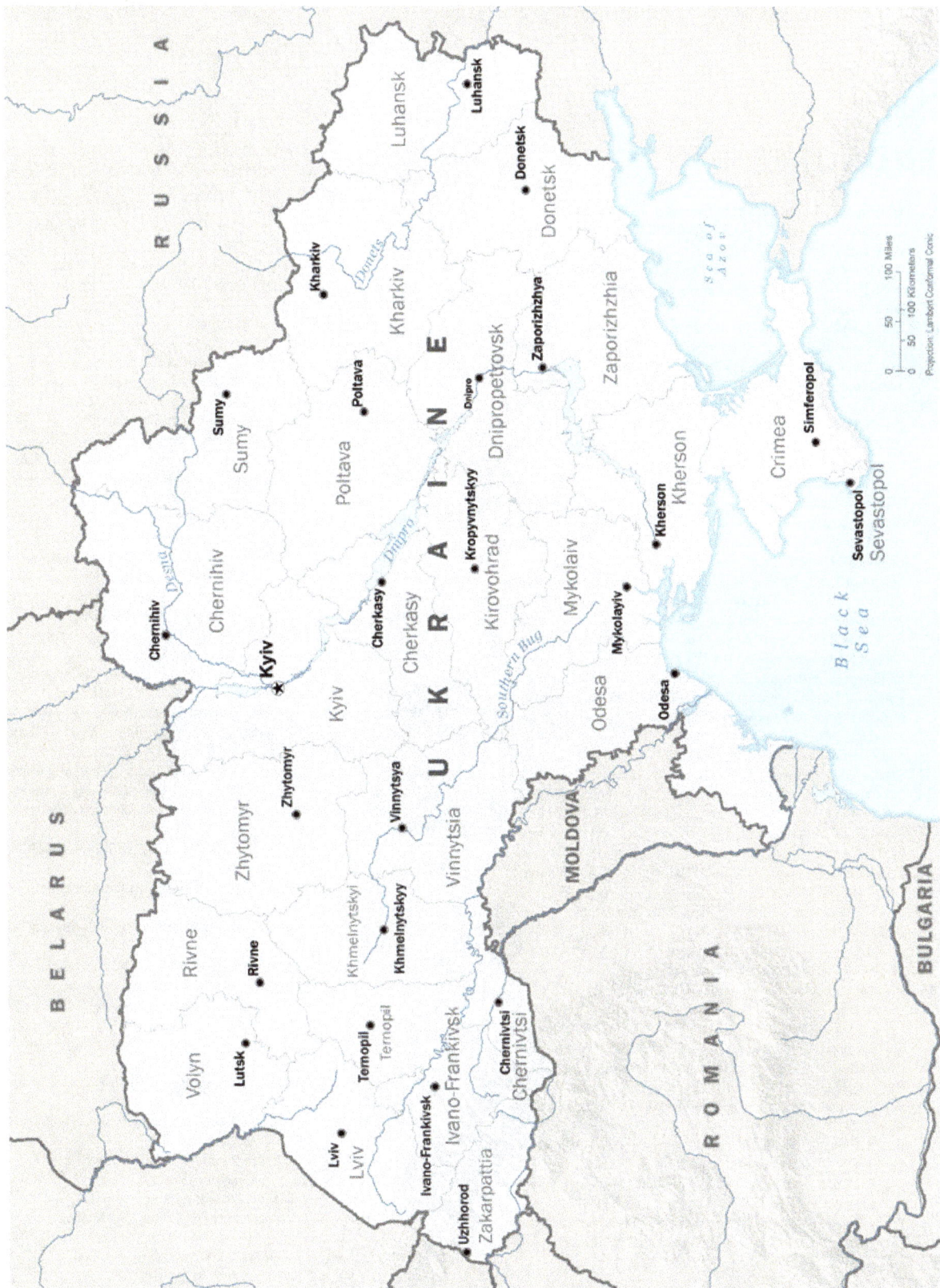

ENDNOTES

1. OUSD(P), response to DoD OIG request for information, 24.1 OAR 001 and 24.1 OAR 002, 12/26/2023; OUSD(P), vetting comment, 4/29/2024.
2. CIA Director William Burns, testimony before the Senate Select Intelligence Committee, "Hearing on Annual Worldwide Threats Assessment," 3/11/2024.
3. Isabel van Brugen, "Ukraine Seeks to Cut Off Putin's Lifeblood with Attacks Inside Russia," Newsweek, 1/25/2024; Svitlana Vlasova and Brad Lendon, "Ukraine's Drones Sink Another Russian Warship, Kyiv Says," CNN, 3/6/2024.
4. Guy Faulconbridge and Tom Balmforth, "Russia Takes Avdiivka from Ukraine, Biggest Gain in Nine Months," Reuters, 2/18/2024; Alex Babenko, "Exhaustion, Dwindling Reserves and a Commander Who Disappeared: How Ukraine Lost Avdiivka to Russia," Associated Press, 3/11/2024.
5. Victoria Butenko, "Zelensky Fires Ukraine's Military Chief in Major Shakeup Nearly Two Years Into War," CNN, 2/8/2024.
6. World Bank, "Ukraine: Third Rapid Damage and Needs Assessment (RDNA3), February 2022–December 2023," 2/15/2024; Yale School of Public Health, "Remote Assessment of Bombardment of Ukraine's Power Generation and Transmission Infrastructure, 1 October 2022 to 30 April 2023–A Conflict Observatory Report," 2/29/2024; Srdjan Nedeljkovic And Yehor Konovalov, "Russia Targets Kyiv with Ballistic Missiles as Fears Increase Of Attacks on Energy Infrastructure, Associated Press, 12/11/2023; Hanna Arhirova, "Russia Steps up its Aerial Barrage of Ukraine as Kyiv Officials Brace for Attacks on Infrastructure," Associated Press, 11/3/2023.
7. State, vetting comment, 4/30/2024.
8. State, cable, "Ukraine: OSN Open Source Review February 15-19, 2024 (DS OPS)," 24 STATE 16574, 2/19/2024. USAID Ukraine, response to USAID OIG request for information, 3/25/2024.
9. USAREUR-AF, response to DoD OIG request for information, 24.2 OAR 063, 4/3/2024.
10. USAREUR-AF, response to DoD OIG request for information, 24.2 OAR 063, 4/3/2024.
11. SAG-U, response to DoD OIG request for information, 24.2 OAR 034, 24.2 OAR 038, and 24.2 OAR 056, 3/29/2024.
12. USTRANSCOM, response to DoD OIG request for information, 24.2 OAR 045, 3/26/2024.
13. Ukraine Supplemental Appropriations Act, 2022, P.L. 117-103, Div N, 3/15/2022; Additional Ukraine Supplemental Appropriations Act, 2022, P.L. 117-128, 5/21/2022; Ukraine Supplemental Appropriations Act, 2023, P.L. 117-180, 9/30/2022; and Additional Ukraine Supplemental Appropriations Act, 2023, P.L. 117-328, Div M, enacted 12/29/2022; Ukraine Security Supplemental Appropriations Act, P.L. 118-50, Div B, enacted 4/24/2024.
14. Lara Seligman, "Pentagon Needs Congress to Hand Over $10B to Replace Weapons Sent to Ukraine," Politico, 3/11/2024.
15. Dan Lamothe, "U.S. Will Send Ukraine $300 Million in Arms as Further Aid Stays Stalled," Washington Post, 3/13/2024.
16. White House, transcript, "Press Briefing by Press Secretary Karine Jean-Pierre and National Security Advisor Jake Sullivan," 3/12/2024.
17. Major General Pat Ryder, transcript, "Pentagon Press Secretary Air Force Maj. Gen. Pat Ryder Holds a Press Briefing," 3/12/2024.
18. SAG-U, response to DoD OIG request for information, 24.2 OAR 061, 3/29/2024.
19. USAREUR-AF, response to DoD OIG request for information, 24.2 OAR 063, 4/3/2024.
20. USEUCOM, response to DoD OIG request for information, 24.2 OAR 019, 4/3/2024; USEUCOM, discussion with DoD OIG staff, Stuttgart, Germany, 12/6/2023.
21. Stefan Wolff and Tetyana Malyarenko, "Ukraine War: Corruption Scandals and High-Level Rifts Could Become an Existential Threat as Kyiv Asks for More Military Aid," The Conversation, 2/1/2024; Peter Dickinson," Wartime Ukraine Ranks Among World's Top Performers in Anti-corruption Index," Atlantic Council, 2/1/2024; Adrian Karatnucky, "How Deep Does Corruption Run in Ukraine?" Foreign Policy, 3/6/2024; George Wright, "Ukraine Says it has Uncovered Major Arms Corruption," BBC, 1/28/2024; Dan Peleschuk, "Ukraine Unveils Corruption Probes into Reconstruction Schemes," Reuters, 11/21/2023.
22. Stefan Wolff and Tetyana Malyarenko, "Ukraine War: Corruption Scandals and High-Level Rifts Could Become an Existential Threat as Kyiv Asks for More Military Aid," The Conversation, 2/1/2024; Peter Dickinson," Wartime Ukraine Ranks Among World's Top Performers in Anti-corruption Index," Atlantic Council, 2/1/2024; Adrian Karatnucky, "How Deep Does Corruption Run in Ukraine?" Foreign Policy, 3/6/2024; George Wright, "Ukraine Says it has Uncovered Major Arms Corruption," BBC, 1/28/2024; Dan Peleschuk, "Ukraine Unveils Corruption Probes into Reconstruction Schemes," Reuters, 11/21/2023.
23. State, response to State OIG request for information, 4/12/2024.
24. State, press release, "Responding to Two Years of Russia's Full-Scale War," 2/23/2024.
25. Treasury, press release, "On Second Anniversary of Russia's Further Invasion of Ukraine and Following the Death of Aleksey Navalny, Treasury Sanctions Hundreds of Targets in Russia and Globally," 2/23/2024.
26. USAID, "Complex Emergency Fact Sheet #5," 3/21/2024; UNHCR, website, "Ukraine Situation Global Report 2022."
27. USAID BHA, response to USAID OIG request for information, 3/11/2024.
28. USAID BHA, response to USAID OIG request for information, 3/11/2024.
29. CRS, "Ukraine: Background, Conflict with Russia, and U.S. Policy," 9/19/2019; State, vetting comment, 4/29/2024.
30. CRS, "Ukraine: Background, Conflict with Russia, and U.S. Policy," 9/19/2019.
31. New York Times, "Maps: Tracking the Russian Invasion of Ukraine," 6/9/2023; State, vetting comment, 4/29/2024.
32. New York Times, "Maps: Tracking the Russian Invasion of Ukraine," 6/9/2023.
33. New York Times, "Maps: Tracking the Russian Invasion of Ukraine," 6/9/2023.
34. Guy Faulconbridge and Tom Balmforth, "Russia Takes Avdiivka from Ukraine, Biggest Gain in Nine Months," Reuters, 2/18/2024; Alex Babenko, "Exhaustion, Dwindling Reserves and a Commander Who Disappeared: How Ukraine Lost Avdiivka to Russia," Associated Press, 3/11/2024.
35. OUSD(P), response to DoD OIG request for information, 24.1 OAR 001 and 24.1 OAR 002, 12/26/2023.

36. CRS, "Russia's War Against Ukraine: Overview of U.S. Assistance and Sanctions," 12/20/2023; Ukraine Supplemental Appropriations Act, 2022, P.L. 117-103, Div N, 3/15/2022; Additional Ukraine Supplemental Appropriations Act, 2022, P.L. 117-128, 5/21/2022; Ukraine Supplemental Appropriations Act, 2023, P.L. 117-180, 9/30/2022; and Additional Ukraine Supplemental Appropriations Act, 2023, P.L. 117-328, Div M, 12/29/2022.

37. Ukraine Security Supplemental Appropriations Act, P.L. 118-50, Div B, 4/24,/2024.

38. Ukraine Security Supplemental Appropriations Act, P.L. 118-50, Div B, 4/24/2024.

39. Ukraine Supplemental Appropriations Act, 2022, P.L. 117-103, Div N, enacted 3/15/2022; Additional Ukraine Supplemental Appropriations Act, 2022, P.L. 117-128, 5/21/2022; Ukraine Supplemental Appropriations Act, 2023, P.L. 117-180, 9/30/2022; and Additional Ukraine Supplemental Appropriations Act, 2023, P.L. 117-328, Div M, 12/29/2022.

40. USAID, vetting comment, 5/9/2024.

41. OUSD(C), vetting comment, 1/30/2024.

42. 22 U.S.C. §2318(a)(1).

43. Additional Ukraine Supplemental Appropriations Act, 2022, P.L. 117-128, enacted 5/21/2022; Consolidated Appropriations Act, 2023, P.L. 117-328, enacted 12/29/2022.

44. OUSD(C), response to DoD OIG request for information, 24.2 OAR 003, 4/3/2024.

45. OUSD(C), vetting comment, 1/30/2024.

46. National Defense Authorization Act for FY 2016, P.L. 114-92, Sec. 1250, "Ukraine Security Assistance Initiative," 11/25/2015.

47. State, vetting comment, 4/30/2024.

48. OUSD(C), response to DoD OIG request for information, 24.2 OAR 003, 4/3/2024.

49. OUSD(P), response to DoD OIG request for information, 24.2 OAR 002, 3/6/2024; OUSD(P), vetting comment, 4/29/2024.

50. OUSD(P), vetting comment, 4/29/2024.

51. OUSD(C), response to DoD OIG request for information, 24.2 OAR 003, 4/3/2024.

52. Arms Export Control Act, as Amended, P.L. 117-263, Sec. 2 [2752] "Coordination With Foreign Policy." 12/23/2022.

53. State, response to State OIG request for information, 3/22/2024; Ukraine Supplemental Appropriations Act, 2022, P.L. 117-103, Div. N, 3/15/2022; the Additional Ukraine Supplemental Appropriations Act, 2022, P.L. 117-128, 5/21/2022; and the Additional Ukraine Supplemental Appropriations Act, 2023, P.L. 117-328, Div. M, 12/29/2023; State, vetting comment, 4/30/2024.

54. State, response to State OIG request for information, 3/22/2024.

55. State, response to State OIG request for information, 4/28/2024.

56. State, response to State OIG request for information, 3/22/2024.

57. State, response to State OIG request for information, 3/22/2024.

58. State, response to State OIG request for information, 3/22/2024.

59. State, response to State OIG request for information, 3/22/2024.

60. State, response to State OIG request for information, 3/22/2024.

61. DoD OIG, "Management Advisory: The Navy's Execution of Funds to Assist Ukraine," DODIG- 2024-069, 3/28/2024.

62. DoD OIG, "Management Advisory: The Navy's Execution of Funds to Assist Ukraine," DODIG- 2024-069, 3/28/2024.

63. State, response to State OIG request for information, 3/25/2024.

64. State, response to State OIG request for information, 3/25/2024.

65. State, response to State OIG request for information, 3/25/2024.

66. State, response to State OIG request for information, 3/25/2024.

67. State, response to State OIG request for information, 3/25/2024.

68. State, response to State OIG request for information, 3/25/2024.

69. USAID Ukraine, response to USAID OIG request for information, 3/25/2024.

70. USAID Ukraine, response to USAID OIG request for information, 3/25/2024.

71. USAID Ukraine, response to USAID OIG request for information, 3/25/2024.

72. USAID Ukraine, response to USAID OIG request for information, 3/25/2024.

73. Ukraine Ministry of Finance, "Technical Guidance Operations Manual for Managing the PEACE in Ukraine Project," 9/14/2022.

74. Ukraine Ministry of Finance, "Technical Guidance Operations Manual for Managing the PEACE in Ukraine Project," 9/14/2022.

75. World Bank, "World Bank Group Financing Support Mobilization to Ukraine Since February 24, 2022," 3/1/2024.

76. USAID Ukraine, response to USAID OIG request for information, 3/25/2024.

77. Ukraine Ministry of Finance, "Technical Guidance Operations Manual for Managing the PEACE in Ukraine Project," 9/14/2022.

78. Ukraine Ministry of Finance, "Technical Guidance Operations Manual for Managing the PEACE in Ukraine Project," 9/14/2022.

79. Ukraine Ministry of Finance, "Technical Guidance Operations Manual for Managing the PEACE in Ukraine Project," 9/14/2022.

80. Ukraine Ministry of Finance, "Technical Guidance Operations Manual for Managing the PEACE in Ukraine Project," 9/14/2022.

81. Ukraine Ministry of Finance, "Technical Guidance Operations Manual for Managing the PEACE in Ukraine Project," 9/14/2022.

82. Ukraine Ministry of Finance, "Technical Guidance Operations Manual for Managing the PEACE in Ukraine Project," 9/14/2022.

83. Ukraine Ministry of Finance, "Technical Guidance Operations Manual for Managing the PEACE in Ukraine Project," 9/14/2022.

84. USAID Ukraine, response to USAID OIG request for information, 3/25/2024; USAID, "Verification Report – Pensions, March-July 2022," 4/1/2022.

85. Ukraine Ministry of Finance, "Technical Guidance Operations Manual for Managing the PEACE in Ukraine Project," 9/14/2022.

86. Ukraine Ministry of Finance, "Technical Guidance Operations Manual for Managing the PEACE in Ukraine Project," 9/14/2022.

87. USAID Ukraine, response to USAID OIG request for information, 3/25/2024.

88. USAID Ukraine, response to USAID OIG request for information, 3/25/2024

89. USAID Ukraine, response to USAID OIG request for information, 3/25/2024.

90. USAID, vetting comment, 4/30/2024.

91. Ukraine Ministry of Finance, "Technical Guidance Operations Manual for Managing the PEACE in Ukraine Project," 9/14/2022.

92. Ukraine Ministry of Finance, "Technical Guidance Operations Manual for Managing the PEACE in Ukraine Project," 9/14/2022.

93. USAID Ukraine, response to USAID OIG request for information, 3/25/2024.

94. USAID Ukraine, response to USAID OIG request for information, 3/25/2024.

95. USAID OIG, "Direct Budget Support: USAID Ensured That the Government of Ukraine Adhered to Required Controls, but Did Not Verify the Accuracy of Salary Expenditures," 2/13/2024.

96. USAID OIG, "Direct Budget Support: USAID Ensured That the Government of Ukraine Adhered to Required Controls, but Did Not Verify the Accuracy of Salary Expenditures," 2/13/2024.

97. USAID OIG, "Direct Budget Support: USAID Ensured That the Government of Ukraine Adhered to Required Controls, but Did Not Verify the Accuracy of Salary Expenditures," 2/13/2024.

98. USAID OIG, "Direct Budget Support: USAID Ensured That the Government of Ukraine Adhered to Required Controls, but Did Not Verify the Accuracy of Salary Expenditures," 2/13/2024.

99. USAID OIG, "Direct Budget Support: USAID Ensured That the Government of Ukraine Adhered to Required Controls, but Did Not Verify the Accuracy of Salary Expenditures," 2/13/2024.

100. USAID OIG, "Direct Budget Support: USAID Ensured That the Government of Ukraine Adhered to Required Controls, but Did Not Verify the Accuracy of Salary Expenditures," 2/13/2024.

101. USAID Ukraine, response to USAID OIG request for information, 12/15/2023.

102. USEUCOM, response to DoD OIG request for information, 24.2 OAR 020, 4/15/2024.

103. State, response to State OIG request for information, 12/22/2023.

104. State, response to State OIG request for information, 3/22/2024.

105. State, response to State OIG request for information, 3/22/2024.

106. State, response to State OIG request for information, 3/22/2024.

107. ODC-Kyiv, response to DoD OIG request for information, 24.2 OAR 025B, 3/26/2024.

108. State, response to State OIG request for information, 12/22/2023.

109. State, response to State OIG request for information, 3/22/2024.

110. State, response to State OIG request for information, 3/22/2024.

111. State, response to State OIG request for information, 3/22/2024.

112. State, vetting comment, 4/30/2024.

113. State, response to State OIG request for information, 3/22/2024.

114. State, response to State OIG request for information, 3/22/2024.

115. State, response to State OIG request for information, 3/22/2024.

116. State, response to State OIG request for information, 3/22/2024.

117. State, response to State OIG request for information, 3/22/2024.

118. USAID Ukraine, response to USAID OIG request for information, 3/25/2024.

119. USAID Ukraine, response to USAID OIG request for information, 3/25/2024.

120. USAID Ukraine, response to USAID OIG request for information, 3/25/2024.

121. OUSD(P), response to DoD OIG request for information, 24.1 OAR 002, 12/26/2023.

122. OUSD(P), response to DoD OIG request for information, 24.1 OAR 001, 12/26/2023; OUSD(P), response to DoD OIG request for information, 24.2 OAR 001, 3/6/2024.

123. USEUCOM, response to DoD OIG request for information, 24.2 OAR 007, 4/3/2024.

124. CIA Director William Burns, testimony before the Senate Select Intelligence Committee, "Hearing on Annual Worldwide Threats Assessment," 3/11/2024.

125. CIA Director William Burns, testimony before the Senate Select Intelligence Committee, "Hearing on Annual Worldwide Threats Assessment," 3/11/2024.

126. Ellie Cook, "Ukraine Trolls Russia Over Black Sea Fleet Ship Loss," Newsweek, 4/15/2024.

127. CIA Director William Burns, testimony before the Senate Select Intelligence Committee, "Hearing on Annual Worldwide Threats Assessment," 3/11/2024.

128. CIA Director William Burns, testimony before the Senate Select Intelligence Committee, "Hearing on Annual Worldwide Threats Assessment," 3/11/2024.

129. Guy Faulconbridge and Tom Balmforth, "Russia Takes Avdiivka from Ukraine, Biggest Gain in Nine Months," Reuters, 2/18/2024; Alex Babenko, "Exhaustion, Dwindling Reserves and a Commander Who Disappeared: How Ukraine Lost Avdiivka to Russia," Associated Press, 3/11/2024.

130. White House, statement, "Readout of President Biden's Call with President Zelenskyy of Ukraine," 2/17/2024.

131. Guy Faulconbridge and Tom Balmforth, "Russia Takes Avdiivka from Ukraine, Biggest Gain in Nine Months," Reuters, 2/18/2024; Alex Babenko, "Exhaustion, Dwindling Reserves and a Commander Who Disappeared: How Ukraine Lost Avdiivka to Russia," Associated Press, 3/11/2024.

132. Guy Faulconbridge and Tom Balmforth, "Russia Takes Avdiivka from Ukraine, Biggest Gain in Nine Months," Reuters, 2/18/2024; Alex Babenko, "Exhaustion, Dwindling Reserves and a Commander Who Disappeared: How Ukraine Lost Avdiivka to Russia," Associated Press, 3/11/2024.

133. DIA, response to DoD OIG request for information, 24.2 OAR 030, 3/27/2024.

134. Institute for the Study of War, "Russian Offensive Campaign Assessment, February 15, 2024," 2/15/2024.

135. Director of National Intelligence Avril Haines, testimony before the Senate Select Intelligence Committee, "Hearing on Annual Worldwide Threats Assessment," 3/11/2024.

136. DIA, response to DoD OIG request for information, 24.2 OAR SUPP002, 4/16/2024.

137. DIA, response to DoD OIG request for information, 24.2 OAR SUPP002, 4/16/2024.

138. DIA, response to DoD OIG request for information, 24.2 OAR SUPP002, 4/16/2024.

139. DIA, response to DoD OIG request for information, 24.2 OAR SUPP002, 4/16/2024.

140. Isabel van Brugen, "Ukraine Seeks to Cut Off Putin's Lifeblood With Attacks Inside Russia," Newsweek, 1/25/2024; Brendan Cole, "Russian Oil Hub in Putin's Home City on Fire After Drone Hit," Newsweek, 1/31/2024.

141. OUSD(P), response to DoD OIG request for information, 24.2 OAR 050, 3/26/2024.

142. Tom Balmforth and Pavel Polityuk, "Ukraine Says it Sank Russian Large Landing Warship in Black Sea," Reuters, 2/14/2024.

143. Tom Balmforth and Pavel Polityuk, "Ukraine Says it Sank Russian Large Landing Warship in Black Sea," Reuters, 2/14/2024; Vasco Cotovio, "Ukraine Says It Sank Russian Warship Off Coast of Crimea and Unleashed 'Massive' Missile Barrage on Peninsula," CNN, 2/1/2024; Svitlana Vlasova and Brad Lendon, "Ukraine's Drones Sink Another Russian Warship, Kyiv Says," CNN, 3/6/2024; DIA, response to DoD OIG request for information, 24.2 OAR SUPP001, 4/16/2024.

144. Svitlana Vlasova and Brad Lendon, "Ukraine's Drones Sink Another Russian Warship, Kyiv Says," CNN, 3/6/2024.

145. DIA, response to DoD OIG request for information, 24.2 OAR SUPP001, 4/16/2024.

146. Victoria Butenko, "Zelensky Fires Ukraine's Military Chief in Major Shakeup Nearly Two Years Into War," CNN, 2/8/2024.

147. Anton Hrushetskyi, "Dynamics of Trust in Social Institutions in 2021-2023," Kyiv International Institute of Sociology, 12/18/2023; Nate Ostiller, "Poll: Ukrainians' Trust in Zelensky Declines to 62%, Trust in Military, Zaluzhnyi Remains High." The Kyiv Independent, 12/18/2023.

148. Konstantin Skorkin, "What Does General Zaluzhny's Dismissal Mean for Ukraine?" Carnegie Endowment for International Peace, 2/10/2024; Peter Dickinson, "Removal of Ukraine's 'Iron General' is One of Zelenskyy's Biggest Gambles," Atlantic Council, 2/8/2024; Anton Hrushetskyi, "Dynamics of Trust in Social Institutions in 2021-2023," Kyiv International Institute of Sociology, 12/18/2023; Nate Ostiller, "Poll: Ukrainians' Trust in Zelensky Declines to 62%, Trust in Military, Zaluzhnyi Remains High." The Kyiv Independent, 12/18/2023.

149. Associated Press, "Ukraine's President Says Dismissed Military Commander Zaluzhnyi Will Be New Ambassador to the UK," 3/8/2024.

150. Valerii Zaluzhnyi, "Ukraine's Army Chief: The Design of War Has Changed," CNN, 2/8/2024.

151. Valerii Zaluzhnyi, "Ukraine's Army Chief: The Design of War Has Changed," CNN, 2/8/2024.

152. Victoria Butenko, "Zelensky Fires Ukraine's Military Chief in Major Shakeup Nearly Two Years Into War," CNN, 2/8/2024.

153. USAREUR-AF, response to DoD OIG request for information, 24.2 OAR 063, 4/3/2024.

154. USAREUR-AF, response to DoD OIG request for information, 24.2 OAR 063, 4/3/2024.

155. USAREUR-AF, response to DoD OIG request for information, 24.2 OAR 063, 4/3/2024.

156. Joint Staff Publication, "Mission Command—2nd Ed." JS J7 Deployable Training Division, 1/2020.

157. USAREUR-AF, response to DoD OIG request for information, 24.2 OAR 063, 4/3/2024; USAREUR-AF, vetting comment, 4/29/2024.

158. USAREUR-AF, response to DoD OIG request for information, 24.2 OAR 063, 4/3/2024.

159. USAREUR-AF, vetting comment, 4/29/2024.

160. SAG-U, response to DoD OIG request for information, 24.2 OAR 034, 3/29/2024.

161. SAG-U, response to DoD OIG request for information, 24.2 OAR 035, 3/29/2024.

162. SAG-U, response to DoD OIG request for information, 24.2 OAR 036, 3/29/2024.

163. SAG-U, response to DoD OIG request for information, 24.2 OAR 036, 3/29/2024.

164. USAREUR-AF, response to DoD OIG request for information, 24.2 OAR 063, 4/3/2024.

165. USAREUR-AF, response to DoD OIG request for information, 24.2 OAR 063, 4/3/2024.

166. Hanna Arhirova and Samya Kullab, "Ukraine Lowers Its Conscription Age to 25 to Replenish Its Beleaguered Troops," Associated Press, 4/3/2024.

167. Xiaofei Xu and Yulia Kesaieva, "Zelensky Signs Law Expanding Draft Age as Ukraine Struggles to Beef Up Its Military," CNN, 4/2/2024.

168. Hanna Arhirova and Samya Kullab, "Ukraine Lowers Its Conscription Age to 25 to Replenish Its Beleaguered Troops," Associated Press, 4/3/2024.

169. Director of National Intelligence Avril Haines, testimony before the Senate Select Intelligence Committee, "Hearing on Annual Worldwide Threats Assessment," 3/11/2024.

170. DIA, response to DoD OIG request for information, 24.2 OAR 030, 3/27/2024.

171. DIA, response to DoD OIG request for information, 24.2 OAR 029, 3/27/2024; RFE/RL, "Kremlin Tasks Senior Ex-Wagner Commander With Forming Volunteer Corps," 9/29/2023.

172. DIA, response to DoD OIG request for information, 24.2 OAR 029, 3/27/2024.

173. DIA, response to DoD OIG request for information, 24.2 OAR 029, 3/27/2024.

174. DIA, response to DoD OIG request for information, 24.2 OAR 029, 3/27/2024.

175. DIA, response to DoD OIG request for information, 24.2 OAR 029, 3/27/2024.

176. Julian E. Barnes and David E. Sanger, "Russia Is Refining Online Operations That Focus on Ukraine Aid," New York Times, 3/28/2024.

177. Julian E. Barnes and David E. Sanger, "Russia Is Refining Online Operations That Focus on Ukraine Aid," New York Times, 3/28/2024.

178. DIA, response to DoD OIG request for information, 24.2 OAR 030, 3/27/2024.

179. State, press release, "Imposing Sanctions on Actors Supporting Kremlin-Directed Disinformation Efforts," 3/20/2024.

180. Tuhina, Gjeraqina. "Two Years into EU Ban, Russia's RT and Sputnik Are Still Accessible Across the EU," RFE/RL, 2/3/2024.

181. Tuhina, Gjeraqina. "Two Years into EU Ban, Russia's RT and Sputnik Are Still Accessible Across the EU," RFE/RL, 2/3/2024.

182. Director of National Intelligence Avril Haines, testimony before the Senate Select Intelligence Committee, "Hearing on Annual Worldwide Threats Assessment," 3/11/2024.

183. DIA, response to DoD OIG request for information, 24.2 OAR 028, 3/27/2024.

184. DIA, response to DoD OIG request for information, 24.2 OAR 028, 3/27/2024.

185. CIA Director William Burns, testimony before the Senate Select Intelligence Committee, "Hearing on Annual Worldwide Threats Assessment," 3/11/2024.

186. DIA, response to DoD OIG request for information, 24.2 OAR 028, 3/27/2024.

187. DIA, response to DoD OIG request for information, 24.2 OAR 030, 3/27/2024.

188. SAG-U, response to DoD OIG request for information, 24.1 OAR 026, 12/27/2023.

189. SAG-U, response to DoD OIG request for information, 24.1 OAR 026, 12/27/2023; SAG-U, vetting comment, 4/29/2024.

190. USAREUR-AF IG and SAG-U IG, discussion with DoD OIG staff, Wiesbaden, Germany, 12/7/2023.

191. SAG-U, response to DoD OIG request for information, 24.2 OAR 033, 3/29/2024.

192. SAG-U, response to DoD OIG request for information, 24.2 OAR 034, 3/29/2024.

193. SAG-U, response to DoD OIG request for information, 24.1 OAR 027, 12/27/2023.

194. USEUCOM, response to DoD OIG request for information, 24.1 OAR 003, 12/25/2023; SAG-U, response to DoD OIG request for information, 24.1 OAR 026, 12/27/2023.

195. SAG-U, response to DoD OIG request for information, 24.1 OAR 026, 12/27/2023.

196. USAREUR-AF IG and SAG-U IG, discussion with DoD OIG staff, Wiesbaden, Germany, 12/7/2023.

197. USAREUR-AF IG and SAG-U IG, discussion with DoD OIG staff, Wiesbaden, Germany, 12/7/2023.

198. USAREUR-AF IG and SAG-U IG, discussion with DoD OIG staff, Wiesbaden, Germany, 12/7/2023.

199. Lara Seligman, "Pentagon Needs Congress to Hand Over $10B to Replace Weapons Sent to Ukraine," Politico, 3/12/2024; Tara Copp and Lolita C. Baldor, "Pentagon to Give Ukraine $300 Million in Weapons Even as It Lacks Funds to Replenish U.S. Stockpile," Associated Press, 3/12/2024.

200. Lara Seligman, "Pentagon Needs Congress to Hand Over $10B to Replace Weapons Sent to Ukraine," Politico, 3/11/2024.

201. White House, transcript, "Press Briefing by Press Secretary Karine Jean-Pierre and National Security Advisor Jake Sullivan," 3/12/2024.

202. Tara Copp and Lolita C. Baldor, "Pentagon to Give Ukraine $300 Million in Weapons Even as It Lacks Funds to Replenish U.S. Stockpile," Associated Press, 3/12/2024.

203. OUSD(P), response to DoD OIG request for information, 24.2 OAR 005, 3/26/2024.

204. DoD, transcript, "Pentagon Press Secretary Air Force Maj. Gen. Pat Ryder Holds a Press Briefing," 3/12/2024.

205. Dan Lamothe, "U.S. Will Send Ukraine $300 Million in Arms as Further Aid Stays Stalled," Washington Post, 3/13/2024.

206. DSCA, Security Assistance Management Manual, Chapter 8: End-Use Monitoring, 12/21/2023; DoD OIG, "Evaluation of the DoD's Enhanced End-Use Monitoring of Defense Articles Provided to Ukraine," DODIG-2024-043, 1/10/2024; 22 U.S.C. §2753-2754.

207. State, response to State OIG request for information, 12/22/2023.

208. ODC-Kyiv, response to DoD OIG request for information, 24.2 OAR 049, 3/26/2024.

209. DSCA, Security Assistance Management Manual, Chapter 8: End-Use Monitoring, 12/21/2023; ODC-Kyiv, response to DoD OIG request for information, 24.2 OAR 048, 3/26/2024.

210. ODC-Kyiv, responses to DoD OIG requests for information, 24.2 OAR 025B, OAR 026B, and OAR 049, 3/26/2024.

211. ODC-Kyiv, response to DoD OIG request for information, 24.2 OAR 026B, 3/26/2024.

212. DoD OIG, "Evaluation of the DoD's Enhanced End-Use Monitoring of Defense Articles Provided to Ukraine," DODIG-2024-043, 1/10/2024.

213. ODC-Kyiv, response to DoD OIG request for information, 24.2 OAR 026B, 3/26/2024.

214. ODC-Kyiv, response to DoD OIG request for information, 24.2 OAR 048, 3/26/2024.

215. ODC-Kyiv, response to DoD OIG request for information, 24.2 OAR 027, 3/26/2024.

216. DoD OIG, "Evaluation of the DoD's Enhanced End-Use Monitoring of Defense Articles Provided to Ukraine," DODIG-2024-043, 1/10/2024.

217. State, vetting comment, 4/30/2024.

218. DoD OIG, "Evaluation of the U.S. European Command's Planning and Execution of Ground Transportation of Equipment to Support Ukraine from Port to Transfer Locations," DODIG-2024-053, 2/8/2024.

219. DoD OIG, "Evaluation of the U.S. European Command's Planning and Execution of Ground Transportation of Equipment to Support Ukraine from Port to Transfer Locations," DODIG-2024-053, 2/8/2024.

220. OUSD(P)RUE, vetting comment, 4/30/2024.

221. ODC-Kyiv, response to DoD OIG request for information, 24.2 OAR 062B, 3/26/2024; OUSD(P)RUE, vetting comment, 4/30/2024.

222. ODC-Kyiv, response to DoD OIG request for information, 24.2 OAR 062B, 3/26/2024; Lara Jakes, "Ukraine Could Deploy F-16s as Soon as July, but Only a Few," New York Times, 3/11/2024.

223. ODC-Kyiv, response to DoD OIG request for information, 24.2 OAR 062B, 3/26/2024.

224. Lara Jakes, "Ukraine Could Deploy F-16s as Soon as July, but Only a Few," New York Times, 3/11/2024.

225. Lara Jakes, "Ukraine Could Deploy F-16s as Soon as July, but Only a Few," New York Times, 3/11/2024.

226. OUSD(P)RUE, vetting comment, 4/30/2024.

227. SAG-U, response to DoD OIG request for information, 24.2 OAR 035, 3/29/2024.

228. USTRANSCOM, response to DoD OIG request for information, 24.2 OAR 045, 3/26/2024.

229. USTRANSCOM, response to DoD OIG request for information, 24.2 OAR 045, 3/26/2024.

230. USTRANSCOM, response to DoD OIG request for information, 24.2 OAR 045, 3/26/2024.

231. USTRANSCOM, response to DoD OIG request for information, 24.2 OAR 045, 3/26/2024.

232. USTRANSCOM, response to DoD OIG request for information, 24.2 OAR 045, 3/26/2024.

233. USEUCOM, response to DoD OIG request for information, 24.2 OAR 043, 4/1/2024.

234. SAG-U, responses to DoD OIG request for information, 24.2 OAR 034, 3/29/2024, and 24.2 OAR 038, 4/1/2024.

235. SAG-U, response to DoD OIG request for information, 24.2 OAR 056, 3/29/2024.

236. DoD OIG, "Evaluation of Sustainment Strategies for the PATRIOT Air Defense Systems Transferred to the Ukrainian Armed Forces," DODIG-2024-056, 2/15/2024; DoD OIG, "Evaluation of the DoD's Sustainment Plan for Bradley, Stryker, and Abrams Armored Weapon Systems Transferred to the Ukrainian Armed Forces," DODIG-2024-057, 2/15/2024.

237. DoD OIG, "Evaluation of the DoD's Sustainment Plan for Bradley, Stryker, and Abrams Armored Weapon Systems Transferred to the Ukrainian Armed Forces," DODIG-2024-057, 2/15/2024.

238. DoD OIG, "Evaluation of Sustainment Strategies for the PATRIOT Air Defense Systems Transferred to the Ukrainian Armed Forces," DODIG-2024-056, 2/15/2024.

239. DoD OIG, "Evaluation of Sustainment Strategies for the PATRIOT Air Defense Systems Transferred to the Ukrainian Armed Forces," DODIG-2024-056, 2/15/2024; DoD OIG, "Evaluation of the DoD's Sustainment Plan for Bradley, Stryker, and Abrams Armored Weapon Systems Transferred to the Ukrainian Armed Forces," DODIG-2024-057, 2/15/2024.

240. DoD OIG, "Evaluation of Sustainment Strategies for the PATRIOT Air Defense Systems Transferred to the Ukrainian Armed Forces," DODIG-2024-056, 2/15/2024; DoD OIG, "Evaluation of the DoD's Sustainment Plan for Bradley, Stryker, and Abrams Armored Weapon Systems Transferred to the Ukrainian Armed Forces," DODIG-2024-057, 2/15/2024.

241. DoD OIG, "Management Advisory: Audit of Remote Maintenance and Distribution Cell-Ukraine Restructuring Contract Award," DODIG-2024-041, 1/9/2024.

242. SAG-U, response to DoD OIG request for information, 24.2 OAR 057, 3/29/2024.

243. SAG-U, response to DoD OIG request for information, 24.2 OAR 057, 3/29/2024.

244. SAG-U, response to DoD OIG request for information, 24.2 OAR 055, 3/29/2024.

245. USAREUR-AF, response to DoD OIG request for information, 24.2 OAR 063, 4/3/2024.

246. ODC-Kyiv, response to DoD OIG request for information, 24.2 OAR 059B, 3/26/2024.

247. SAG-U, response to DoD OIG request for information, 24.2 OAR 059, 3/29/2024.

248. SAG-U, response to DoD OIG request for information, 24.2 OAR 055, 3/29/2024.

249. SAG-U, response to DoD OIG request for information, 24.2 OAR 040, 3/29/2024.

250. SAG-U, response to DoD OIG request for information, 24.2 OAR 041, 3/29/2024.

251. SAG-U, response to DoD OIG request for information, 24.2 OAR 036, 3/29/2024.

252. USAREUR-AF, response to DoD OIG request for information, 24.2 OAR 058, 4/3/2024; SAG-U, vetting comment, 4/29/2024.

253. DoD OIG, "Management Advisory: Leahy Vetting of DoD-Trained Ukrainian Armed Forces," DODIG-2024-046, 1/18/2024.

254. DoD OIG, "Management Advisory: Leahy Vetting of DoD-Trained Ukrainian Armed Forces," DODIG-2024-046, 1/18/2024.

255. DoD OIG, "Management Advisory: Leahy Vetting of DoD-Trained Ukrainian Armed Forces," DODIG-2024-046, 1/18/2024.

256. State, transcript, " Special Online Briefing with Ambassador Julianne Smith, U.S. Permanent Representative to NATO," 2/13/2023.

257. USEUCOM, response to DoD OIG request for information, 24.2 OAR 019, 4/3/2024; USEUCOM, discussion with DoD OIG staff, Stuttgart, Germany, 12/6/2023; USEUCOM, vetting comment, 5/9/2024.

258. USEUCOM, response to DoD OIG request for information, 24.2 OAR 019, 4/3/2024; USEUCOM, discussion with DoD OIG staff, Stuttgart, Germany, 12/6/2023.

259. SAG-U, vetting comment, 4/29/2024.

260. SAG-U, response to DoD OIG request for information, 24.2 OAR 061, 3/29/2024.

261. USAREUR-AF IG and SAG-U IG staff, discussion with DoD OIG staff, Wiesbaden, Germany, 12/7/2023.

262. SAG-U, response to DoD OIG request for information, 24.2 OAR 061, 3/29/2024.

263. SAG-U, response to DoD OIG request for information, 24.2 OAR 061, 3/29/2024.

264. SAG-U, response to DoD OIG request for information, 24.2 OAR 060, 3/29/2024.

265. ODC-Kyiv, response to DoD OIG request for information, 24.2 OAR 054B, 3/26/2024.

266. SAG-U, response to DoD OIG request for information, 24.2 OAR 056, 3/29/2024.

267. State, response to State OIG request for information, 3/24/2024.

268. State, response to State OIG request for information, 3/24/2024.

269. State, response to State OIG request for information, 3/24/2024.

270. State, response to State OIG request for information, 3/24/2024.

271. State, response to State OIG request for information, 4/12/2024.

272. State, response to State OIG request for information, 4/12/2024.

273. State, response to State OIG request for information, 4/12/2024.

274. State, response to State OIG request for information, 4/12/2024.

275. State, response to State OIG request for information, 4/12/2024.

276. Eve Sampson and Samuel Granados, "Ukraine is Now the Most Mined Country. It Will Take Decades to Make Safe," Washington Post, 7/22/2023; Michael Drummond, "Ukraine War: How Hidden Landmines, Tripwires and Booby Traps Pose Lethal Danger for Years to Come," Sky News, 1/29/2023; Gerry Doyle, Han Huang, and Jackie Gu, "What Lies Beneath," Reuters, 7/28/2023

277. State, response to State OIG request for information, 3/22/2024.

278. State, responses to State OIG requests for information, 3/22/2024 and 4/4/2024.

279. State, response to State OIG request for information, 3/22/2024.

280. State, response to State OIG request for information, 3/22/2024.

281. State, response to State OIG request for information, 3/22/2024.

282. State, response to State OIG request for information, 3/22/2024.

283. State, response to State OIG request for information, 3/22/2024.

284. State, response to State OIG request for information, 3/22/2024.

285. State, response to State OIG request for information, 3/22/2024.

286. State, response to State OIG request for information, 4/28/2204.

287. State, response to State OIG request for information, 4/28/2204.

288. State, response to State OIG request for information, 3/22/2024.

289. State, response to State OIG request for information, 3/22/2024.

290. State, response to State OIG request for information, 3/22/2024.

291. State, response to State OIG request for information, 4/28/2204.

292. State, responses to State OIG request for information, 3/22/2024 and 4/28/2024.

293. State, response to State OIG request for information, 3/22/2024.

294. State, response to State OIG request for information, 3/22/2024.

295. USAID Ukraine, response to USAID OIG request for information, 3/25/2024.

296. USAID Ukraine, response to USAID OIG request for information, 3/25/2024.

297. USAID Ukraine, response to USAID OIG request for information, 3/25/2024.

298. USEUCOM, response to DoD OIG request for information, 24.2 OAR 012, 4/1/2024.

299. Matthew Lee and Lorne Cook, "Sweden Officially Joins NATO, Ending Decades of Post-World War II Neutrality," Associated Press, 3/7/2024.

300. NATO, website, "The North Atlantic Treaty," undated.

301. Matthew Lee and Lorne Cook, "Sweden Officially Joins NATO, Ending Decades of Post-World War II Neutrality," Associated Press, 3/7/2024.

302. Phelan Chatterjee, "How Sweden and Finland Went from Neutral to NATO," BBC News, 7/11/2023.

303. USEUCOM, response to DoD OIG request for information, 24.2 OAR 007, 4/3/2024.

304. USEUCOM, response to DoD OIG request for information, 24.2 OAR 007, 4/3/2024.

305. NATO, fact sheet, "Steadfast Defender 24," 3/8/2024.

306. NATO, fact sheet, "Steadfast Defender 24," 3/8/2024.

307. USEUCOM, response to DoD OIG request for information, 24.2 OAR 065, 4/1/2024.

308. State, "Integrated Country Strategy-Ukraine," 8/29/2023.

309. USAID Ukraine, "Country Development Cooperation Strategy 2019-2024, Extended Through Jan 9, 2026," 1/4/2024.

310. USAID Ukraine, response to USAID OIG request for information, 3/25/2024.

311. USAID Ukraine, response to USAID OIG request for information, 3/25/2024.

312. Embassy Kyiv, cable, "Ukraine: Scenesetter for OIG Visit to Ukraine January 29-31," 24 KYIV 150 1/27/2024,

313. Matthew Mpoke Bigg, "Ukraine Accuses Defense Company of Embezzling $40 Million," New York Times, 1/28/2024; Joanna Kakissis, "How Much Progress has Ukraine's Government Made Against Corruption?" National Public Radio, 10/10/2023.

314. Peter Dickinson, "Wartime Ukraine Ranks Among World's Top Performers in Anti-corruption Index," Atlantic Council, 2/1/2024.

315. Adrian Karatnycky, "How Deep Does Corruption Run in Ukraine?" Foreign Policy, 3/6/2024; GRECO, Group of States Against Corruption, "Fourth Evaluation Round, Corruption Prevention in Respect of Members of Parliament Judges and Prosecutors," 3/24/2023; State, vetting comment, 5/1/2024.

316. War.Ukraine (Official government website), "Digitalization has Become an Invariable Companion in the Fight for Transparency in Ukraine, and Here's Why," 12/8/2023.

317. Peter Dickinson, "Wartime Ukraine Ranks Among World's Top Performers in Anti-corruption Index," Atlantic Council, 2/1/2024; Adrian Karatnycky, "How Deep Does Corruption Run in Ukraine?" Foreign Policy, 3/6/2024; State, vetting comment, 5/1/2024.

318. Stefan Wolff and Tetyana Malyarenko, "Ukraine War: Corruption Scandals and High-Level Rifts Could Become an Existential Threat as Kyiv Asks for More Military Aid," The Conversation, 2/1/2024; Peter Dickinson, "Wartime Ukraine Ranks Among World's Top Performers in Anti-corruption Index," Atlantic Council, 2/1/2024; Adrian Karatnycky, "How Deep Does Corruption Run in Ukraine?" Foreign Policy, 3/6/2024; George Wright, "Ukraine Says it has Uncovered Major Arms Corruption," BBC, 1/28/2024; Dan Peleschuk, "Ukraine Unveils Corruption Probes into Reconstruction Schemes," Reuters, 11/21/2023.

319. Newsweek, "Zelensky's Corruption Problem," 1/28/2024; Stefan Wolff and Tetyana Malyarenko, "Ukraine War: Corruption Scandals and High-Level Rifts Could Become an Existential Threat as Kyiv Asks for More Military Aid," The Conversation, 2/1/2024; Peter Dickinson, "Wartime Ukraine Ranks Among World's Top Performers in Anti-corruption Index," Atlantic Council, 2/1/2024; Adrian Karatnycky, "How Deep Does Corruption Run in Ukraine?" Foreign Policy, 3/6/2024; George Wright, "Ukraine Says it has Uncovered Major Arms Corruption," BBC, 1/28/2024; Dan Peleschuk, "Ukraine Unveils Corruption Probes into Reconstruction Schemes," Reuters, 11/21/2023.

320. Stefan Wolff and Tetyana Malyarenko, "Ukraine War: Corruption Scandals and High-Level Rifts Could Become an Existential Threat as Kyiv Asks for More Military Aid," The Conversation, 2/1/2024; Peter Dickinson, "Wartime Ukraine Ranks Among World's Top Performers in Anti-corruption Index," Atlantic Council, 2/1/2024; Adrian Karatnycky, "How Deep Does Corruption Run in Ukraine?" Foreign Policy, 3/6/2024; George Wright, "Ukraine Says it has Uncovered Major Arms Corruption," BBC, 1/28/2024; Dan Peleschuk, "Ukraine Unveils Corruption Probes into Reconstruction Schemes," Reuters, 11/21/2023.

321. State, vetting comment, 5/1/2024.

322. Embassy Kyiv, cable, "Ukraine: INL Assistance Boosts Ukraine's Ability to Hold Corrupt Actors Accountable," 24 KYIV 200, 2/6/2024, and State, vetting comment, 4/29/2024.

323. Embassy Kyiv, cable, "Ukraine: INL Assistance Boosts Ukraine's Ability to Hold Corrupt Actors Accountable," 24 KYIV 200, 2/6/2024.

324. Embassy Kyiv, cable, "Ukraine: INL Assistance Boosts Ukraine's Ability to Hold Corrupt Actors Accountable," 24 KYIV 200, 2/6/2024.

325. State, response to State OIG request for information, 4/12/2024.

326. State, response to State OIG request for information, 4/12/2024.

327. State, response to State OIG request for information, 4/12/2024.

328. State, response to State OIG request for information, 4/12/2024. and 4/29/2024.

329. USAID Ukraine, response to USAID OIG request for information, 3/25/2024.

330. U.S. Mission to the EU, cable, "Scenesetter for Special Representative Penny Pritzker's February 15-16 Visit to Brussels," 24 USEU BRUSSELS 142, 2/12/2024; State, vetting comment, 5/1/2024.

331. State, response to State OIG request for information, 4/28/2024.

332. State, response to State OIG request for information, 4/12/2024.

333. State, response to State OIG request for information, 4/12/2024.

334. State, response to State OIG for information, 4/12/2024.

335. State, response to State OIG for information, 4/12/2024 and 4/29/2024.

336. State, response to State OIG for information, 4/12/2024.

337. State, response to State OIG for information, 4/12/2024.

338. State, response to State OIG request for information, 4/12/2024.

339. State, response to State OIG request for information, 3/22/2024.

340. State, response to State OIG request for information, 3/22/2024.

341. State, response to State OIG request for information, 3/22/2024.

342. State, response to State OIG request for information, 3/22/2024.

343. USAID Ukraine, response to USAID OIG request for information, 3/25/2024.

344. USAID Ukraine, response to USAID OIG request for information, 3/25/2024.

345. USAID Ukraine, response to USAID OIG request for information, 3/25/2024.

346. USAID Ukraine, response to USAID OIG request for information, 3/25/2024.

347. USAID Ukraine, response to USAID OIG request for information, 3/25/2024.

348. USAID Ukraine, response to USAID OIG request for information, 3/25/2024.

349. USAID Ukraine, response to USAID OIG request for information, 3/25/2024.

350. USAID Ukraine, response to USAID OIG request for information, 3/25/2024.
351. USAID Ukraine, response to USAID OIG request for information, 3/25/2024.
352. USAID Ukraine, response to USAID OIG request for information, 3/25/2024.
353. USAID Ukraine, response to USAID OIG request for information, 3/25/2024.
354. USAID Ukraine, response to USAID OIG request for information, 3/25/2024; Telegram, Danylo Hetmantsev, 3/20/2024.
355. USAID Ukraine, response to USAID OIG request for information, 3/25/2024.
356. USAID Ukraine, response to USAID OIG request for information, 3/25/2024.
357. USAID Ukraine, response to USAID OIG request for information, 3/25/2024.
358. USAID Ukraine, response to USAID OIG request for information, 3/25/2024.
359. USAID Ukraine, response to USAID OIG request for information, 3/25/2024.
360. USAID Ukraine, response to USAID OIG request for information, 3/25/2024.
361. USAID Ukraine, response to USAID OIG request for information, 3/25/2024.
362. USAID Ukraine, response to USAID OIG request for information, 3/25/2024.
363. USAID Ukraine, response to USAID OIG request for information, 3/25/2024.
364. State, response to State OIG request for information, 3/22/2024.
365. State, response to State OIG request for information, 12/22/2023.
366. State, responses to State OIG request for information, 12/22/2023 and 3/22/2024.
367. State, response to State OIG request for information, 3/22/2024.
368. State, response to State OIG request for information, 3/22/2024.
369. State, response to State OIG request for information, 3/22/2024.
370. State, response to State OIG request for information, 3/22/2024.
371. State, response to State OIG request for information, 3/22/2024.
372. World Bank, "Ukraine: Third Rapid Damage and Needs Assessment (RDNA3), February 2022–December 2023," 2/15/2024; Yale School of Public Health, "Remote Assessment of Bombardment of Ukraine's Power Generation and Transmission Infrastructure, 1 October 2022 to 30 April 2023–A Conflict Observatory Report," 2/29/2024; Srdjan Nedeljkovic and Yehor Konovalov, "Russia Targets Kyiv with Ballistic Missiles as Fears Increase of Attacks on Energy Infrastructure, Associated Press, 12/11/2023; Hanna Arhirova, "Russia Steps up its Aerial Barrage Of Ukraine as Kyiv Officials Brace for Attacks on Infrastructure," Associated Press, 11/3/2023.
373. World Bank, "Ukraine: Third Rapid Damage and Needs Assessment (RDNA3), February 2022–December 2023," 2/15/2024; Yale School of Public Health, "Remote Assessment of Bombardment of Ukraine's Power Generation and Transmission Infrastructure, 1 October 2022 to 30 April 2023–A Conflict Observatory Report," 2/29/2024; Srdjan Nedeljkovic and Yehor Konovalov, "Russia Targets Kyiv with Ballistic Missiles as Fears Increase of Attacks on Energy Infrastructure," Associated Press, 12/11/2023; Hanna Arhirova, "Russia Steps up its Aerial Barrage Of Ukraine as Kyiv Officials Brace for Attacks on Infrastructure," Associated Press, 11/3/2023.

374. State, cable, "Ukraine: OSN Open Source Review February 15-19, 2024 (DS OPS)," 24 STATE 16574, 2/19/2024.
375. State, cable, "Ukraine: OSN Open Source Review February 15-19, 2024 (DS OPS)," 24 STATE 16574, 2/19/2024.
376. USAID Ukraine, response to USAID OIG request for information, 3/25/2024.
377. USAID Ukraine, response to USAID OIG request for information, 3/25/2024.
378. Ambassador Bridget Brink (@USAmbKyiv), tweet, 3/22/2024, 1:28 PM; USAID Ukraine, response to USAID OIG request for information, 3/25/2024.
379. USAID Ukraine, response to USAID OIG request for information, 3/25/2024.
380. USAID Ukraine, response to USAID OIG request for information, 3/25/2024.
381. Svitlana Vlasova, Christian Edwards, and Caitlin Danaher, "Russian Airstrikes Destroy Kyiv's Largest Power Plant," CNN, 4/12/2024.
382. State, cable, "Ukraine: OSN Open Source Review February 15-19, 2024 (DS OPS)," 24 STATE 16574, 2/19/2024; State, vetting comment, 4/23/2024.
383. State, cable, "Ukraine: OSN Open Source Review February 15-19, 2024 (DS OPS)," 24 STATE 16574, 2/19/2024; State, vetting comment, 4/23/2024.
384. World Bank, "Ukraine: Third Rapid Damage and Needs Assessment (RDNA3), February 2022–December 2023," 2/15/2024.
385. World Bank, "Ukraine: Third Rapid Damage and Needs Assessment (RDNA3), February 2022–December 2023," 2/15/2024.
386. USAID Ukraine, response to USAID OIG request for information, 3/25/2024.
387. USAID Ukraine, response to USAID OIG request for information, 3/25/2024.
388. Embassy Kyiv, cable, "Ukraine: U.S. Assistance Success Stories–January 2024." 24 KYIV 260, 2/16/2024.
389. Embassy Kyiv, cable, "Ukraine: U.S. Assistance Success Stories–January 2024." 24 KYIV 260, 2/16/2024.
390. State, response to State OIG request for information, 3/22/2024.
391. USEUCOM, response to DoD OIG request for information, 24.2 OAR 006, 4/1/2024.
392. State, response to State OIG request for information, 3/22/2024.
393. State, response to State OIG request for information, 3/22/2024.
394. State, response to State OIG request for information, 3/22/2024.
395. State, response to State OIG request for information, 3/24/2024.
396. State, response to State OIG request for information, 3/22/2024.
397. State, response to State OIG request for information, 3/22/2024 and 4/11/2024.
398. State, response to State OIG request for information, 3/22/2024; World Bank, website, "Ukraine Relief, Recovery, Reconstruction, and Reform Trust Fund," undated.
399. State, response to State OIG request for information, 3/22/2024.
400. State, response to State OIG request for information, 3/22/2024.
401. State, response to State OIG request for information, 3/22/2024.
402. State, response to State OIG request for information, 3/22/2024.
403. Multilateral Investment Guarantee Agency, website, "About Us," undated.

404. Multilateral Investment Guarantee Agency, website, "Support to Ukraine's Reconstructions and Economy Trust Fund (SURE TF)," undated.

405. State, response to State OIG request for information, 3/22/2024.

406. UN OCHA, "Humanitarian Needs and Response Plan for Ukraine," 1/3/2024.

407. USAID BHA, response to USAID OIG request for information, 3/11/2024.

408. USAID BHA, response to USAID OIG request for information, 3/11/2024.

409. USAID, Localization at USAID: The Vision and Approach, 8/2022.

410. UN OCHA, "Humanitarian Needs and Response Plan for Ukraine," 1/3/2024; USAID, "Complex Emergency Fact Sheet #2," 2/23/2024.

411. UN OCHA, "Humanitarian Needs and Response Plan for Ukraine," 1/3/2024; USAID, "Complex Emergency Fact Sheet #5," 3/21/2024.

412. USAID, "Complex Emergency Fact Sheet #5," 3/21/2024; UNHCR, website, "Ukraine Situation Global Report 2022."

413. USAID, "Complex Emergency Fact Sheet #2," 2/23/2024.

414. USAID, "Complex Emergency Fact Sheet #2," 2/23/2024; USAID BHA, response to USAID OIG request for information, 03/11/2024.

415. USAID, "Complex Emergency Fact Sheet #5," 3/21/2024; USAID BHA, response to USAID OIG request for information, 03/11/2024.

416. USAID, "Complex Emergency Fact Sheet #2," 2/23/2024.

417. USAID, "Complex Emergency Fact Sheet #5," 3/21/2024.

418. USAID BHA, response to USAID OIG request for information, 3/11/2024.

419. USAID BHA, response to USAID OIG request for information, 3/11/2024.

420. USAID BHA, response to USAID OIG request for information, 3/11/2024.

421. USAID BHA, response to USAID OIG request for information, 3/11/2024.

422. USAID BHA, response to USAID OIG request for information, 3/11/2024.

423. USAID BHA, response to USAID OIG request for information, 3/11/2024.

424. USAID BHA, response to USAID OIG request for information, 3/11/2024.

425. USAID BHA, response to USAID OIG request for information, 3/11/2024.

426. USAID BHA, response to USAID OIG request for information, 3/11/2024.

427. USAID BHA, response to USAID OIG request for information, 3/11/2024.

428. USAID Ukraine, response to USAID OIG request for information, 3/25/2024.

429. USAID Ukraine, response to USAID OIG request for information, 3/25/2024.

430. USAID Ukraine, response to USAID OIG request for information, 3/25/2024.

431. USAID Ukraine, response to USAID OIG request for information, 3/25/2024.

432. USAID Ukraine, response to USAID OIG request for information, 3/25/2024.

433. USAID Ukraine, response to USAID OIG request for information, 3/25/2024.

434. USAID Ukraine, response to USAID OIG request for information, 3/25/2024.

435. USAID Ukraine, response to USAID OIG request for information, 3/25/2024.

436. USAID Ukraine, response to USAID OIG request for information, 3/25/2024.

437. USAID Ukraine, response to USAID OIG request for information, 3/25/2024.

438. USAID Ukraine, response to USAID OIG request for information, 3/25/2024.

439. USAID Ukraine, response to USAID OIG request for information, 3/25/2024.

440. USAID Ukraine, response to USAID OIG request for information, 3/25/2024.

441. USAID Ukraine, response to USAID OIG request for information, 3/25/2024.

442. USAID BHA, response to USAID OIG request for information, 3/11/2024.

443. USAID BHA, response to USAID OIG request for information, 3/11/2024.

444. USAID BHA, response to USAID OIG request for information, 3/11/2024.

445. USAID BHA, response to USAID OIG request for information, 3/11/2024.

446. USAID BHA, response to USAID OIG request for information, 3/11/2024.

447. State, response to State OIG request for information, 12/22/2023.

448. USAID BHA, response to USAID OIG request for information, 3/11/2024.

449. USAID BHA, response to USAID OIG request for information, 3/11/2024.

450. USAID BHA, response to USAID OIG request for information, 3/11/2024.

451. State, response to State OIG request for information, 3/22/2024.

452. State, responses to State OIG request for information, 3/22/2024 and 4/3/2024.

453. State, response to State OIG request for information, 3/22/2024.

454. State, response to State OIG request for information, 3/22/2024.

455. State, response to State OIG request for information, 3/22/2024.

456. State, response to State OIG request for information, 3/22/2024.

457. State, response to State OIG request for information, 3/22/2024.

458. State, responses to State OIG request for information, 3/22/2024 and 4/29/2024.

459. State, response to State OIG request for information, 3/22/2024.

460. State, response to State OIG request for information, 3/22/2024.

461. State, response to State OIG request for information, 3/22/2024.

462. State, response to State OIG request for information, 3/22/2024.

463. State, responses to State OIG request for information, 3/22/2024 and 4/29/2024.

464. State, response to State OIG request for information, 3/22/2024.

465. State, response to State OIG request for information, 3/22/2024.

466. State, response to State OIG request for information, 3/22/2024.

467. State, response to State OIG request for information, 3/22/2024.

468. State, response to State OIG request for information, 3/22/2024.

469. State, response to State OIG request for information, 3/22/2024.
470. State, response to State OIG request for information, 3/22/2024.
471. State, response to State OIG request for information, 3/22/2024.
472. State, response to State OIG request for information, 3/22/2024.
473. State, memorandum, "Strategic Planning Guidelines for Embassy Kyiv M/E Missions," 12/4/2023.
474. State, memorandum, "Strategic Planning Guidelines for Embassy Kyiv M/E Missions," 12/4/2023.
475. State, memorandum, "Strategic Planning Guidelines for Embassy Kyiv M/E Missions," 12/4/2023.
476. State, response to State OIG request for information, 3/22/2024.
477. State, response to State OIG request for information, 3/22/2024.
478. State, response to State OIG request for information, 3/22/2024.
479. State, response to State OIG request for information, 3/22/2024.
480. USAID BHA, response to USAID OIG request for information, 3/11/2024.
481. State, response to State OIG request for information, 3/22/2024.
482. State, response to State OIG request for information, 3/22/2024.
483. State, response to State OIG request for information, 3/22/2024.
484. Embassy Kyiv, cable, "Ukraine: FY24 Quarter 2 Accountability and Oversight of U.S. Foreign Assistance Programs," 24 KYIV 332, 3/4/2024.
485. Embassy Kyiv, cable, "Ukraine: FY24 Quarter 2 Accountability and Oversight of U.S. Foreign Assistance Programs," 24 KYIV 332, 3/4/2024.
486. State, response to State OIG request for information, 3/22/2024.
487. State, responses to State OIG request for information, 3/22/2024 and 4/17/2024.
488. State, response to State OIG request for information, 3/22/2024.
489. State, response to State OIG request for information, 3/22/2024.
490. State, response to State OIG request for information, 3/24/2024.
491. State, vetting comment, 5/9/2024
492. State, response to State OIG request for information, 12/22/2023; and MSI, website, "Ensuring U.S. Government Funding Is Achieving Results in Ukraine," undated.
493. State, fact sheet, "EUR/ACE MEASURE Contract Fact Sheet," undated.
494. State, response to State OIG request for information, 3/22/2024.
495. State, response to State OIG request for information, 3/22/2024.
496. State, response to State OIG request for information, 3/22/2024.
497. State, cable, "USOSCE Permanent Council Statement on Russian Federation's Ongoing Aggression in Ukraine." 24 STATE 14924, 2/13/2024.
498. State, "Ukraine Assistance Strategy, Version 2, January 2023–December 2025." 11/15/2023.
499. State, response to State OIG request for information, 3/22/2024.
500. State, response to State OIG request for information, 3/22/2024.
501. State, response to State OIG request for information, 3/22/2024.
502. State, response to State OIG request for information, 3/22/2024.
503. Embassy Kyiv, cable, "Ukraine: U.S. Assistance Success Stories: January 2024," 24 KYIV 260, 2/16/2024.
504. Embassy Kyiv, cable, "Ukraine: U.S. Assistance Success Stories: January 2024," 24 KYIV 260, 2/16/2024.
505. USAGM, website, "Mission," undated.
506. USAGM, response to State OIG request for information, 4/3/2024.
507. State, press release, "Building a More Resilient Information Environment," 3/18/2024.
508. USAGM, response to State OIG request for information, 4/3/2024.
509. USAGM, response to State OIG request for information, 4/3/2024.
510. USAGM, response to State OIG request for information, 4/3/2024.
511. USAGM, response to State OIG request for information, 4/3/2024.
512. USAGM, response to State OIG request for information, 4/3/2024.
513. USAGM, "USAGM Ukraine Supplemental Funding Report, 60-Day Update, February 7, 2024," 2/7/2024.
514. USAGM, "USAGM Ukraine Supplemental Funding Report, 60-Day Update, February 7, 2024," 2/7/2024.
515. USAGM, response to State OIG request for information, 4/3/2024.
516. USAGM, response to State OIG request for information, 4/3/2024.
517. USAGM, response to State OIG request for information, 4/3/2024.
518. USAGM, response to State OIG request for information, 4/3/2024.
519. USAGM, response to State OIG request for information, 4/3/2024.
520. USAGM, response to State OIG request for information, 4/3/2024.
521. USAGM, response to State OIG request for information, 4/3/2024.
522. USAGM, response to State OIG request for information, 4/3/2024.
523. USAGM, "USAGM Ukraine Supplemental Funding Report, 60-Day Update, February 7, 2024," 2/7/2024.
524. USAGM, "USAGM Ukraine Supplemental Funding Report, 60-Day Update, February 7, 2024," 2/7/2024.
525. USAGM, "USAGM Ukraine Supplemental Funding Report, 60-Day Update, February 7, 2024," 2/7/2024.
526. USAGM, vetting comment, 4/29/2024.
527. USAGM, vetting comment, 4/29/2024.
528. USAGM, vetting comment, 4/29/2024.
529. USAGM, response to State OIG request for information, 4/3/2024.
530. USAGM, response to State OIG request for information, 4/3/2024.
531. USAGM, response to State OIG request for information, 4/3/2024.
532. Associated Press, "Court Orders a Detained Russia-US Journalist to Remain in Custody for Two More Months," 4/1/2024.
533. USAGM, response to State OIG request for information, 4/3/2024.
534. USAGM, response to State OIG request for information, 4/3/2024.
535. USAGM, response to State OIG request for information, 4/3/2024.
536. USAGM, response to State OIG request for information, 4/3/2024.
537. Reuters, Guy Faulconbridge, "Who Was Alexei Navalny and What Did He Say of Russia, Putin, and Death?" 2/17/2024.
538. Adrian Karatnycky, "Russia is Back to the Stalinist Future," Foreign Policy, 3/24/2024.
539. USAGM, response to State OIG request for information, 4/3/2024; and Aditi Sangal, Adrienne Vogt, and Leinz Vales, CNN, "U.S. Ambassador to Russia Joins Mourners Outside Church for Navalny's Funeral in Moscow," 3/1/2024.
540. USAGM, response to State OIG request for information, 4/3/2024.
541. USAGM, response to State OIG request for information, 4/3/2024.
542. USAGM, response to State OIG request for information, 4/3/2024.
543. USAGM, response to State OIG request for information, 4/3/2024.
544. USAGM, response to State OIG request for information, 4/3/2024.
545. USAGM, response to State OIG request for information, 4/3/2024.
546. USAGM, response to State OIG request for information, 4/3/2024.
547. USAGM, response to State OIG request for information, 4/3/2024.
548. State, website, "About Us—Global Engagement Center," undated.
549. State, response to State OIG request for information, 3/22/2024.
550. State, response to State OIG request for information, 3/22/2024.
551. State GEC, "More than a Century of Antisemitism: How Successive Occupants of the Kremlin Have Used Antisemitism to Spread Disinformation and Propaganda," 1/25/2024.
552. State, response to State OIG request for information, 3/22/2024.

553. State, press release, "Building a More Resilient Information Environment," 3/18/2024.

554. State, press release, "Imposing Sanctions on Actors Supporting Kremlin-Directed Disinformation Efforts," 3/20/2024.

555. State, press release, "Imposing Sanctions on Actors Supporting Kremlin-Directed Disinformation Efforts," 3/20/2024.

556. State, response to State OIG request for information, 3/22/2024.

557. State, response to State OIG request for information, 3/22/2024.

558. State, response to State OIG request for information, 3/22/2024.

559. BridgeUSA, "BridgeUSA," 4/11/2024.

560. State, response to State OIG request for information, 3/22/2024.

561. State, response to State OIG request for information, 3/22/2024.

562. State, fact sheet, "Russia's Filtration Operations and Forced Relocations," undated.

563. State, press release, "Invocation of the OSCE Moscow Mechanism to Examine Reports of the Russian Federation's Arbitrary Detention of Civilians in Ukraine," 2/29/2024.

564. State, fact sheet, "Responding to Two Years of Russia's Full-Scale War," 2/23/2024.

565. State, fact sheet, "Responding to Two Years of Russia's Full-Scale War," 2/23/2024.

566. State, fact sheet, "Responding to Two Years of Russia's Full-Scale War," 2/23/2024.

567. State GEC, press release, "The Kremlin's War Against Ukraine's Children," 8/24/2024.

568. State GEC, press release, "The Kremlin's War Against Ukraine's Children," 8/24/2024.

569. Polina Nikolskaya and Mari Salto, "Posterchild for Russia's Removal of Ukraine Orphans Says He Was Coached, Threatened," Reuters, 3/19/2024.

570. Polina Nikolskaya and Mari Salto, "Posterchild for Russia's Removal of Ukraine Orphans Says He Was Coached, Threatened," Reuters, 3/19/2024.

571. State, press release, "Crimes Against Humanity in Ukraine," 2/18/2024.

572. State, press release, "Crimes Against Humanity in Ukraine," 2/18/2024.

573. State, press release, "Responding to Two Years of Russia's Full-Scale War," 2/23/2024.

574. State, fact sheet, "Responding to Two Years of Russia's Full-Scale War," 2/23/2024.

575. State, press release, "The United States Joins the International Coalition for the Return of Ukrainian Children," 3/7/2024.

576. State, press release, "The United States Joins the International Coalition for the Return of Ukrainian Children," 3/7/2024.

577. State, response to State OIG request for information, 3/22/2024.

578. State, response to State OIG request for information, 3/22/2024.

579. State, press release, "Invocation of the OSCE Moscow Mechanism to Examine Reports of the Russian Federation's Arbitrary Detention of Civilians in Ukraine," 2/29/2024.

580. State, press release, "Invocation of the OSCE Moscow Mechanism to Examine Reports of the Russian Federation's Arbitrary Detention of Civilians in Ukraine," 2/29/2024.

581. State, press release, "Invocation of the OSCE Moscow Mechanism to Examine Reports of the Russian Federation's Arbitrary Detention of Civilians in Ukraine," 2/29/2024.

582. State, press release, "Invocation of the OSCE Moscow Mechanism to Examine Reports of the Russian Federation's Arbitrary Detention of Civilians in Ukraine," 2/29/2024.

583. Embassy Kyiv, cable, "Ukraine: Scenesetter for OIG Visit to Ukraine January 29-31," 24 KYIV 150, 1/27/2024

584. State, press release, "Launch of the Atrocity Crimes Advisory Group (ACA) for Ukraine," 3/25/2022 and 4/28/2024.

585. Embassy Kyiv, cable, "Ukraine: Scenesetter for OIG Visit to Ukraine January 29-31," 24 KYIV 150, 1/27/2024.

586. Embassy Kyiv, cable, "Ukraine: Scenesetter for OIG Visit to Ukraine January 29-31," 24 KYIV 150, 1/27/2024.

587. State, cable, "War Bulletin 18:00 CET, 6 January," 24 FTR 2454.

588. State, response to State OIG request for information, 3/22/2024.

589. State, responses to State OIG request for information, 4/12/2024 and 4/28/2024.

590. State, response to State OIG request for information, 4/12/2024.

591. State, response to State OIG request for information, 4/28/2024.

592. State, response to State OIG request for information, 4/12/2024.

593. State, response to State OIG request for information, 4/12/2024.

594. State, response to State OIG request for information, 4/12/2024.

595. State, responses to State OIG request for information, 4/12/2024 and 4/28/2024.

596. DHS OIG, response to DoD OIG request for information, 24.2 WOG DHS 08, 4/8/2024.

597. State, press release, "Launch of the Atrocity Crimes Advisory Group (ACA) for Ukraine," 3/25/2022.

598. Crimes Advisory Group for Ukraine: "What We Do," website, 4/12/2024, Crimes Advisory Group for Ukraine, "Who We Are," website, 4/12/2024.

599. State, response to State OIG request for information, 3/22/2024.

600. State, response to State OIG request for information, 4/28/2024.

601. State, response to State OIG request for information, 3/22/2024.

602. State, response to State OIG request for information, 3/22/2024.

603. State, response to State OIG request for information, 3/22/2024.

604. State, response to State OIG request for information, 3/22/2024.

605. State, response to State OIG request for information, 3/22/2024.

606. State, response to State OIG request for information, 3/22/2024.

607. State, response to State OIG request for information, 3/22/2024.

608. State, response to State OIG request for information, 3/22/2024.

609. State, response to State OIG request for information, 3/22/2024.

610. State, response to State OIG request for information, 3/22/2024.

611. CRS, "Russia's War on Ukraine: Financial and Trade Sanctions," 2/22/2023.

612. CRS, "Russia's War on Ukraine: Financial and Trade Sanctions," 2/22/2023.

613. CRS, "Russia's War on Ukraine: Financial and Trade Sanctions," 2/22/2023.

614. CRS, "Russia's War on Ukraine: Financial and Trade Sanctions," 2/22/2023.

615. CRS, "Russia's War on Ukraine: Financial and Trade Sanctions," 2/22/2023.

616. State, cable, 24 STATE 16226, 2/16/2024.

617. State, cable, 24 STATE 16226, 2/16/2024.

618. State, cable, 24 STATE 16226, 2/16/2024.

619. State, website, "How the United States is Holding Russia and Belarus to Account," 2/23/2024.

620. State, website, "How the United States is Holding Russia and Belarus to Account," 2/23/2024.

621. Treasury OIG, response to DoD OIG request for information, 24.2 WOG TREAS 08, 4/4/2024.

622. Treasury, press release, "On Second Anniversary of Russia's Further Invasion of Ukraine and Following the Death of Aleksey Navalny, Treasury Sanctions Hundreds of Targets in Russia and Globally," 2/23/2024.

623. State, press release, "Responding to Two Years of Russia's Full-Scale War on Ukraine and Navalny's Death," 2/23/2024.

624. State, press release, "Responding to Two Years of Russia's Full-Scale War on Ukraine and Navalny's Death," 2/23/2024.

625. Treasury, press release, "On Second Anniversary of Russia's Further Invasion of Ukraine and Following the Death of Aleksey Navalny, Treasury Sanctions Hundreds of Targets in Russia and Globally," 2/23/2024.

626. Treasury, press release, "On Second Anniversary of Russia's Further Invasion of Ukraine and Following the Death of Aleksey Navalny, Treasury Sanctions Hundreds of Targets in Russia and Globally," 2/23/2024.

627. Treasury, press release, "On Second Anniversary of Russia's Further Invasion of Ukraine and Following the Death of Aleksey Navalny, Treasury Sanctions Hundreds of Targets in Russia and Globally," 2/23/2024.

628. Treasury, press release, "On Second Anniversary of Russia's Further Invasion of Ukraine and Following the Death of Aleksey Navalny, Treasury Sanctions Hundreds of Targets in Russia and Globally," 2/23/2024; State, vetting comment, 4/29/2024.

629. State, response to State OIG request for information, 3/24/2024, and Federal Register, website, "Taking Additional Steps With Respect to the Russian Federation's Harmful Activities," 12/26/2023.

630. State, cable, 24 STATE 16226, 2/16/2024.

631. State, cable, "Pre-notification of Further Designations Against the Russian Federation," 24 STATE 18204, 2/23/2024.

632. Steve Feldstein and Fiona Brauer, "Why Russia Has Been So Resilient to Western Export Controls," Carnegie Endowment for International Peace, 3/11/2024.

633. Dalton Bennett, Mary Ilyushina, Lily Kuo, and Pei-Lin Wu, "Precision Equipment for Russian Arms Makers Came from U.S.-allied Taiwan," Washington Post, 2/1/2024. Andrey Zayakin and Yian Lee, "Taiwan Has Become the Russian Arms Industry's Main Source for High Precision Machine Tools," Insider, 1/26/2024.

634. State, cable, "Pre-notification of Further Designations Against the Russian Federation," 24 STATE 18204, 2/23/2024.

635. Andrey Zayakin and Yian Lee, "Taiwan Has Become the Russian Arms Industry's Main Source for High Precision Machine Tools," Insider, 1/26/2024.

636. European Council, Council of the European Union, "Infographic—Impact of Sanctions on the Russian Economy," 12/10/2023.

637. Andrey Zayakin and Yian Lee, "Taiwan has Become the Russian Arms Industry's Main Source for High Precision Machine Tools," Insider, 1/26/2024.

638. Andrey Zayakin and Yian Lee, "Taiwan has Become the Russian Arms Industry's Main Source for High Precision Machine Tools," Insider, 1/26/2024.

639. State, response to State OIG request for information, 3/22/2024.

640. State, response to State OIG request for information, 3/22/2024.

641. State, response to State OIG request for information, 3/22/2024.

642. State, website, "How the United States is Holding Russia and Belarus to Account," 2/23/2024.

643. State, website, "How the United States is Holding Russia and Belarus to Account," 2/23/2024.

644. DoJ OIG, response to DoD OIG request for information, 24.2 WOG DOJ 05, 4/11/2023.

645. DoJ OIG, response to DoD OIG request for information, 24.2 WOG DOJ 05, 4/11/2023.

646. State, response to State OIG request for information, 3/22/2024.

647. State, response to State OIG request for information, 3/22/2024.

648. State, response to State OIG request for information, 3/22/2024.

649. State, response to State OIG request for information, 3/22/2024.

650. European Council, Council of the European Union, "Infographic—Impact of Sanctions on the Russian Economy," 12/10/2023.

651. State, response to State OIG request for information, 3/22/2024.

652. Tim Lister, "Russia Boasts it is Beating Sanctions, but its Longer-term Prospects are Bleak," CNN, 1/29/2024.

653. Tim Lister, "Russia Boasts it is Beating Sanctions, but its Longer-term Prospects are Bleak," CNN, 1/29/2024.

654. Daria Mosolova, "Russian Copycats Fill Market Gaps Left by Western Brands," Financial Times, 12/22/2023.

655. Treasury, press release, "Global Advisory on Russian Sanctions Evasion Issued Jointly by the Multilateral REPO Task Force," 3/9/2023.

656. White House, press release, "Fact Sheet: Biden Administration Expands U.S. Sanctions Authorities to Target Financial Facilitators of Russia's War Machine," 12/22/2023.

657. State, response to State OIG request for information, 3/22/2024.

658. State, response to State OIG request for information, 3/22/2024.

659. State, response to State OIG request for information, 3/22/2024.

660. Graeme Wood, "A Suspicious Pattern Alarming the Ukrainian Military," The Atlantic, 3/18/2024.

661. Graeme Wood, "A Suspicious Pattern Alarming the Ukrainian Military," The Atlantic, 3/18/2024.

662. European Council, Council of the European Union, "Infographic—Impact of Sanctions on the Russian Economy," 12/10/2023.

663. Tim Lister, "Russia Boasts it is Beating Sanctions, but its Longer-term Prospects are Bleak," CNN, 1/29/2024.

664. Valerii Zaluzhnyi, "Ukraine's Army Chief: The Design of War Has Changed," CNN, 2/8/2024.

665. Tim Lister, "Russia Boasts it is Beating Sanctions, but its Longer-term Prospects are Bleak," CNN, 1/29/2024.

666. Tim Lister, "Russia Boasts it is Beating Sanctions, but its Longer-term Prospects are Bleak," CNN, 1/29/2024.

667. State, cable, 24 STATE 5178, 1/18/2024.

668. Statista, website, "Average Monthly Brent Crude Oil Price from March 2022 to March 2024," Statista, 4/25/2024.

669. State, cable, 24 STATE 5178, 1/18/2024.

670. Treasury, press release, "New U.S. Department of the Treasury Price Cap Analysis Shows That Increased Sanctions Enforcement is Forcing Russia to Sell Oil at a Steeper Discount and Limiting Russian Revenue," 2/23/2024.

671. State, response to State OIG request for information, 3/22/2024.

672. State, response to State OIG request for information, 3/22/2024.

673. State, response to State OIG request for information, 3/22/2024.

674. State, response to State OIG request for information, 3/22/2024.

675. Tim Lister, "Russia Boasts it is Beating Sanctions, but its Longer-term Prospects are Bleak," CNN, 1/29/2024; European Council, Council for the European Union, "Infographic—Impact of Sanctions on the Russian Economy," 12/10/2023.

676. Tim Lister, "Russia Boasts it is Beating Sanctions, but its Longer-term Prospects are Bleak," CNN, 1/29/2024.

677. European Council, Council of the European Union, "Infographic—Impact of Sanctions on the Russian Economy," 12/10/2023.

678. European Council, Council of the European Union, "Infographic—Impact of Sanctions on the Russian Economy," 12/10/2023.

679. State, response to State OIG request for information, 3/22/2024.

680. State, vetting comment, 4/29/2024.

681. State, vetting comment, 4/29/2024.

682. State, vetting comment, 4/29/2024.

683. DEA, response to DoD OIG request for information, 24.2 WOG DEA 01-03, 4/11/2024.

684. DEA, response to DoD OIG request for information, 24.2 WOG DEA 01-03, 4/11/2024.

685. DEA, response to DoD OIG request for information, 24.2 WOG DEA 01-03, 4/11/2024.

686. DEA, response to DoD OIG request for information, 24.2 WOG DEA 01-03, 4/11/2024.

INSPECTOR GENERAL HOTLINE

The United States is committed to supporting the Ukrainian people during Russia's war of aggression. We are dedicated to providing oversight of the funds and resources American taxpayers have provided in support of Ukraine.

We encourage you to confidentially report any of the following suspected activities related to the programs or operations of the U.S. Department of Defense, the U.S. Department of State (including the U.S. Agency for Global Media), and the U.S. Agency for International Development to the appropriate Hotline listed below.

Corruption
Sexual Exploitation and Abuse
Fraud, Waste, Abuse, Mismanagement
Trafficking In Persons

dodig.mil/hotline	stateoig.gov/hotline	oig.usaid.gov/report-fraud
+1 703-604-8799 or +1 800-424-9098	+1 202-647-3320 or +1 800-409-9926	+1 202-712-1070